G000145091

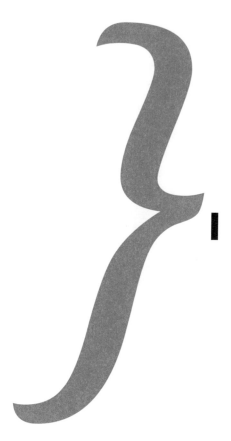

REASON™ 4
IGNITE!
The Visual Guide
for New Users

Matt Piper

COURSE TECHNOLOGY
CENGAGE Learning™

Australia • Brazil • Japan • Korea • Mexico • Singapore • Spain • United Kingdom • United States

COURSE TECHNOLOGY
CENGAGE Learning™

Reason 4 Ignite!
Matt Piper

Publisher and General Manager,
Course Technology PTR: Stacy L. Hiquet

Associate Director of Marketing: Sarah Panella

Manager of Editorial Services: Heather Talbot

Marketing Manager: Mark Hughes

Executive Editor: Mark Garvey

Project Editor: Jenny Davidson

Technical Reviewer: Michael Prager

PTR Editorial Services Coordinator: Erin Johnson

Copy Editor: Gene Redding

Interior Layout: Shawn Morningstar

Cover Designer: Mike Tanamachi

Indexer: Sharon Shock

Proofreader: Heather Urschel

© 2008 Course Technology, a part of Cengage Learning

ALL RIGHTS RESERVED. No part of this work covered by the copyright herein may be reproduced, transmitted, stored, or used in any form or by any means graphic, electronic, or mechanical, including but not limited to photocopying, recording, scanning, digitizing, taping, Web distribution, information networks, or information storage and retrieval systems, except as permitted under Section 107 or 108 of the 1976 United States Copyright Act, without the prior written permission of the publisher.

Reason is a trademark of Propellerhead Software AB.

For product information and technology assistance, contact us at

**Cengage Learning Customer & Sales Support,
1-800-354-9706**

For permission to use material from this text or product, submit all requests online at
cengage.com/permissions

Further permissions questions can be emailed to
permissionrequest@cengage.com

Library of Congress Control Number: 2007938245
ISBN-13: 978-1-59863-478-5
ISBN-10: 1-59863-478-X

Course Technology
25 Thomson Place
Boston, MA 02210
USA

Cengage Learning is a leading provider of customized learning solutions with office locations around the globe, including Singapore, the United Kingdom, Australia, Mexico, Brazil, and Japan. Locate your local office at:
international.cengage.com/region

Cengage Learning products are represented in Canada by Nelson Education, Ltd.

For your lifelong learning solutions, visit **courseptr.com**
Visit our corporate website at **cengage.com**

Printed in the United States of America
2 3 4 5 6 7 11 10 09

This book is dedicated with love to Mom.

Acknowledgments

I want to thank the wonderful people at Course Technology who were so helpful during the course of writing this book. Jenny Davidson, you were such a pleasure to work with. Mark Garvey, your enthusiasm and support for my writing means a lot. Michael Prager, I was thrilled when I found out you would be technical reviewer for my book. Thanks for the great job you did. Gene Redding, you made some excellent catches while copy editing this book (including a couple of important technical bits), which really saved the day.

I want to give a huge thanks to Michael Lindqvist of Propellerhead. You made me feel I was a welcome part of the beta team, responding thoughtfully and good-humoredly to all my messages/posts, even though you were no doubt crazy-busy heading up the testing of the software prior to its release (both the initial release and the update). Also, thanks to Timothy Self at Propellerhead. Your initial encouragement was a major factor in my decision to take on this project for Course Technology.

Getting to write about software I love to use, with support from the cool company that created it, in addition to the support from Course Technology, turned a potentially daunting task into something very positive and enjoyable.

About the Author

Matt Piper has indulged his passion for music technology as a recording engineer, music producer, studio owner, musician/composer, and experimental music promoter since moving to Los Angeles in 1991. He joined the Course Technology family in 2005 with the publication of *Reason 3 Power!*, which he co-authored with Michael Prager. In 2006, he authored *Using Reason's Virtual Instruments: Skill Pack*, an in-depth study of synthesis and how to make your own patches in Reason. Piper can currently be found in music venues around town using his laptop and other electronics to make strange psychedelic sounds with various improvisational groups.

} Contents

CONTENTS ⟩

CONTENTS }

✳ ✳ ✳

} Introduction

If Reason 4 is the first music production program you have ever purchased, then you could not have started with a more fun-to-learn program. And even if you already have other music production software and are just now adding Reason to your arsenal, there has never been a better time to join the ranks of the thousands of musicians and producers all over the world making music with Reason. Reason 4 is without a doubt the most exciting version of Reason yet.

Developed by the Propellerhead Company in Sweden, Reason is one of the most popular and best-selling music production software products of all time. This is no doubt due in large part to Reason's massive variety of sounds, combined with exceptional ease of use. Not to mention, Reason has traditionally been very stable software that packs an amazing punch without putting too heavy a hit on your computer. Even moderately fast computers can achieve great results with a towering rack full of Reason synths, drum machines, samplers, loop players, and effects. This is still true in this latest version, even with all the cool new features!

Reason 4 is perhaps the biggest leap forward since Reason was created. The program has become quite a bit more powerful, and I have to say, much more enjoyable and exciting to work with. Reason 4 includes the addition of an amazing-sounding, colossal synthesizer called Thor. It also adds an arpeggiator, so if you like, you can simply hold down any chord on your MIDI keyboard and hear your favorite Reason synth outputting the individual notes of the chord separately and in perfect time, in whatever automatic pattern you have selected. In addition to these new features, the Sequencer has been completely (and very smartly) remade, so it is much easier and more enjoyable to work with. It even supports tempo automation and time signature automation! Also added is the ReGroove Mixer, which allows hands-on control of the groove/timing relationships within and between the separate elements of your song in a way that has never existed before in any music software to my knowledge. It allows you to make these adjustments in real time as your song is playing, so you can get the rhythmic feel just right, on the spot!

Now that you have heard a little about what Reason 4 can do for you, here's a little bit about what this book can do for you. First off, you should know that this book is by no means a reworking of (or a replacement for) the Reason manual. Don't get me wrong: The manual that comes with Reason is an excellent resource that I encourage you to make the most of. But this book is something entirely different. It is a way to get your hands onto Reason 4, and to drop you right into the action (with some guidance!) so that before you know it, you are really in the Reason groove! This book is not hard work. You will not find long lists of features and difficult theoretical explanations to wrap your head around. Instead, in each chapter you will immediately be led through relatively short groups of simple, fool-proof steps. And at the end of each short exercise, something cool will happen that you can easily hear. Instant gratification! You will easily understand what's going on because you will hear the results, and experience in real time what it feels like to make Reason work for you!

Although this book is aimed at beginners, if you are indeed new to Reason, I am here to tell you that once you've gone through all the exercises in this book, you will not be a beginner anymore! My hope is that by the time you read it cover to cover, not only will you be very comfortable working with Reason, but you will also have a few nifty tricks up your sleeve that will impress even the most experienced Reason users. Of course, the main goal is to just start making music with Reason, and have fun while you do it. So jump right in!

1 } Getting to Know Reason 4

Congratulations. You've got yourself some top-notch music production software, and it's not hard to learn. You've got a book in your hand that will give you a substantial head start and really save you some time in the learning process. To that end, Chapters 2 through 9 will focus on a particular bit of Reason and will go pretty deep into each area.

The purpose of this first chapter is much like the purpose of the practice mode on a video game, where you can get used to controlling the vehicle without anyone shooting at you. I'd like to help you get a feel for the basic functions in Reason that you'll be using for the rest of the book and also point out a couple of important settings that you should really be aware of in order to get the most out of Reason 4 (and have the best experience possible with this book).

In this chapter you will learn how to:

* Set your Reason preferences so that you can get the most out of this book
* Add devices to the Reason rack
* Use the 14-channel Reason Mixer
* Use the Reason Sequencer

Don't Install from the Reason 4.0 DVD

What? Don't install from this beautiful DVD that I just took out of the pretty black box? That's right. Why? Because by the time you read this, Propellerhead will have already released an update for registered users, and the update will work better than version 4.0. As I type this, version 4.0.1 is already being tested, and by the time you read this, the latest available version may be newer than that. Trust me: No matter how awesome the software company is (and Propellerhead is a very cool company), the original release version usually has some bugs, or bits that "weren't quite ready" when the software first came out. So please register yourself and your software at www.propellerheads.se. Then log in and download the latest update for Reason 4. After you run the installer you downloaded and launch Reason for the first time, it will ask you to put in the pretty black DVD, and it will install your Reason Factory sound bank and Orkester ReFills from the DVD. By the way, if you already installed from the disc, don't worry. All you have to do is uninstall and then download and install the latest version from www.propellerheads.se.

Important General Settings

Here are a few settings that will help you as you use Reason. They are also settings that I used when creating the tutorials in this book, so if you set them the same way, we can both be on the same page and avoid unnecessary confusion.

1. Open the Reason preferences (from the Edit menu if you're using Windows, or from the Reason menu if you're using Mac) and make sure you're on the General page.

2. Set Editing: Mouse Knob Range to Very Precise. That way you can select very specific values when you move knobs and faders on the Reason devices.

3 The box next to Show Parameter Value Tool Tip should always be checked. That way, when you let your cursor rest over a control on a Reason device, a red text box will appear, telling you the full name of the control and the exact value it is set to.

4 The box next to Show Automation Indication should always be checked, so if you record automation on a knob, fader, or other control, there will be a green outline around it to show it is automated (and will move by itself at some point during song playback).

5 Default Song should be set for Empty Rack, because nearly all the exercises in this book will start with an empty rack.

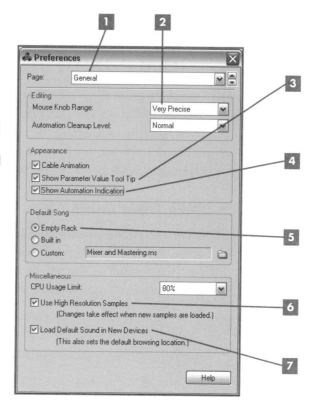

6 Use High Resolution Samples should be checked, because we want everything to sound as good as possible at all times.

7 Load Default Sound in New Devices should be checked while you are using this book, since that's the way I had it set as I constructed the exercises.

For information regarding settings on the rest of the Preferences pages (including Audio preferences and Keyboards and Control Surfaces), you would do best to consult the Reason Operation Manual and the manual for your specific audio interface or MIDI device. There are just too many possible configurations to try to cover in this book.

Getting to Know the Reason Rack

One of the great things about Reason is the way devices are arranged and connected the same way they would be in a real studio rack. This makes the logic simple to understand and will be very familiar to anyone who has worked in a recording studio or who has connected guitar pedals or modular synthesizers, for that matter.

Rack Front and Back

In the demo song you are about to open, you will see that several of the devices in the Reason rack are folded. This means that their size is minimized so that you can see as many devices as possible at one time on the screen. You will unfold a few of them in the following exercise.

1 From the File menu, select Open and browse to Reason (Program/Application Folder) > Demo Songs > eXode - Radiant Emission.rps and open that song.

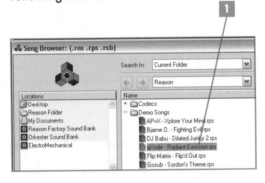

2 Click OK to close the Song Information window.

3 Click the triangle/arrow on the left of the Reason hardware device to unfold it. This device represents the connection between the rest of the rack and your sound card and MIDI devices.

4 Unfold the MClass Mastering Suite Combinator to see all the fancy gold devices being used to put the final audio processing on this song.

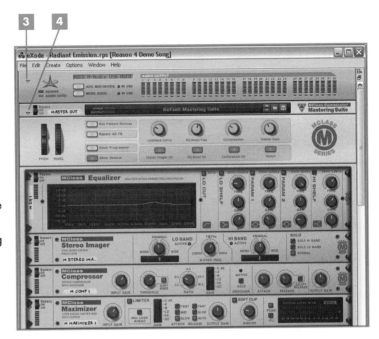

5 Press the Tab key on your computer keyboard to flip the Reason rack around, and enjoy the hot cable-swinging action. Then drag the vertical scrollbar down until you see Remix. Remix is also referred to as Mixer 14:2.

6 Unfold Mixer 14:2 (Remix).

7 Click on the cable plugged into the Channel 8 Left Audio input, and drag and connect it to the Channel 9 Left Audio input. This is how you make connections on the back of the Reason rack.

Before moving on, here's one last word about folding. You will notice that to the left of each track in the Reason Sequencer, there is a fold/unfold triangle as well. It serves the same purpose as in the rack. It allows you to fold an item to save space when you are not editing it or unfold it when you need to see the details. But before getting into the Reason Sequencer, let's create some devices in the rack.

Creating Devices

For the next exercise, you will want to start with an empty rack, either by launching Reason or by selecting New (Ctrl+N) from the File menu. If you have Default Song set for Empty Rack on the General page of your Reason preferences as instructed in the "Important General Settings" section at the start of this chapter, you should be good to go. The purpose of this exercise is to show you the different ways to create devices in the Reason rack.

1 From the Create menu, select Mixer 14:2.

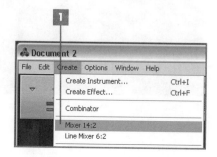

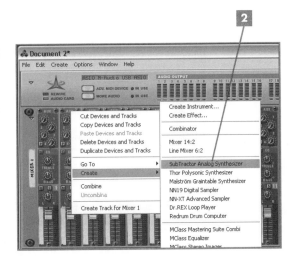

2 Right-click on Mixer 14:2, and a menu (known as a context menu) will pop up. From that menu, mouse over Create and select SubTractor Analog Synthesizer.

3 From the Window menu, select Show Tool Window. (Or you could use the F8 key, which is the keyboard shortcut for this same function.)

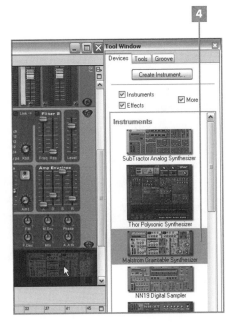

4 Drag a Malström Graintable Synthesizer from the Tool window and drop it under the Subtractor in the rack.

5 From the Create menu, select Create Instrument.

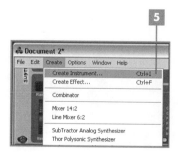

6 Now instead of choosing a specific device, you will be choosing a specific sound (which could come from any instrument). Expand the Bass folder, then expand the Synth Bass folder, then double-click on Attack Bass.thor.

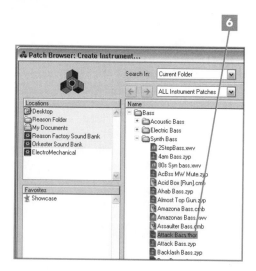

7 Now that you have created an instance of Thor, drag the vertical scrollbar up to the top of the page, and you will see that all three devices you created have been automatically routed to the first three channels on Mixer 14:2.

8 Press the Tab key on your computer keyboard to flip your rack around.

The reason I wanted you to flip the rack around in Step 8 is so that you could see the cables connecting the three instruments to the mixer, as well as the cables connecting the master outputs of the mixer to outputs 1 and 2 of your sound card, by way of the Reason hardware device.

Mixer 14:2 (Remix)

The Mixer 14:2 is the 14-channel mixer you will be using at least one instance of in all your Reason songs. It is laid out like a pretty standard analog mixer. In the next exercise, you will get a feel for its various functions.

Mute, Solo, Pan, and Volume

1 From the File menu, select Open and browse to Reason (Program/Application folder) > Demo Songs > Turbotito - Sydney Heat.rps, and open that song. Then click OK to close the Song Information window with the nice photo of Filip Nikolic in his techno-color dream coat.

2 Click the Play button on the Reason Transport, and you will hear the song start playing.

3 Click the Mute button on Channel 2. This will mute the drums, and you will not hear them anymore. Once you are satisfied that this works, click the Mute button again to unmute the drums.

4 Turn the Channel 1 Pan knob all the way to the left, then all the way to the right, and then back to center. You should hear the synth bass move from left to right and then back to center in the stereo field.

5 Turn up the Channel 1 fader to a value of 80, exactly even with the Channel 2 (drums) Level slider. Now the pumping bass track is overpowering.

6 On your computer keyboard, press Ctrl+Z to undo that last step. The Channel 1 Level slider should return to its original lower position. Although it's faster to use Ctrl+Z, you could also choose Undo Change Channel 1 Level from the Edit menu.

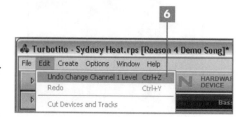

7 Slowly turn the Master Fader all the way down and then back up again. The whole mix should come down and then back up again.

EQ and Auxiliary Send/Return

Of course, EQ stands for equalizer and refers to the Bass and Treble knobs on each channel. Anyone who has ever owned a home stereo is familiar with that. However, if you've never used a professional mixing console, you may not be familiar with auxiliary sends and returns. Each of the four Auxiliary Send knobs on each channel allows you to send the audio signal from that channel into an effects device such as a reverb or delay. Those Aux Send knobs control how loud of a signal you are sending to the effects device. The signal coming back from the effects device comes through the Auxiliary Return, and the four Auxiliary Return knobs control how much audio signal from the effects device will be sent to the Master Output L/R of the mixer. The next exercise picks up where the last one left off, still using the Turbotito - Sydney Heat demo song.

1. With the Turbotito - Sydney Heat demo song playing, turn the Channel 2 Treble knob all the way down. Nothing will happen.

2. Now click the Channel 2 EQ On/Off knob. Now the treble is turned down.

3. Turn the Channel 2 Treble knob all the way up and then back to center.

4. Click the Channel 2 Solo button. Now every track except for Channel 2 is muted.

5. Turn the Channel 2 Aux (Auxiliary) Send 1 knob all the way up. Since Aux Return 1 is coming from the RV7000 Reverb, you will hear reverb applied to the drums.

II

❄ ❄ ❄

Sequencing in Reason/Reason Transport Controls

Since there are so many facets to the sequencer and what it can do, rather than going into overwhelmingly exhaustive detail in a single chapter, I am taking the approach of introducing a new slice of sequencer functionality in each chapter, in sections such as "Sequencing with Dr.REX" and "Sequencing with Subtractor." I think this will be a more fun and natural way to learn, and my expectation is that by the end of the book you will be quite comfortable with Reason 4's sequencer.

Loop On/Off, Click, and Left/Right Locators

1 From the File menu, select Open and browse to Reason (Program/Application folder) > Demo Songs > eXode - Radiant Emission.rps, and open that song. Then click OK to close the Song Information window.

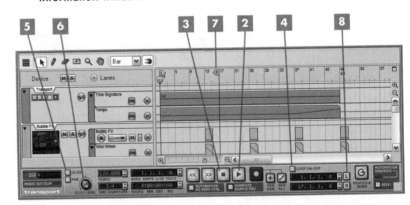

2 Click Play on the Reason Transport, and let the song play until about bar 17 or so.

3 Click Stop twice (once to stop playback, and once to return the song position marker to bar 1).

4 Click the Loop On/Off button to turn looping on, and then click Play.

5 As the playback loops the bars between the left and right locators, activate the Click button.

6 Turn the volume of the Click up and down using the Click Level knob.

7 Drag the right locator over to bar 17. Now your loop is twice as long as it was.

8 Click the Go to Left Locator button (labeled L), and the song position marker will jump to the left locator, continuing playback from that point.

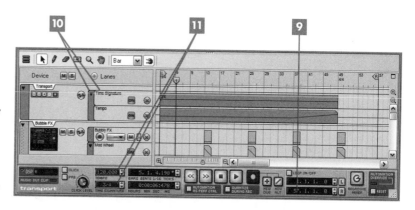

9 Click on the first number (17) in the right locator window, type in 57, and press Enter on your computer keyboard. Now the right locator is at bar 57.

10 Listen to the song all the way from bar 1 through bar 57. Notice that the first Sequencer track is labeled Transport and contains a lane labeled Time Signature and another labeled Tempo.

11 Also notice the green outlines around the Tempo and Time Signature display windows in the Reason Transport. This indicates that these parameters have had automation recorded for them, so that they will automatically change during the song.

As you listen to the Radiant Emissions demo song for this exercise, you will hear the tempo ramp up as you watch the upward line at the end of the Tempo lane in the Transport track. You will also hear the time signature change from 3/4 to 4/4 at bar 49. You will see these changes displayed in the Tempo and Time Signature windows in the Reason Transport. In Reason 4, it is very easy to do tempo and time signature changes.

Zooming, Scrolling, Hand Tool, and Magnifying Glass Tool

The next exercise should help you get comfortable with the tools you will use in order to see just what you need to see in the Reason Sequencer. This exercise picks up where the last exercise left off.

1 With the Radiant Emissions demo song still loaded and playback stopped, drag the horizontal scrollbar all the way to the right (bar 217), and you will see the end marker. The end marker determines the actual end point when you export your song as an audio file.

2 Slowly drag the vertical scroll-bar all the way to the bottom, and you will see that there is a whole lot of this sequence you haven't seen yet.

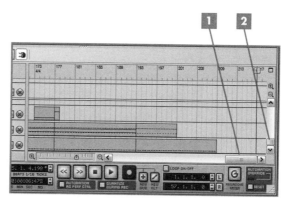

3 To see more of the sequence, drag the top of the Reason Sequencer upwards almost all the way to the top of the window, just under the first RV7000 Advanced Reverb.

4 Click the Vertical Zoom In button a few times, and you will see the Sequencer tracks get taller, so you can see more vertical detail.

5 Click the Horizontal Zoom In button a few times to see more horizontal detail.

6 Select the Hand tool.

7 Click (and hold) in the middle of the Sequencer window, and you will be able to drag the entire sequence up and down, left and right, and round and round. It's like controlling the horizontal and vertical scrollbars at the same time.

8 Select the Magnifying Glass tool.

9 Ctrl+click in the middle of the Sequencer window several times until you can see all the tracks again. (Without holding down Ctrl, clicking with the Magnifying Glass tool zooms in both horizontally and vertically; Ctrl+click zooms out.)

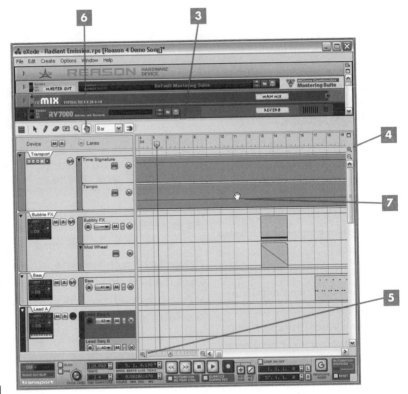

10 This next trick is where it's really nice to have two LCD computer monitors: Click the button in the upper right corner of the Reason rack.

In Step 10 above, after you click the button, you will have two windows: a separate Sequencer window and a separate rack window. It's really helpful to have two LCD monitors, so you can have the sequencer on one monitor and the rack on the other.

Time Signature and Snap to Grid

The Radiant Emission demo song starts off with a time signature of 3/4 and eventually changes to a time signature of 4/4. If the time signature is 4/4, the first number in the time signature means that there are four beats in a bar (or measure), and the second number means that a 1/4 note equals one beat. With a time signature of 3/4, the first number means that there are three beats in a bar (or measure), and the second number again means that a 1/4 note equals one beat. If you chose a time signature of 6/8, that would mean that there are six beats per bar and a 1/8 note equals one beat.

The following exercise picks up where the last exercise left off. You will be focusing on the Sequencer window.

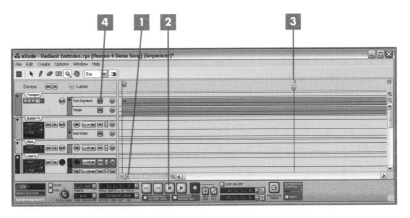

1 Drag the horizontal magnification slider all the way to the left for maximum magnification.

2 Click the Stop button on the Reason Transport until the song position marker is at bar 1.

3 Drag the song position marker to bar 2. Since Snap is set to Bar, you will not be able to leave the song position marker anywhere between bars 1 and 2.

4 Turn off the Time Signature lane. Since the Time Signature lane had set the time for 3/4, and you turned it off, now the song is at its default time signature of 4/4.

5 Set the Snap value to 1/2. Then drag the song position marker between bars 1 and 2, and you will see that it stops at the 1/2 note as well.

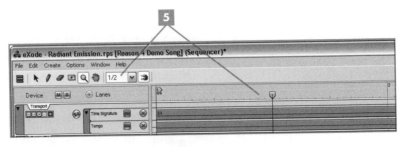

6 Turn off Snap to Grid. Now you can leave the song position marker at any point between bars 1 and 2.

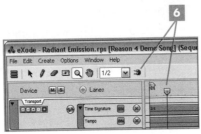

7 Click the Snap to Grid button to turn it back on, and set the Snap value to 1/16. Then move the song position marker back and forth, and you will see that it can be left at any 1/16 note.

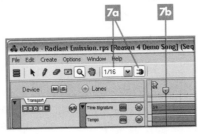

Editing Tools: Selection, Pencil, Razor, and Eraser

The following exercise picks up where the last exercise left off and again focuses on the Sequencer window.

1 With Snap to Grid still activated, set the Snap value for 1/16 and select the Pencil tool.

2 Click once at bar 1 on the Sequencer track labeled Bass. You have just created a clip with a duration of 1/16 note.

3 Starting at the second 1/4 note from bar 1 (that's three 1/16 notes from the end of the clip you drew), draw a clip that is one 1/4 note long.

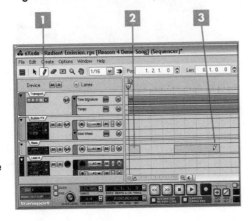

4 Choose **your** Selection tool.

5 Click **once on the** first clip **you** drew to select it. Then click on the arrow **on its right side, and** drag **it to the** right **so that the end of the first clip touches the beginning of the second clip. Now you have two clips that each last a 1/4 note.**

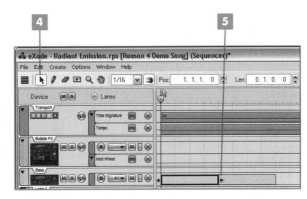

6 Select **your** Razor tool.

7 Slice **each** clip **in its middle. Now you have four 1/8-note clips.**

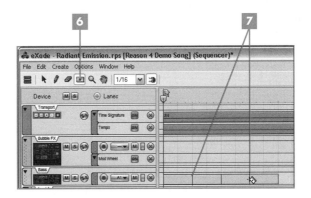

8 Choose **the** Selection tool. **Then, while** holding **down the Ctrl** button, click **on each** clip **so that all four are selected.**

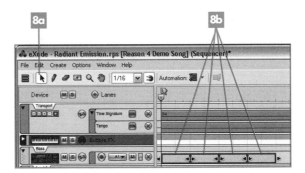

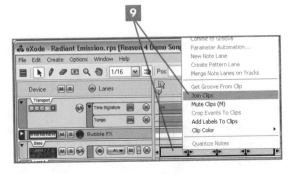

9 Right-click on one of the clips and choose Join Clips from the context menu.

10 Double-click on the clip, and now you can see the Key Edit window, where you can draw in notes with your Pencil tool if you want.

11 Click the Arrange/Edit Mode button to go back to the Arrange mode.

12 Select the Erase tool.

13 Click on your clip, and it will be erased.

You will get plenty of practice with the Key Edit window later in this book, but for now I just wanted to show it to you. Now you can see that Snap to Grid affects how the song position marker can be moved, how clips can be resized, as well as has how the Pencil tool works. It also affects how you move the left and right locators, and it makes it easy to move clips and drop them exactly on the bar or beat you want.

Recording Automation in the Reason Sequencer

This sounds very fancy, but it's really quite easy. Pretty much every little move that can be made in Reason can be automated, which means that the move can be recorded and then played back automatically. You will see multiple examples of this throughout the book. Right now, here's an easy one. You are going to automate a Solo button on the Mixer 14:2.

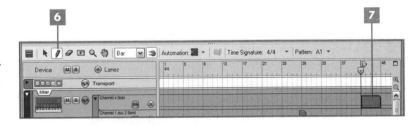

1 From the File menu, select Open and browse to Reason (Program/Application folder) > Demo Songs > Turbotito - Sydney Heat.rps and open that song, then click OK to close the Song Information window.

2 Move the left locator to bar 41.

3 Click the Go to Left Locator button.

4 Click the little triangle to the left of the Mixer track in the Reason Sequencer (to unfold the track).

5 Right-click on the Channel 4 Solo button, and choose Edit Automation from the context menu. A Channel 4 Solo lane will appear on the top of the Mixer Sequencer track. Channel 4 is labeled Blip Gates.

6 Select the Pencil tool.

7 Draw a clip on the Channel 4 Solo automation lane from bar 41 to bar 45, then hold down the Alt key (to temporarily turn your Pencil back into a Selection tool) and double-click on the clip.

8 Set the Snap value to Bar.

9 Click once in the upper left corner of your clip to create an automation point. This will turn on the Channel 4 Solo button.

10 Click once in the lower right corner of your clip to make another automation point. This will turn off the Channel 4 Solo button.

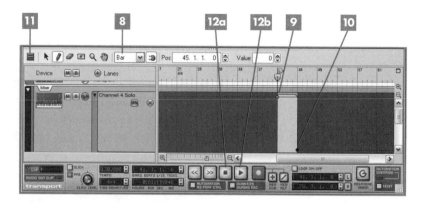

11 Click the Arrange/Edit Mode button twice to change back to Arrange mode.

12 Click the Stop button so that the song position marker returns to bar 1. Then click the Play button and listen.

When you listen to the song, you should hear everything but the Blip Gates drop out right at bar 41 and then come back in dramatically at bar 45. The way we did this was very precise and efficient. Another way you could have done this (instead of drawing in the automation) would be to select the Mixer Sequencer track, click Record, and then hit the Channel 4 Solo button at the appropriate moments and record the automation live.

Picking up where the last exercise left off, let's automate a fade out.

1 Right-click on the Master Fader and select Edit Automation from the context menu.

2 Draw a clip with your Pencil tool starting at bar 61 and ending at bar 73, then hold down the Alt key (to temporarily turn your Pencil back into a Selection tool) and double-click on the clip.

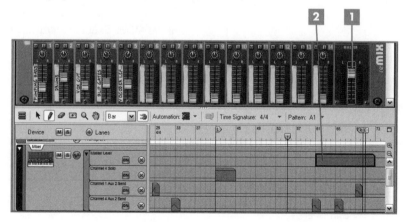

3 Click once in the upper left corner of your clip (at bar 61) to create an automation point.

4 Click once at the bottom of the clip at bar 69 (a little bit to the left of the right locator and end marker) to create another automation point.

5 Click the Arrange/Edit Mode button twice to change back to Arrange mode.

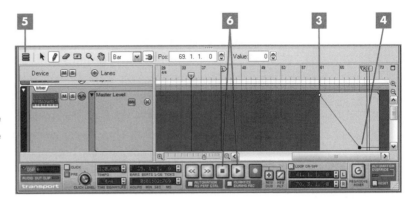

6 Click the Stop button once or twice so that the song position marker returns to bar 1. Then click the Play button and listen.

Again, you could have simply moved the Master Fader with your mouse while recording the automation on the Mixer track in the Sequencer, but drawing it in is more smooth and precise. If you want to get fancy and make a fade that's tapered at the end, you could add an extra automation point or two toward the bottom of the clip in the second half of the fade so that the first half of the fade is faster while the second half fades more gradually.

You could automate a tempo change the exact same way as you created the fade in the exercise above: by right-clicking on the Tempo window and choosing Edit Automation. In fact, you can easily automate nearly anything that can be done in Reason.

Read the Fabulous Manual (RTFM)

If you get stuck anywhere in this book, and something you are trying to do isn't working even though you have reviewed my steps, please refer to the Reason Operation Manual. It is a .pdf file found in the Documentation folder in your Reason program folder.

❋ ❋ ❋

The Operation Manual is a very helpful resource. It is your friend in times of need. It will get you unstuck. Find the chapter dealing with the device that is giving you trouble, or look up a key word in the index. The Help manual, which is accessible from the Help menu inside of Reason, is the same thing as the Operation Manual, but without pictures. I am a big fan of PDF manuals. They allow me to use the Search function. I just type in a word relating to my problem and generally find my answer very easily by clicking the little binoculars icon in my PDF viewer (Adobe Acrobat or Foxit Reader). If somehow you don't have a PDF viewer (and your computer doesn't know what program to use to open PDF files), both the viewers I mentioned are available for free download. Just do a Google search and download directly from the Adobe or Foxit Web site.

Propellerhead Online Support

Another resource that is very helpful is the Reason Web site. It really is a good idea to register your copy of Reason at www.propellerheads.se. Then you can access all the helpful articles in their Support section. I have found answers there to the most odd and specialized technical problems that you could imagine. I have been surprised more than once to find a very specific answer to something I thought was a very strange or difficult problem. As a last resort, I have had good results e-mailing their tech support through the support section of the Propellerhead Web site. You may have to wait a day or two for a response (different time zones), but the responses I have received have been very thoughtful, detailed, and helpful.

All right. Now that you've gotten your feet wet, it's time to jump into learning the big gun in Reason's beat-production arsenal: Dr.Rex.

2 Dr.Rex

No device in Reason can help you put together a song more quickly and effortlessly than Dr.Rex. Load a few instances of Dr.Rex into your Reason song, and before you know it you will have some very full sounding, grooving rhythmic and bass content in your track.

Dr.Rex is designed for the sole purpose of playing and manipulating REX loops. REX loops are audio files that have been "sliced up" using another Propellerhead program called ReCycle. Dozens of these REX loops are included in your Reason Factory Sound Bank. In a REX file, the audio file is typically sliced on the attacks, or transients, of the audio waveform. So if a drumbeat is made into a REX file, usually a slice will be made of each beat of the rhythm (although you will find instances where more than one beat is included in a single slice). Slicing up the audio this way allows the tempo at which the REX file is played back to be changed without altering pitch or significantly changing the audio quality of the loop. It also allows you to change the pitch of the entire loop or of individual slices without changing the tempo. In these respects a REX loop is similar to an Acidized Wave file (as would be used in Sony Acid software) or a Wave file imported into Ableton Live software.

A trick that makes REX loops so useful is that they also contain MIDI information. Each slice in a REX file is assigned a MIDI note value. This means that in addition to simply playing a REX loop "as is," the individual slices can be triggered by playing a MIDI keyboard or by drawing in notes in the Reason Sequencer. Having the slices controlled by MIDI allows you to easily cut out slices you don't want or rearrange them any way you like within your MIDI sequence.

In this chapter you will learn how to:

❄ Change the sound and feel of drum and instrument loops using the synth parameters in Dr.Rex

❄ Sequence a song in five minutes using Dr.Rex

❄ Use the Reason Sequencer to automate the Dr.Rex synth parameters

❄ Use the Scream 4 Sound Destruction Unit to mutilate a Dr.Rex drum loop

Digging into Dr.Rex

Dr.Rex is immediately fun to groove with, and the best way to get to know how to use it is to actually start using it! So let's load up Dr.Rex and try some of its key features.

1 Start with an empty rack (File > New). Click and drag Mixer 14:2 from the Devices Tool window into the Reason rack.

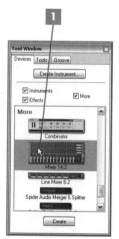

2 Drag Dr.Rex from the Devices Tool window into the Reason rack, placing it directly below Mixer 14:2.

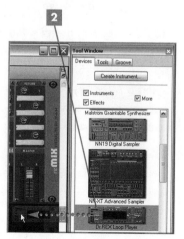

Dr.Rex Key Features Exercise

3 Click **Dr.Rex's** Preview button to hear the loop that has been loaded by default, which is called Hhp65_FoSho_136_Chrnc.rx2. Note that clicking the Preview button a second time will stop the loop, but please let it play for now.

4 Click in the Tempo window of the Reason Transport and drag up until you have set the value to 136 bpm, which is the loop's original tempo (notice that 136 is included in the filename).

5 As the loop continues to play, drag Dr.Rex's Transpose knob to the right and left and hear the pitch of the loop change. You will also see the highlighted key on the keyboard display above the Transport knob change. The default value is zero, so you can return the knob to zero when you are done playing with it.

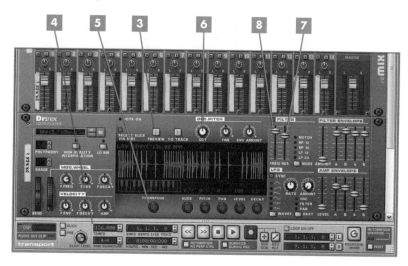

6 Now play with the Oscillator Octave knob, turning it back and forth as the loop plays. This will be similar to Transpose, except that you will be jumping by octaves (12 semitones) instead of by single semitone increments. Return the knob to 12 o'clock (a value of 4) when you are done.

7 Move the Filter Resonance (Res) fader about 3/4 of the way to the top (to a value of about 91).

8 Now move the Filter Frequency (Freq) fader up and down within the upper third of its path of travel (between values of 127 and about 80). You can do this creatively and in rhythm. Nice filter sweep!

Note that when using the Tool window to create new devices, you can double-click on the device in the Tool window instead of dragging it into the rack, if you prefer. In that case, the new device will be inserted below whatever device was last highlighted in the rack.

Auditioning Loops Inside Dr.Rex

As you learned in the previous exercise, all you have to do to hear the REX loop that is currently loaded into Dr.Rex is to click the Preview button located above the Waveform Display. The loop will continue to play until you click the Preview button again.

You can also preview the currently loaded REX loop by playing the D0 key on your MIDI keyboard. When you preview in this manner, the loop will play only once. With either method, the loop will play back at the song tempo set in the Reason Transport panel rather than the loop's original tempo (the tempo at which the loop was recorded).

Auditioning Loops Inside the Loop Browser

You can also audition loops before you load them into Dr.Rex. This is done with the REX File Browser, which you open by clicking on the Browse Loop button. Note that when the Preview button on the top of Dr.Rex is engaged, if you open the REX File Browser and audition a loop within the File Browser, Autoplay will be automatically (and irrevocably) engaged, the currently loaded loop will stop playing, and the loop you select in the REX File Browser will begin playing in sync with your track at the Reason Song Tempo rather than at its original tempo. However, if Dr.Rex's Preview button is not engaged, loops will audition at their original tempo within the REX File Browser rather than the Song Tempo.

Auditioning loops in the REX Loop Browser using the synchronized Preview function while your track plays is extremely useful. You can very quickly and easily hear which loops fit best in your song. Let's give it a spin. I have a feeling once you have tried this out, you will be using the feature quite a bit in your music production.

1. Start with an empty rack. Click and drag Mixer 14:2 from the Devices Tool window into the Reason rack.

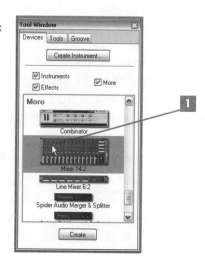

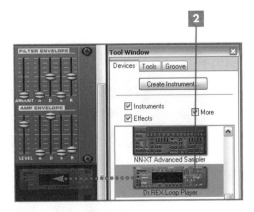

2 Drag Dr.Rex from the Devices Tool window into the Reason rack, placing it directly below Mixer 14:2. Then drag a second Dr.Rex from the Devices Tool window into the Reason rack, placing it directly below the first Dr.Rex.

3 Open the REX Loop Browser by clicking on the Browse Loop button of the top Dr.Rex (the button has a folder icon).

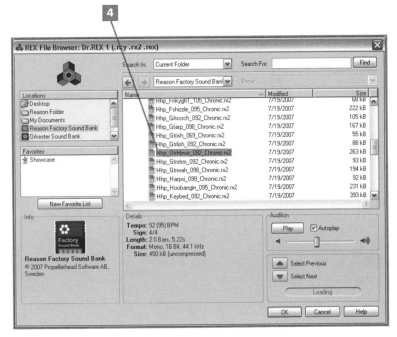

4 Browse to Reason Factory Sound Bank > Dr Rex Instrument Loops > Various Hip Hop Loops and click only once on the file named Hhp_GtrMinor_092_Chronic. rx2. If there is a checkmark next to Autoplay, you will hear the loop play once. The 092 in the filename refers, of course, to the original tempo. Even though your song tempo is 120, you hear the loop audition at its original slower tempo of 92. Click OK to load the loop into the top Dr.Rex.

5 Set your song tempo to 92 in the Reason Transport panel.

6 Select the Sequencer track labeled Dr.REX 1 by clicking on the Dr.REX 1 device icon.

7 Click the To Track button on the top Dr.Rex. The MIDI information for the loop should appear on the top Reason Sequencer track. Press the Play button on the Reason Transport panel.

8 If the buzz on the loop bothers you, turn down the Filter Freq slider on the top Dr.Rex until it sounds OK to you.

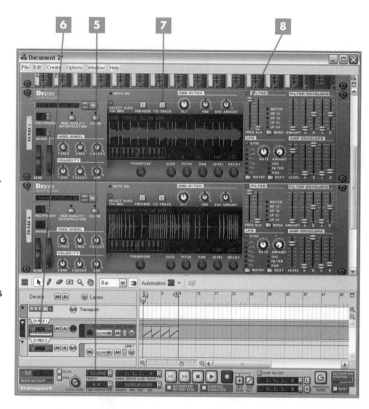

9 Turn down Channel 1 on the mixer to a value of 74 (almost halfway down) so that the guitar loop doesn't drown out the drums.

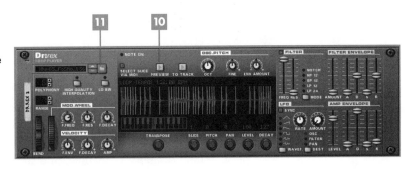

10 Click the Preview button on the bottom Dr.Rex.

11 The default loop doesn't match too well, so click the Browse Loop button on the bottom Dr.Rex to open the REX File Browser. The guitar loop on the top Dr.Rex should still be playing.

12 Browse to Reason Factory Sound Bank > Dr Rex Drum Loops > Abstract HipHop. Now, one at a time, start clicking once on each file in the Abstract HipHop folder. Notice that regardless of their original tempo, all the loops play back in perfect sync with your 92 bpm guitar loop. Some of them fit better than others, but now do you see how easy it is to find the right one? When you find the one you like, just click OK to select it.

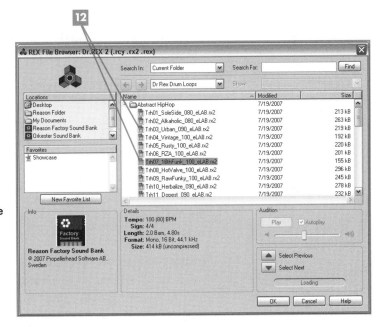

Slick Moves with Envelopes and LFO

If you are new to the world of synthesizers (virtual or otherwise), then terms like Filter Envelope, Amp Envelope, and LFO (low frequency oscillator) may sound a bit perplexing. In reality, the concepts are actually pretty simple, and we can explore them together hands-on, one bite-sized piece at a time.

Amp Envelope

When dealing with audio and synthesizers, think of an envelope as the shape of an event over time. You know that an amplifier makes things louder (it increases the audio volume). So when we talk about the Amp Envelope, we are talking about the shape of the volume of the sound over time. Think of the shape of the sound of an ocean wave coming into shore. The volume fades in, reaches a peak, and then recedes. Now think of a snare drum hit. The initial sound is immediate and will normally ring out for only a relatively short time thereafter. Finally, think of striking and holding a note on a piano. The initial attack (beginning of the sound) is immediate like the drum hit, but the decay (how long it takes the note to fade into silence) is much longer than with a drum.

A very common type of envelope used to control both filters and amplifiers in synthesizers is an ADSR (Attack, Decay, Sustain, and Release) Envelope. With Dr.Rex drum loops, the two controls that you will probably use the most are Attack and Decay. Decay is especially useful with the Amp Envelope because it can be used to tighten up a drum beat. How? As stated in the preceding paragraph, decay is simply how long it takes a note to fade into silence once it has been played. A snare drum with a long decay will continue to ring out after it has been hit. A snare drum with a short decay setting will not.

Attack, on the other hand, is how long it takes a note or sound to reach its full volume once it has been played. An ambient synth pad may have a long attack (the sound takes a few seconds to fade in or swell), while an unprocessed drum hit will have almost zero attack (a very short attack). The following exercise will give you an idea of what I'm talking about.

1 Load up another Reason rack with Mixer 14:2 followed by Dr.Rex underneath. Click the Preview button on Dr.Rex.

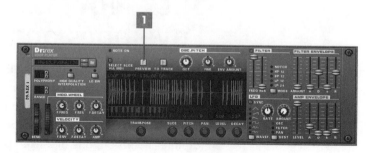

2 As the loop plays, slowly move the Amp Decay slider down all the way to the bottom. As you approach a Decay value of zero, you will hear the duration of the individual beats become very short, giving the loop a more glitchy sound. When you are done, move the Decay slider all the way back to the top.

3 Move the Amp Attack slider up to a value of 40, and slowly move it up and down between values of 40 and 30. You will hear that the attack (the very first part of each beat) is quiet, resulting in an effect somewhat similar to backwards masking (listening to a recording in reverse).

4 Leave the Amp Attack at a value of 30, and turn the Amp Decay slider all the way down for an interesting effect. You will hear a range of subtly different effects if you move the Amp Attack slider between 40 and 20.

5 If this sounds too quiet, you can turn the Amp Level up all the way. Remember to turn it back down to its default value of 100 when you're done to avoid any loud surprises later!

Filter Envelope

To make electronic music, you will want to become familiar with using filters. They sound cool and are a big part of the fun—especially low-pass filters (which allow low frequencies to pass but filter out high frequencies). One very nice effect that can be done with filters is to gradually change the frequency of the filter over time. You will do some slower filter sweeps a bit later in this chapter. In this exercise, you will see Dr.Rex's Filter Envelope do a very fast filter sweep for you each time a new REX slice (beat) is triggered.

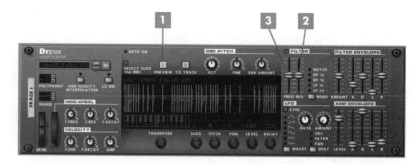

1 Load up a new Reason rack with Mixer 14:2 followed by Dr.Rex underneath. Click the Preview button on Dr.Rex.

2 Turn the Filter Resonance (RES) slider up halfway.

3 Slowly turn the Filter Frequency (FREQ) slider down halfway.

4 Slowly turn the Filter Envelope Amount slider up halfway.

5 Slowly turn the Filter Envelope Attack slider up to a value of 30 (about 1/4 of the way up) and listen to the effect. Then slowly turn it back down to zero.

6 Slowly turn the Filter Envelope Decay slider down to zero and then back up again. Listen to the effect as you slowly move this control. You can experiment with different combinations of the Attack and Decay sliders in the Filter Envelope.

LFO

In a synthesizer, an oscillator produces waveforms. It produces the basic sound, which is then processed by other parts of the synthesizer. Within the range of human hearing, different waveforms have different sounds. A sine wave (for example) has a very mellow sound, while an unfiltered sawtooth wave has a crisp, cutting sound full of harmonics. A low frequency oscillator (LFO) uses the same waveforms but usually produces them at frequencies well below the range of human hearing. Instead of being amplified as a sound source, the signal from the LFO is used to affect something else (like filter frequency, stereo pan, or the pitch of the audio oscillator). You will learn more about the different basic waveforms and get a clear picture of the differences between them in Chapter 4, "SubTractor." Right now, let's jump in and see how easy it is to set up Dr.Rex's LFO to do some really cool things to your REX loops!

Using the LFO to Control the Filter Frequency

In this first example, we will use the LFO to *modulate* (or change) the filter frequency. You will clearly hear the shape of a few of the different waveforms as we do this.

1 Load up another Reason rack with Mixer 14:2 followed by Dr.Rex underneath. Press Play on the Reason Transport, and then press the Preview button on Dr.Rex to hear the default loop.

2 Turn the Filter Resonance slider up halfway.

3 Turn on the LFO sync button. It will light up red. Since the track is playing, the LFO will sync to the track.

4 Turn the LFO Rate knob down to 8/4. Since you have the LFO Sync active, 8/4 actually refers to the musical time division (it will take the LFO eight 1/4 notes to sweep though its waveform once).

5 Change the LFO destination to Filter. You can do this by clicking directly on the word Filter or by clicking the Dest button until you see the little red light next to Filter.

6 Select the second waveform (inverse sawtooth) by clicking on it.

7 Turn the LFO Amount knob up to 3 o'clock. Now you can hear the filter frequency "ramp up" every eight beats. It ramps up in the same shape as the waveform you selected.

8 Now click on the third waveform (sawtooth), and you will hear the filter frequency ramp down in that shape.

9 Finally, change the LFO destination to Osc by clicking on it. Now you can hear the LFO actually change the pitch of the drum loop! (You can try this with the other waveforms too if you like.)

Please note: The reason I wanted you to click the Play button in Step 1 is so that you can hear the LFO properly synced, with the bottom of the filter sweep on the first beat of the eight-bar phrase. If the Play button is not engaged, you will hear the beat playing and the LFO doing something, but the LFO will not be properly synced.

Using the LFO to Control Stereo Panning

The next example is similar, and it is a pretty slick trick. This time, you will use the LFO to modulate the stereo pan of the loop. The effect will be very much like turning your home stereo's balance knob back and forth or turning the pan knob back and forth on a mixing console. Here, it will be very precise and right on the beat.

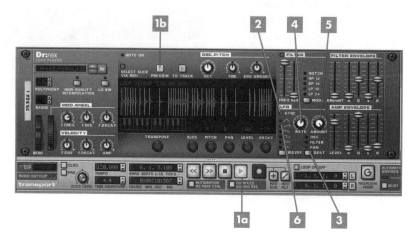

1 Load up a new Reason rack with Mixer 14:2 followed by Dr.Rex underneath. Press Play on the Reason Transport, and then press the Preview button on Dr.Rex to hear the default loop.

2 Turn on the LFO sync button. It will light up red. Since the track is playing, the LFO will sync to the track.

3 Change the LFO destination to Pan.

4 Turn the LFO Rate knob up to 1/4.

5 Turn the LFO Amount knob up all the way.

6 Make sure the first waveform (triangle) is selected. You should hear some extreme, beat-synced stereo panning going on now.

Modifying Individual Slices

In Dr.Rex's Waveform Display, it is possible to modify attributes of each individual slice rather than change one or more of those parameters for the entire loop. The parameters that can be modified for individual slices are Pitch, Pan, Level, and Decay. In the following exercise, you will adjust Pitch and Pan.

1 Load up another Reason rack with Mixer 14:2 followed by Dr.Rex underneath.

2 Open the REX File Browser by clicking the folder icon. Browse to Reason Factory Sound Bank > Dr Rex Instrument Loops > Guitar Loops > Ac Guitar Strum 070 bpm. Select the REX file named AcGt_Slow_Cm_070.rx2. Then click OK in the lower right corner of the REX File Browser.

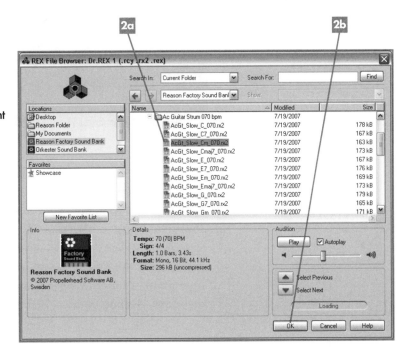

35

❋ ❋ ❋

3 In the Reason Transport, turn the tempo down to 70.

4 Click the Preview button on Dr.Rex to hear the loop.

5 Click on the first slice to select it (although it should already be selected by default).

6 Turn the pitch for this slice down to -1.

7 Turn the Slice Pan knob all the way to the left (value of –64).

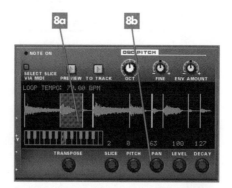

8 Click on the second slice to select it, and turn the Slice Pan knob all the way to the right.

Of course, if one slice in a loop is too loud or too quiet, you can select it and then adjust the Slice Level knob to a comfortable setting. Or if you want to tighten up a drum hit, for example, you can turn down the decay for that slice. By the way, if you want to listen to an individual slice, you can Alt+click on it. A little speaker icon will appear over the slice, and you will hear it play each time you click your mouse. Alternatively, you can trigger each slice with your MIDI keyboard, starting on note C1 and moving up in semitone steps.

Sequencing with Dr.Rex

Sequencing with Dr.Rex is easy and fun. In fact, Dr.Rex does a good bit of the sequencing for you by way of its To Track button. The only way to actually hear your loop play automatically in your song when you press Play on the Reason Transport panel is to copy the REX loop to the corresponding Reason Sequencer track. The easiest way to do this is to click the To Track button located above Dr.Rex's Waveform Display. Then the MIDI notes corresponding to each slice in the REX loop will be pasted on the Sequencer track assigned to Dr.Rex. You will get to try this in the next exercise, and you will see how easy it is.

Sequence a Song in Five Minutes

To introduce you to sequencing with Dr.Rex, I'd like to give you a taste of how Dr.Rex can help you throw down some music for a TV commercial in five minutes or less. Although this exercise has several steps, it is not at all difficult and should very quickly give you an idea of how easy it is to create music using Dr.Rex.

1 Load up a Reason rack with an instance of Mixer 14:2, and then drag in three instances of Dr.Rex, one after the other.

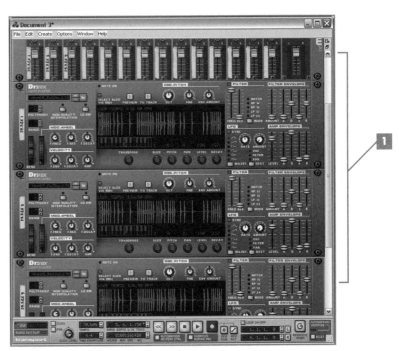

2 Open the REX File Browser of the top Dr.Rex by clicking the folder icon. Browse to Reason Factory Sound Bank > Dr Rex Instrument Loops > Various Hip Hop Loops. Double-click on the first REX file, which is Hhp_Basstarr_093_Chrnc.rx2.

3 Open the REX File Browser of the middle Dr.Rex by clicking the folder icon. Browse to Reason Factory Sound Bank > Dr Rex Drum Loops > Hip Hop. Double-click on the REX file named Hhp18_Furios_093_Chronic.rx2.

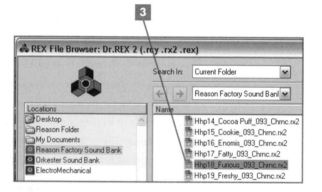

4 Open the REX File Browser of the bottom Dr.Rex by clicking the folder icon. Browse to Reason Factory Sound Bank > Dr Rex Instrument Loops > Scratch Loops. Double-click on the REX file named Scratch_Sine1_085_MajicM.rx2. (I am noticing some rather suggestive filenames in these REX file folders!)

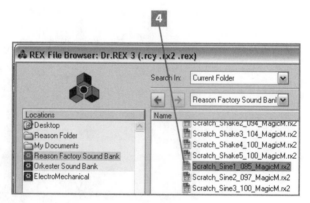

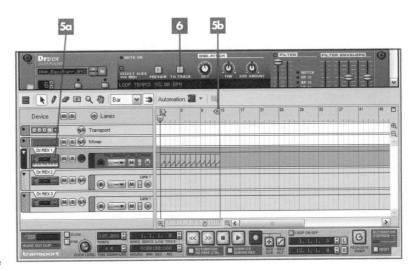

5 Select the Dr.REX 1 track in Reason Sequencer by clicking on it once (you can click on the little picture of Dr.Rex). Leave your left locator at bar 1 and drag your right locator to bar 13.

6 On the top Dr.Rex, click on the To Track button. The MIDI notes controlling each slice of the loop will be pasted on the Sequencer track, spanning the bars between the left and right locators.

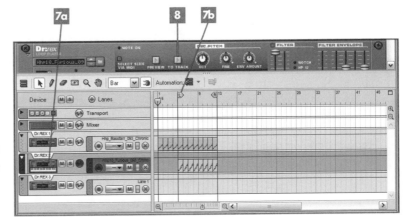

7 Select the Dr.REX 2 track in Reason Sequencer by clicking on it once. Drag your left locator to bar 5 and leave the right locator at bar 13.

8 On the middle Dr.Rex, click on the To Track button. Again, the MIDI notes corresponding to each slice in the loop will be pasted on the Sequencer track, spanning the distance between the left and right locators.

9 Select the Dr.REX 3 track in Reason Sequencer by clicking on it once. Drag the left locator to bar 9 and leave the right locator at bar 13.

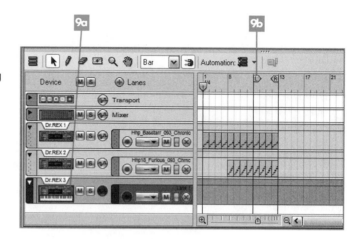

10 On the bottom (third) Dr.Rex, turn the Amp Envelope Level slider down to 70, and then click on the To Track button.

11 On the Reason Sequencer, turn Tempo down to 105.

12 Drag the left locator to bar 1. Press the Play button on the Reason Transport and listen to what you've got.

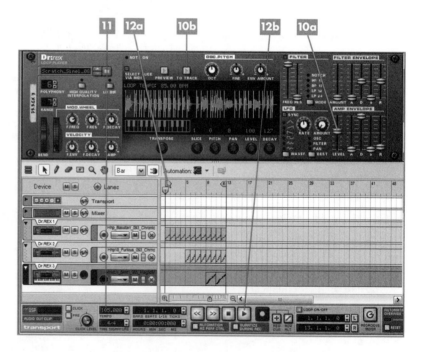

Dr.Rex can really make music production a modular process, plugging in a guitar part here and a bass part there, quickly culminating in a complete song. Your Reason Factory Sound Bank includes plenty of acoustic, electric, and wah-wah guitar REX loops, as well as keyboard parts and tons of drumbeats.

Look at the little song you just made in the previous exercise. Notice that at the top of each Dr.Rex Waveform Display, the original Loop Tempo of the REX File is listed in beats per minute (bpm). The first two loops have original Loop Tempos of 93 bpm, while the third has an original Loop Tempo of 85 bpm. Yet they are all playing back in perfect sync with each other at your specified Song Tempo of 105 bpm! See how easy this is? You can grab musical puzzle pieces out of the REX Loops box, and Dr.Rex makes them fit! And if you find that the rhythmic content fits perfectly, but some of the loops are in the wrong key, you can easily fix that by adjusting the pitch of the overall loop or of an individual slice that may be causing a harmonic clash.

❄ **AN IMPORTANT NOTE ABOUT THE TO TRACK BUTTON**

Anyone reading this who has experience using previous versions of Reason probably knows that in those older versions, if you used the To Track button in Dr.Rex while you had the wrong track selected in the sequencer (a Malström track, for example), you would receive a warning that you were about to "create data on a track that plays another device than the one selected." You could then slap yourself on the forehead (if necessary), click Cancel, and select the appropriate Dr.Rex track in the sequencer before clicking To Track again. That warning is no more! Apparently, a sufficient number of users were annoyed by the warning to cause Propellerhead to remove it. The training wheels are off! Unfortunately, I was one of the people who really needed that warning, and I copy data to the wrong track in Reason 4 daily. No big deal, though! Just select the data and drag and drop it onto the correct track, or choose Undo from the Edit menu and try again.

Transposing Loops

As you saw in the previous exercise, it is easy to put together several different Dr.Rex instrument loops to make a song. Obviously, if you put together several different loops (guitar, keyboard, and bass, for example), you may end up in a situation where one or more of the loops are not in the correct key. This is very easy to fix.

1 Load up another Reason rack with Mixer 14:2 followed by Dr.Rex underneath. Then drag one more Dr.Rex into your rack beneath the first one.

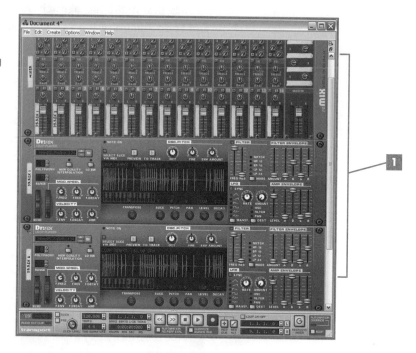

2 In the top Dr.Rex, click the Browse Loop button and browse to Reason Factory Sound Bank > Dr Rex Instrument Loops > Various Hip Hop Loops. Double-click on the first REX file, which is Hhp_Basstarr_093_Chrnc.rx2. It's the same bass loop we used before.

3 In the Reason Transport, turn Tempo down to 100.

4 In the second Dr.Rex, load the following loop: Reason Factory Sound Bank > Dr Rex Instrument Loops > Guitar Loops > WahWah 085 bpm > Gt_Wah_A7_02_085.rx2.

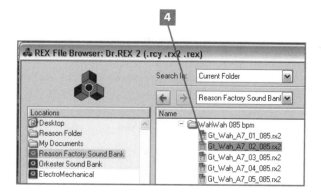

5 Click the Preview buttons on both instances of Dr.Rex. You will hear that the loops are playing in time, but they are not in tune with each other.

6 Turn the bottom Dr.Rex's Transpose knob up to a value of 4, or for the same effect, click on E above middle C on the keyboard display below the Dr.Rex Waveform Display. That sounds better, doesn't it?

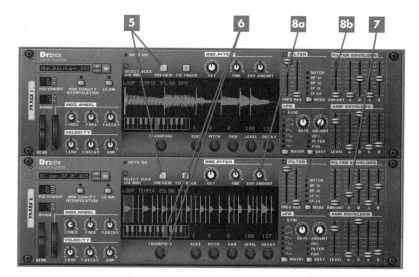

7 As a crazy (but admittedly unrelated) bonus trick, turn the bottom Dr.Rex's Filter Envelope Attack slider up to 32.

8 Now turn the bottom Dr.Rex's Oscillator Envelope Amount knob up to a value of 22 (a bit past 1 o'clock). Sounds like someone is scratching the wah-wah part. The Filter Envelope is controlling the pitch of the loop! (Hint: If you set the Filter Type for Notch instead of LP 12, it sounds even more like scratching a record.)

Just the Slices You Want

Now you are about to get a taste of how editable and customizable these REX loops can be. In the next exercise, you will send a REX loop to a Sequencer track, cut out the slices you don't want, and leave the ones you do want.

1. Load up another Reason rack with Mixer 14:2 followed by Dr.Rex underneath.

2. Click on Dr.Rex's Browse Loop button and load the following drum loop: Reason Factory Sound Bank > Dr Rex Drum Loops > Abstract HipHop > Trh04_Vintage_100_eLAB.rx2.

3. Click Dr.Rex's To Track button to send the MIDI data to the sequencer.

4. You should see the loop copied four times between bars 1 through 9 in the Reason Sequencer. Double-click on the fourth group to edit it.

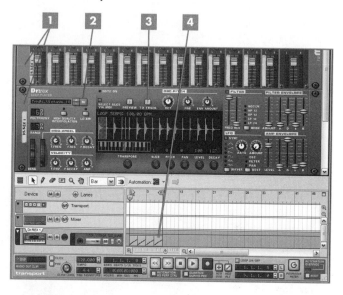

5. What you see now is the REX Lane Editor and Velocity Lane Editor. Grab the top of the sequencer and drag it upward until you can see all 17 slices of the REX loop. If you have two LCD monitors, you may wish to detach the sequencer so that you can see it on your second monitor.

6. Select the Erase tool (click on it once).

7 Drag the horizontal scrollbar at the bottom of the sequencer so that the highlighted slices (the ones you are editing) are right up against the numbered slice list so that it is easier on your eyes and brain.

8 Move your mouse to the bottom of the slice list. Click and hold the mouse as you drag upward slowly through the slice list. Your cursor will turn into a little speaker icon, and you will hear each slice.

9 Locate each cymbal slice (those that contain no drum sound but cymbal). Each time you find a cymbal slice, erase it with the Erase tool. Either you can click directly on a slice (with the lower left edge of the Erase tool) or, if you have trouble with that, you can click and drag around or through the slice, and when you let go of the mouse button, the slice will disappear.

10 Once you have removed the cymbal slices (slice numbers 4, 5, 6, 9, 13, 14, and 17), click the Edit/Arrange View button to return to the Arrange view. Then press Play. When the fourth copy of the REX loop plays, you will hear everything but the cymbals!

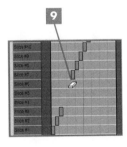

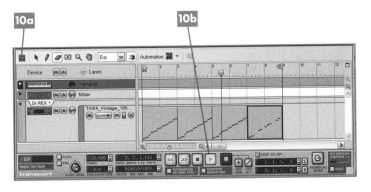

Of course, you can move those notes anywhere you want, in any order, as long as they are within the active range of notes in the loop. In this way you could totally change the rhythm if you want to. By the way, I used the zoom buttons so that you could see more detail in the Arrange view in that last screenshot.

Shortening Note Lengths

You already know how to turn down the Amp Envelope Decay (or individual slice decay) to make a note or drumbeat shorter and tighter. However, if you use the controls in Dr.Rex, then that entire track will have those changes applied throughout. But what if you want only one short section of a Dr.Rex track to have shorter notes? A good way to do this is to shorten the MIDI note lengths in the sequencer.

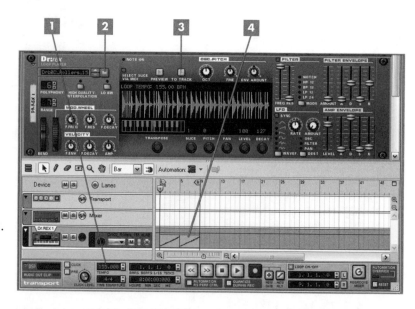

1 In a fresh Reason rack with Mixer 14:2 followed by Dr.Rex underneath, raise the tempo on the Reason Transport to 155 bpm.

2 Load the following loop into Dr.Rex: Reason Factory Sound Bank > Dr Rex Drum Loops > Drum N Bass > Drb02_Rollers_155_eLab.rx2.

3 Click on Dr.Rex's To Track button.

4 Double-click on the second group of MIDI data on Dr.Rex's Sequencer track. The REX lane and Velocity lane will become visible.

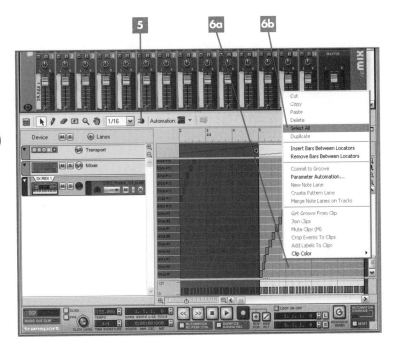

5 Click on the Snap to Grid button so that it is deactivated (not outlined).

6 Right-click in the highlighted area (the area you are editing) of the REX lane and choose Select All from the context menu.

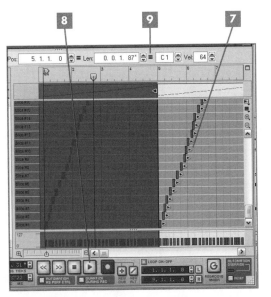

7 Mouse over the right edge of any note (over the black arrow). Your cursor will turn into a double-ended arrow. Click and drag all the way to the left. It will be a short distance, but it will make all the notes a little shorter.

8 Press Play on the Reason Transport and watch the song position marker. The first group of notes in the sequencer will sound normal, and the second group will sound shorter and choppier. Kinda cool, right?

9 If you want to make the notes even shorter, turn off the Match Values button (looks like an equals symbol) between the Note Length and Note Value menus and then move on to Step 10.

10 Turn Note Length down to 0.0.0.80 by clicking and dragging down on the rightmost group of numbers in the Note Length window or by double-clicking in the Note Length window and typing the value in manually. Of course, you can even go shorter than that if you want, but at some point the loop will lose its punch if you go too short.

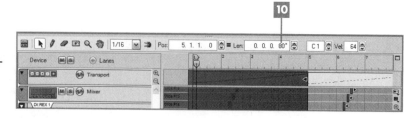

Automating a Filter Sweep in the Sequencer

At the beginning of this chapter, you moved the Filter Frequency slider up and down slowly while a drum loop played. Reason allows you to record this action into the sequencer (or draw it into the sequencer). In fact, you can record adjustments of almost any Dr.Rex parameter into the sequencer. Here's how:

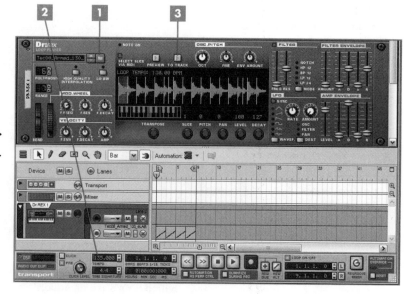

1 In a fresh Reason rack with Mixer 14:2 followed by Dr.Rex underneath, load the following loop into Dr.Rex: Reason Factory Sound Bank > Dr Rex Drum Loops > Techno > Tec08_Armed_130_eLAB.rx2.

2 Turn the tempo up to 135 in the Reason Transport panel.

3 Click the To Track button on Dr.Rex.

4 Click the New Dub button in the Reason Transport panel.

5 Turn the Filter Resonance slider up halfway.

6 Turn the Filter Freq slider all the way down.

7 Make sure Loop is off.

8 Click the Precount button (labeled Pre) on the Reason Transport panel to give yourself four beats to get set before recording commences!

9 Press Record and immediately do Step 10.

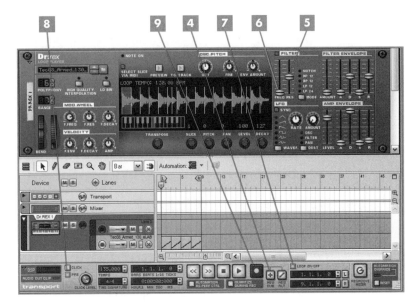

10 Very slowly ease the Filter Freq slider upward so that it is all the way up by the end of bar 8.

11 Press Stop twice to stop recording and to return the song position marker to the beginning of the loop. Then press Play and listen to what you've got.

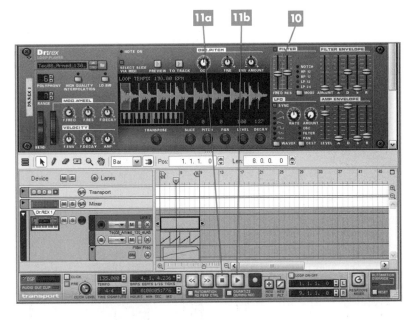

As you play this loop, notice the green outline around the Filter Frequency slider indicating that you have automated that parameter. Also notice that there is a new lane in the sequencer labeled Filter Freq. The next little exercise picks up where the previous exercise left off. You are about to smooth out your filter sweep.

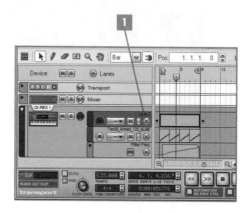

1 Click the Delete Note lane (X marks the spot) on Lane 2. Ignore the warning message (click Continue). We didn't really need that lane. I just used the New Dub feature to keep things as clean and organized as possible.

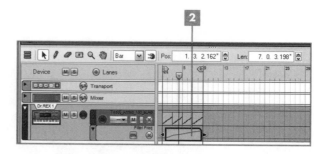

2 Double-click on the grouped information in the Filter Freq lane.

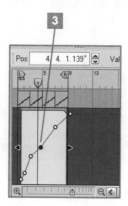

3 Notice all the little dots charting your not-completely-smooth filter sweep! (Mine wasn't perfect either!) One by one, click on each dot and then press Delete on your computer keyboard, leaving only the start and end points.

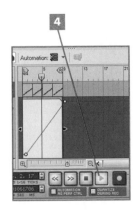

4 Look at your perfect linear filter sweep. If you are not already playing the loop, press the Play button and hear the precise filter sweep you have created.

Here is yet a third way to make this sweep. Again, the next little exercise picks up where the previous exercise left off.

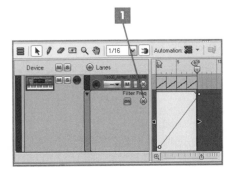

1 Click the Delete Automation Lane button on the Filter Freq Automation lane. Click Continue when the warning message pops up.

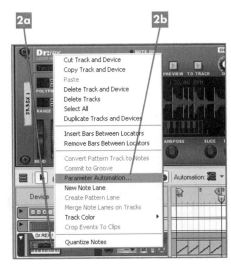

2 Right-click on the Dr.Rex icon in the sequencer and select Parameter Automation from the context menu.

3 Click in the Filter Freq checkbox and click OK.

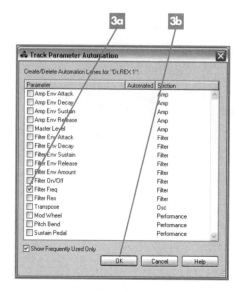

4 Select the Pencil tool.

5 Click and drag the Pencil tool so that you create a group spanning bars 1 through 8 in your new Filter Freq Automation lane.

6 Select the Selection tool.

7 Double-click the new group you created.

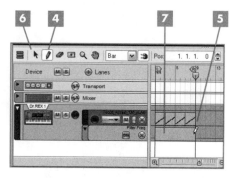

8 Select the Pencil tool again and draw a diagonal line upwards from left to right in the Filter Freq Automation lane.

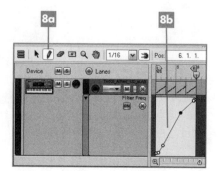

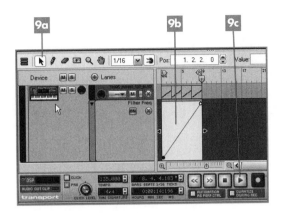

9. Select the Selection tool, and again click on and delete the dots one by one so that you are left with only the end points and a perfect diagonal line. Then press Play.

OK, I'm sure some of you DJs and electronic music producers out there are probably pretty smooth on your manual filter sweeps, but these are great techniques for creating any gradual change in filter frequency, volume, or other parameter over any period of time you wish.

Yes, Dr.Rex Does Respond to Velocity

When most people hear the word "velocity," they think about how fast an object is moving. But when someone playing a MIDI key-board or drum pad thinks about velocity, he thinks about how hard a note is struck. It makes sense because the faster your hand moves toward the key or pad, the harder contact you will make. That velocity information is recorded along with the rest of the MIDI information, including which note was played and for how long.

A little earlier, you learned how to use the Level knob under Dr.Rex's Waveform Display to adjust the volume of a single slice. As a useful alternative, the following exercise will show you how to use velocity to control the volume of REX slices.

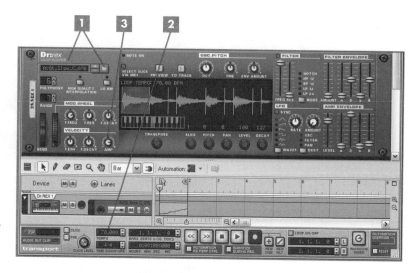

1 In a fresh Reason rack with Mixer 14:2 followed by Dr.Rex underneath, load the following loop into Dr.Rex: Reason Factory Sound Bank > Dr Rex Instrument Loops > Guitar Loops > Ac Guitar Strum 070 bpm > AcGt_Slow_C_070.rx2.

2 In the Reason Transport panel, slow down the tempo to 70 bpm, but don't play the loop.

3 Play your MIDI keyboard between notes C1 and E1 (the first few notes of the loop). Notice that however hard or soft you play, you hear the notes at the same volume. Now, in the Velocity section of Dr.Rex, turn the Amp knob halfway to the right. If you play your keyboard some more, you will notice that the notes are louder or quieter, depending on how hard or softly you play.

4 Click on the Horizontal Zoom In button until eight bars take up the whole sequencer window. You'll have to drag the horizontal scrollbar to the left so you can see the left and right locators.

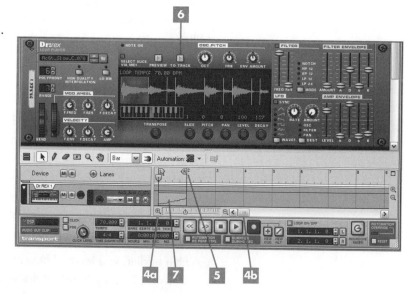

5 Move the right locator to bar 2.

6 Click Dr.Rex's To Track button.

7 Double-click on the grouped MIDI information on the Dr.Rex Sequencer track.

8 Now you are in Edit mode. Click on the Horizontal Zoom In button until the note and velocity info takes up the whole sequencer window. You'll have to drag the horizontal scrollbar to the left so you can see the left and right locators.

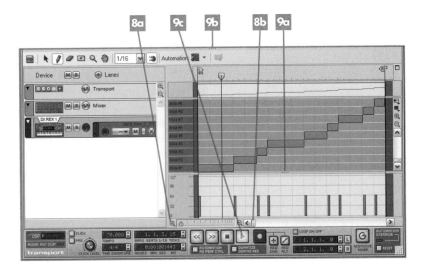

9 Drag up the top of the Velocity lane so you can see more detail, and drag up the top of the sequencer window so you can see all nine REX slices. Then press Play. The loop sounds a little quiet because Dr.Rex is now sensitive to velocity, and by default these notes are all at half-volume (64 on a scale of 0 to 127).

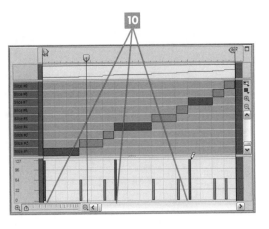

10 Use the Pencil tool to raise the velocity of slices 1, 4, and 7 all the way to the top while the loop plays. Hear the difference?

Now you can see how easy it is to use velocity with Dr.Rex!

❄ **ANOTHER NOTE ABOUT TO TRACK**

It is important to note that once you have copied your REX loop data to a
Sequencer track using Dr.Rex's To Track button, if you subsequently load a
different loop into the same Dr.Rex, it will not play back properly with your
sequence because the information copied to your Sequencer track applied
only to the loop loaded at the time you clicked To Track, but it will not match
perfectly with the newly loaded loop. You may come up with some happy
accidents this way, however. Of course, all you have to do to make things
right is to delete the data from the sequencer and then click To Track again
after you've loaded the new loop into Dr.Rex.

Dr.Rex, Meet Effects!

Throughout this book, you will be introduced to one or more effects
at the end of almost every chapter so that by the end of the book
you will be using the Reason effects like a pro! The effect *du jour*
(for this chapter) is the Scream 4 Sound Destruction Unit. Let's
check it out.

1 In a new Reason rack with
Mixer 14:2 followed by
Dr.Rex underneath, load the
following loop into Dr.Rex:
Reason Factory Sound Bank >
Dr Rex Drum Loops > Acoustic
> Hip Hop > Ahp02_Live_
078_Chronic.rx2.

2 Set the tempo in the Reason
Transport to 95 bpm.

3 Click the Preview button on
Dr.Rex to hear the loop.

4 Drag Scream 4 Distortion from the Devices Tool window and drop it
directly under Dr.Rex. You should immediately hear the effect of the
Scream 4 default patch (called EasyFuzz).

5 Use the (unlabeled) Damage Type knob-style selector switch to try each distortion type. Notice that Tape isn't as ugly as the rest and makes the drums sound huge. The Scream selection at the bottom sounds especially interesting, and the Digital choice directly above it shreds the sound all to hell!

6 Experiment with the P1 and P2 knobs (P stands for *parameter*). They will have a different effect depending on which Damage (distortion) type you have chosen.

7 You can also experiment with the Damage Control knob, which controls the amount of Damage.

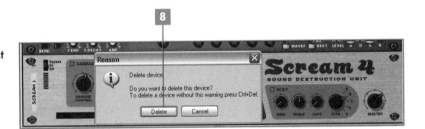

8 Now, click on Scream to select it, and then press the Delete key on your computer keyboard. Reason will ask you if you really want to delete the device, and you will say yes by clicking Delete on the Warning menu.

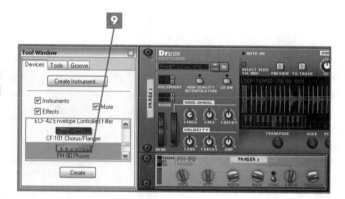

9 Drag PH-90 Phaser from the Device Tool window and drop it directly under Dr.Rex. Wow! That's a different effect!

I know we were talking about Scream 4, but I thought it would be nice to invite a surprise visitor! I wanted to introduce you to the PH-90 Phaser, and that seemed like an easy place to drop it in. Phaser (or phase shifter) sounds great on drums and also works very well for guitar or electric piano.

The effects we just added were added as *insert effects*, which means we added them directly between the sound source (Dr.Rex) and the mixer. Insert effects are usually used when you want the entire sound to be processed, with no dry (unprocessed) signal coming through. Compressors and limiters, for example, are always used as insert effects. Later on, you will learn about *send effects*, which are used when you want to vary the mix of wet (processed) and dry (unprocessed) signal (such as when you want to add just a little bit of reverb to a vocal).

If you made it through all those exercises, you should be pretty much ready to rock with Dr.Rex. Now it's time to check out the other major player in Reason's beat factory: Redrum!

3 } Redrum

In Chapter 2, you learned about using Dr.Rex to add pre-existing drum loops and musical grooves to your music. Now you are about to learn how to make your own beats from scratch with Redrum!

Redrum has a familiar look reminiscent of classic drum machines such as the Roland TR808 or 909. Like those classic drum machines, Redrum offers Step programming with a row of 16 Step buttons. Unlike those old drum machines, Redrum is infinitely flexible, allowing you to load as many different sounds as there are Wave and AIFF files in the world (well, not all at the same time). You can mix and match samples to create your own drum kits, which you can then save as Redrum patches. You can instantly create fully random drum patterns that can serve as starting points for your creative process. Once you get into Redrum, you will find it is easy to use and an essential tool for producing electronic music with Reason.

In this chapter you will learn how to:

❋ Program your own beats using Redrum's internal pattern-based sequencer

❋ Automate pattern changes so that all the drum patterns you use in a song will automatically start at the correct time as your song plays

❋ Use the Reason Sequencer to control Redrum

❋ Customize your Redrum drum kits by swapping out individual samples and by adjusting various parameters on each drum channel

❄ **PLEASE SAVE YOUR WORK**

The exercises in this chapter will build on each other. The beat you make in the first exercise will be used again in the next exercise, and so on. Although having to start over can be great practice, it can also be frustrating if it wasn't on purpose, so to avoid losing your work, please save as you go. Once you complete the first exercise, please click File > Save As and name the Reason Song Redrum_Ignite. Then, as you do more exercises that build on this beat during the chapter, you can save as Redrum_Ignite_2, Redrum_Ignite_3, etc.

Making Beats with Redrum's Pattern Section

Although Redrum can be played with a MIDI controller or the Reason Sequencer just like any of the other Reason instruments, part of the real fun of Redrum is using it like a classic drum machine, and that means creating beats using Redrum's built-in pattern-based programmer. When creating patterns this way, each Step in the pattern is represented by one of Redrum's 16 Step buttons.

Programming Your First Redrum Pattern

This exercise will demonstrate how easy it is to program a beat inside of Redrum. Let's try it!

1 In an empty Reason rack, drag in a Mixer 14:2 and an instance of Redrum underneath. Then click on Redrum's Patch Browser button and select Reason Factory Sound Bank > Redrum Drum Kits > RnB Kits > RnB Kit 02.drp.

2 Turn the Tempo down to 80 in the Reason Transport panel.

3 Click the Select button on Channel 8 of Redrum. As you can see by looking at the top of the channel, a hi-hat cymbal sample is loaded into this channel (the name displayed in the sample display window is Hh_Sexy.wav).

4 Click on Step buttons 1, 3, 5, 7, 9, 11, 13, and 15. This will create an eighth-note hi-hat pattern, since every other sixteenth-note is played.

5 Click Run to hear what you are doing. If you count your hi-hat pattern out loud, it will sound like "1 and 2 and 3 and 4 and... ."

6 Click the Select button on Channel 2 of Redrum so that you can create a snare drum part. Then click Step button 5 and Step button 13. This actually puts a snare drum on beats 2 and 4 of your drum pattern.

7 Now let's add the bass drum (or kick drum). Click the Select button on Channel 1 of Redrum, and then click Step buttons 1, 8, 9, and 16.

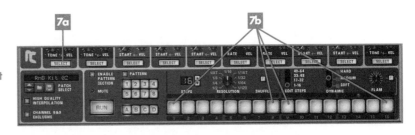

If your beat sounds right, please click File > Save As and name the Reason Song Redrum_Ignite. We'll be using this beat later. In fact, if you are moving on to the next exercise right now, just leave it open, please!

Shuffle

Adding Shuffle gives your rhythms a "swing" feel. The specific way this works is that when Shuffle is activated, all sixteenth notes that fall between eighth notes are delayed to a degree determined by the Global Shuffle Amount knob on the far left of the ReGroove Mixer. A couple of famous (older) examples of shuffles used in popular music are "Rosanna" by Toto and "Fool in the Rain" by Led Zeppelin. By the end of this short, easy exercise, it will be very clear how Shuffle can be used in a hip-hop groove.

1 Open the Redrum_Ignite song you saved in the last exercise, or if you still have the last exercise open, just pick up where you left off. Click Run so you can hear your beat.

2 Click the Shuffle button. You now should be hearing a little bit of shuffle applied to the bass drum.

3 In the Reason Transport panel, click the ReGroove Mixer button. The ReGroove Mixer should open up.

4 Slowly turn up the Global Shuffle Amount knob all the way, and you will hear Steps 9, 12, and 16 of the bass drum pattern played later and later. Then turn the knob back to about 3 o'clock (70%), which I think is a good amount of shuffle for this beat.

Steps 9, 12, and 16 of the bass drum pattern are sixteenth notes that fall between eighth notes. This is easy to see if you click on the Select button on Redrum's Channel 1. Those three notes are being played a little later now than they were before they got shuffled. Go ahead and click File > Save if you want to have this beat shuffled next time you open the song.

The full name for the Shuffle button is Pattern Shuffle. This is because it will apply shuffle only to patterns being played back in Redrum's Pattern section. It will not affect any MIDI information already in the sequencer (such as if you have used Copy Pattern to Track or otherwise recorded something in the sequencer that is playing through Redrum). If you do use Copy Pattern to Track to copy a Redrum pattern to the Reason Sequencer while the Shuffle button is engaged, the information copied to the sequencer will be "shuffled." So when you look at the MIDI notes in the sequencer in Edit mode, you will see that any sixteenth notes that fall between eighth notes are delayed to a degree determined by the Global Shuffle Amount knob. Also, be aware that ReGroove's Global Shuffle knob only affects Redrum's Pattern section. It does not "shuffle" anything in the Reason Sequencer, even if the track in the sequencer is playing Redrum.

Auditioning Redrum Patches (Drum Kits)

The next short exercise will show you a nice way to find the perfect drum kit for your beat.

1. Open the Redrum_Ignite song you saved in the last exercise and click Run so you can hear the beat.

2. Click Redrum's Browse Patch button.

3 Click on various drum kits in any folder you like within Factory Sound Bank > Redrum Drum Kits. Some of the kits may take a few seconds to load, but once a kit is loaded, you will automatically hear it playing the current pattern.

4 If you agree that I have already selected the perfect pattern for this beat (ha ha!) then click Cancel, and no changes will be made.

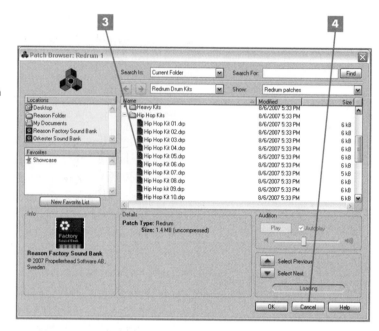

Loading Individual Samples on a Channel

What if you like the sound of your kit, except that one drum is not quite right? Redrum has got you covered. Samples can be loaded on individual Redrum channels by clicking the Browse Sample button with the folder icon on it.

1 With your Redrum Ignite song still open, click the Trigger Drum button on the top of Channel 3. You will hear some sort of weird snare drum (which almost sounds like a hand clap to me!).

2 Click the up/down arrows to the left of the Browse Sample button on Channel 3 to scroll up and down through samples in the current folder. Each time you click the up or down arrow, click the Trigger Drum button to hear the new sample.

3a To see all the available samples currently loaded into memory, click in the Sample Display window.

3b Notice the Open Browser selection at the top of the context menu that appears. It has the same function as clicking the Browse Sample button. Click on any drum sample in the list to select it.

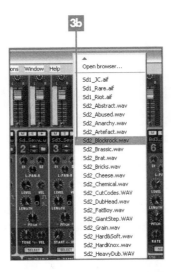

4 Click Channel 3's Browse Sample button. From here you can select any sample from any of your Reason ReFills (or from anywhere in your hard drive, for that matter).

Adding Dynamics to Your Patterns

See that little Dynamics switch on the bottom right of Redrum? By default (that is, when a new Redrum is first dragged into the Reason rack), that switch is set to its Medium position. So every Step button you click on plays its sound at medium volume and lights up amber. If you had it in the Soft position and clicked a Step button, it would light up yellow and play a little softer. In the next exercise, you'll see some pads light up rosy red (or is it pink?) as we make those drum hits loud!

1. Open the Redrum_Ignite song you saved in the last exercise, and click Run so you can hear the beat.

2. Click the Select button on Redrum Channel 2 so that you can edit the snare drum.

3. Move the Dynamics switch into the Hard position.

4. Click once on Steps 5 and 13. The Step buttons should change color from amber to red, and you will hear the snare drum get louder.

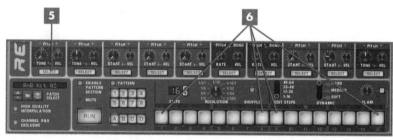

5. Click the Select button on Channel 1 so that you can edit the bass drum.

6. Click once on Steps 1, 8, 9, and 16. Now the bass drum is louder.

You can go ahead and save again when you are done with this. Of course, you could have made any of these Steps softer by moving the Dynamics switch to the Soft position and then clicking on the Step buttons. If you accidentally clicked an extra time on any of the Step buttons, you probably saw the light go off altogether. You activate as well as deactivate the Step buttons by clicking on them.

Stringing Patterns Together

You've been working with this pattern for a while, and if you're like me, you might be thinking it could use a little something extra. In the next exercise, you will make a new pattern that complements this pattern.

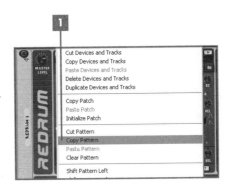

1 Open the Redrum_Ignite song you saved in the last exercise. Right-click anywhere on Redrum, and select Copy Pattern from the menu that pops up. This copies the pattern to the Clipboard, just like copying something to the Clipboard in Microsoft Word, Adobe Photoshop, or any other similar program.

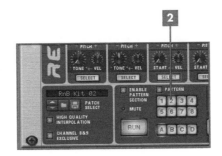

2 Click on the number 2 Pattern Select button. This is an empty pattern.

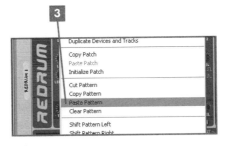

3 Right-click anywhere on Redrum and choose Paste Pattern from the context menu. The pattern that had already been saved as pattern number 1 is copied to pattern number 2 as well.

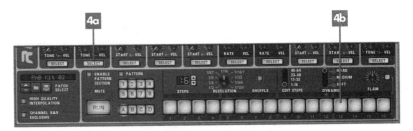

4 Click the Select button on Channel 2 so that you can edit the snare drum. Then click once on Step button 13 to deactivate that Step.

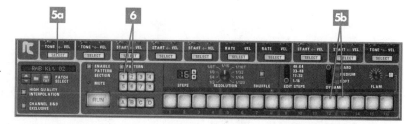

5 Click the Select button on Channel 1 to edit the bass drum. Then click on Step buttons 12 and 13.

6 Click on the number 1 Pattern Select button. Then click Run, and as soon as the beat starts, click Pattern Select button number 2. As soon as that pattern starts, click on Pattern 1 again, and so on.

If you get the timing right, you should hear each pattern once before it switches to the other pattern, and the beat should make sense. Go ahead and save the song.

If you had clicked Record on the Reason Transport during the last exercise, you could have recorded yourself making those pattern changes. Then when you played back the sequence, the pattern changes would happen automatically just as you recorded them. Personally, I get confused switching those patterns manually while the track plays, and I usually mess it up. So next I'm going to show you a much easier way to make the patterns switch back and forth in perfect time.

Automating Pattern Changes

Before you start the next exercise, I want to mention that even though you see only eight Pattern Select buttons, below those Pattern Select buttons are four Bank Select buttons (A, B, C, and D). So you actually have eight patterns for Bank A, eight patterns for Bank B, and so on, for a total of 32 patterns in just one instance of Redrum. In the next exercise, we will continue to stick with Bank A, since we are still dealing with only two patterns and do not really need any other banks.

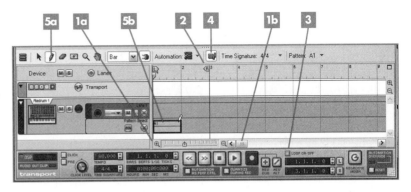

1. Open the Redrum_Ignite song you saved in the last exercise. Then, in the Reason Sequencer, click the Horizontal Zoom-In button a few times until you have a nice big display. Drag the horizontal scrollbar all the way to the left, so you can see bar 1.

2. Drag the right locator over to bar 3.

3. Click the Loop On/Off button to turn looping on (it should light up green).

4. Click the Create Pattern Lane button.

5. Select the Pencil tool. Then click once inside bar 1 in the Pattern Select lane. You have just drawn in Redrum Pattern selection for Bank A, Pattern 1.

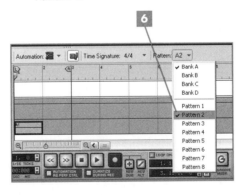

6. Choose Bank A, Pattern 2 from the Pattern Select drop-down menu.

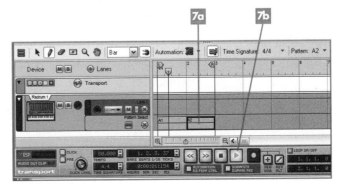

7. With your Pencil tool still selected, click inside of bar 2 in the Pattern Select lane. Redrum should switch to Pattern A2 when the sequencer plays bar 2. Click Play to hear your loop and the automated pattern change.

69
❀ ❀ ❀

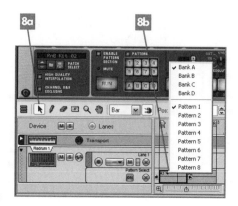

8 Choose your Selection tool (looks like a cursor). Click inside bar 1 in the Pattern Select lane, then click the drop-down arrow next to where it says A1. Notice that you can select any pattern here, the same way you could in the Pattern Select drop-down menu you saw when you had the Pencil tool selected. Don't make any change, though.

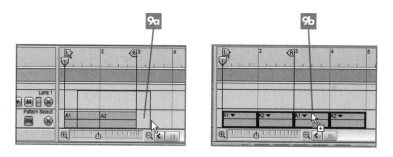

9 Now, just to practice copy/paste in the Reason Sequencer, click and drag your mouse to create a square covering bars 1 and 2 (9a). (Alternatively, you could hold the Shift key while clicking on both bars.) Now that both bars are selected, hold down Ctrl and click on and drag the two bars of information over onto bars 3 and 4 (9b). Don't let go of Ctrl until after you have released the mouse button.

What you did in Step 8 is something you will be doing with all your Sequencer tracks, no matter what instrument they are controlling. As in a Microsoft Word document, you can cut, copy, and paste to save time. Since your songs will usually last more than three minutes (instead of only two bars!), you will do this to extend drum beats and bass lines through your songs. Also, anything that repeats (such as a verse or chorus section) can be copied and pasted throughout the song.

The exercise you just finished is the last one I will ask you to save for this chapter. You will not have to refer back to your Redrum Ignite song from here on out. The other exercises are standalone exercises.

Making Patterns with More than 16 Steps

In the previous exercise, we put together two one-bar patterns to make a two-bar loop. Each pattern had the default 16 Steps and used a resolution of 1/16, so each Step equals a sixteenth note. In the following exercise, you will make a single pattern that lasts two bars (32 Steps at 1/16 resolution).

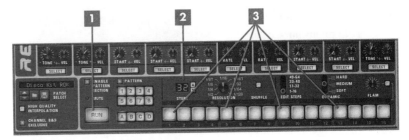

1 Start with an empty rack. Create an instance of the reMix Mixer and then create an instance of Redrum. Click the Run button on Redrum.

2 By default, Disco Kit RDK should be loaded, and the Channel 1 Select button should be lit so that you can edit the bass drum. Turn the pattern length up to 32 Steps (either by using the up/down arrows or by clicking and dragging inside the display window).

3 Click on Step buttons 1, 5, 9, and 13. You will hear the kick drum on those four beats and then silence for the next four beats.

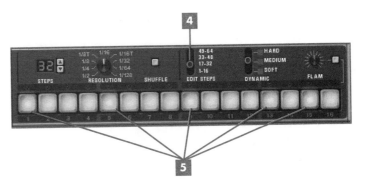

4 Move the Edit Steps switch into the 17–32 position. Previously, you were editing the first group of 16 Steps. Now you will work with the second group of 16 Steps.

5 Click on Step buttons 1, 5, 9, 13, and 15. Now you will hear a four-on-the-floor bass drum pattern with a little pick-up beat at the end of bar 2.

Electro-Fun: Randomize Pattern

Redrum's Randomize Pattern function is truly one of my very favorite parts of working with Redrum. It is so cool we simply must play with it right now!

1 Start with an empty rack. Create an instance of the reMix Mixer 14:2, and then create an instance of Redrum. Turn up the song tempo to 133 in the Reason Transport panel.

2 Open Redrum's Patch Browser and select Reason Factory Sound Bank > Redrum Drum Kits > Electronic Kits > Electronic Kit 6.drp.

3 Turn up the bass drum volume by turning the Channel 1 Level knob up to 86 (about 2 o'clock).

4 Right-click on Redrum (Ctrl+click, Mac) and then select Randomize Pattern from the pop-up menu. Note that Randomize Pattern is also available in the Edit menu.

5 Click Run to hear the pattern.

6 Make sure the Select button on Channel 1 is lit. This is, of course, the bass drum. Then move the Dynamic switch to the Hard position.

7 Click and drag across all 16 Step buttons twice so they are all white (inactive). You should not hear the kick drum any more.

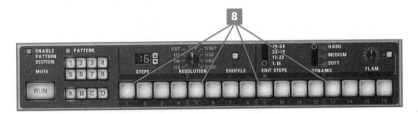

8 Now click on Step buttons 1, 5, 9, and 13 so that you have a four-on-the-floor bass drum pattern.

Now what can make the above exercise extra fun and useful is to select Pattern 2 on Redrum and then repeat Steps 4 through 8. You can easily create a whole bank (eight patterns) of intelligent sounding (but actually random!) patterns this way with a four-on-the-floor bass drum pattern holding it all together. You could also add other elements, such as a steady hi-hat pattern, while leaving the complexity of the random pattern for the rest of the drums in the kit.

The next short exercise picks up where the last exercise left off (so you should already have Redrum in your rack, with a randomized pattern and a four-on-the-floor bass drum pattern).

1 Right-click on Redrum and select Copy Pattern from the context menu.

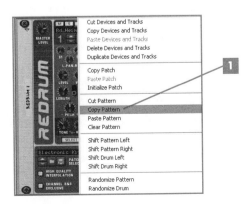

❉ ❉ ❉

2 Select Pattern 2, then right-click on Redrum and select Paste Pattern from the context menu.

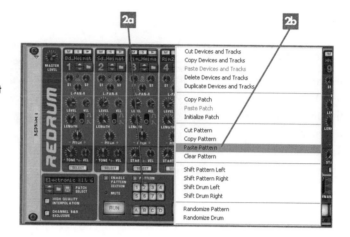

3 With Channel 1 selected (bass drum), click on the number 15 Step Button to create a little pick-up note on the bass drum.

4 Select Pattern 1 and click Run. As Redrum plays, alternate between Pattern 1 and Pattern 2 by using the Pattern Select buttons. You will hear the same rhythm, but without the bass drum pick-up note on Pattern 1, and with the pick-up note on Pattern 2.

Randomize Pattern is a great way to experiment. If you don't like the first random pattern you hear, simply roll the dice again by selecting Randomize Pattern again! It's a great way to stimulate the creative process, and it can result in many happy accidents! And if you want to tweak these random beats in the Reason Sequencer, you can always choose Copy Pattern to Track from Redrum's Edit or context menu, similar to what you did with Dr.Rex (Copy REX Loop to Track). Finally, please note that Randomize Drum is also available from the Edit and context menus. As the name suggests, Randomize Drum merely randomizes the currently selected drum channel, instead of randomizing the whole pattern.

Flam

When you double-strike a drum, this is known as a flam. In Redrum, applying Flam to a step entry will add a second hit to the drum beat very soon after the first hit. The delay between these two hits is determined by the Flam Amount knob. The Flam Amount knob is a global control, which will affect the amount of Flam for all drums in all patterns to which Flam is applied.

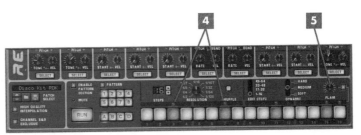

1 In an empty Reason rack, drag in a Mixer 14:2 and an instance of Redrum underneath. Click Run.

2 Click the Select button on Channel 2. Click Step buttons 3 and 7. You will hear two snare hits.

3 Click the Edit Flam button, which will light up red. Then click on Step buttons 11 and 15. You will hear the Flam effect on these two hits and notice that the red LED above these steps is lit constantly to indicate flam.

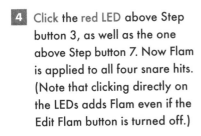

4 Click the red LED above Step button 3, as well as the one above Step button 7. Now Flam is applied to all four snare hits. (Note that clicking directly on the LEDs adds Flam even if the Edit Flam button is turned off.)

5 Now slowly turn the Flam knob all the way to the right to hear the delay between the initial drum hit and the flam hit increase, then slowly turn it all the way to the left to hear the delay decrease.

Flam can be used to accent certain notes and can also be used to create drum rolls (or cymbal rolls). You will also do a little trick with it in the Pattern Resolution exercise that follows.

Pattern Resolution

The length (or note value) of each step is determined by the Pattern Resolution setting. The default is 1/16, meaning that each step is one sixteenth note. You can program different Pattern Resolution settings for each pattern within a single instance of Redrum. Although changing this setting while playing back a pattern will cause the pattern to play back more rapidly or more slowly, it has no effect on the Reason song tempo. You could use lower resolutions such as 1/8 or 1/4 for simple patterns. In the following exercise, you will use a very high resolution to make a snare roll that might be suitable for certain brands of electronic music (though the particular snare sound we will use may not be the hippest for this!).

1. In an empty Reason rack, drag in a Mixer 14:2 and an instance of Redrum underneath. Click Run.

2. Turn the Pattern Length up to 64 steps.

3. Turn the Pattern Resolution up to 1/64.

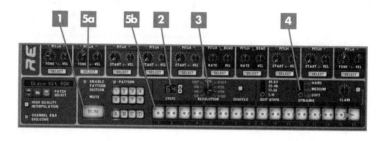

4. Set the Dynamic switch to the Soft position.

5. Click the Channel 2 Select button, and then click and drag across all 16 Steps. They should all be lit up yellow.

6. Move the Edit Steps button to the 17–32 position.

7. Set the Dynamic switch to the Medium position. Then click and drag across all 16 Step buttons to activate them.

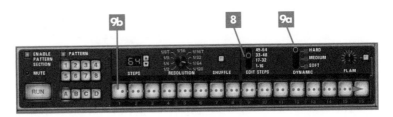

8 Move the Edit Steps button to the 33–48 position.

9 Set the Dynamic switch to the Hard position. Then click and drag across all 16 Step buttons to activate them.

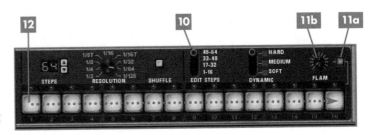

10 Move the Edit Steps button to the 49–64 position.

11 Click the Edit Flam button and turn Flam almost all the way to the left, to a value of 6 or so.

12 Click and drag across all 16 Step buttons to activate them.

Of course, unless you are some kind of deviant, you probably wouldn't want to let this pattern loop over and over. Rather, it would be a one-bar roll that you could throw in once leading into another pattern. And as I have stated, that other pattern could be of any resolution you want.

✳ RUN / ENABLE PATTERN SECTION / PATTERN ENABLE

The Run button is used to start and stop playback of Redrum's Pattern section. When the Enable Pattern Section button is engaged, the Run button will automatically engage whenever you press Play on the Reason Transport panel. You can also click the Run button at any time, whether your Reason song is playing or not. In either case, when Run is engaged, you will see the Step lights move from left to right. If the sounds in Redrum are going to be triggered by note info from the Reason Sequencer, a MIDI controller, or a CV device (instead of using the Pattern section), then you will want to turn off Enable Pattern Section. If Enable Pattern Section is turned off, clicking the Run button will have no effect.

In order to actually hear any patterns you have created, you must also engage the Pattern Enable button. This button (merely labeled Pattern) mutes and unmutes pattern playback starting on the next downbeat according to the time signature selected in the Reason Transport panel. This is a useful feature when you have more than one Redrum in your rack and wish to bring them in and out of the mix alternately.

Using the Reason Sequencer with Redrum

We have already used the Pattern Lane in the Reason Sequencer to control pattern changes. What we have not done yet is to turn off Redrum's Pattern section entirely and sequence purely in the Reason Sequencer. I think a big part of the fun of Redrum is using its built-in pattern-based sequencer, but playing on pads (like an Akai MPC or an M-Audio Trigger Finger or Axiom) or playing on a MIDI keyboard comes quite naturally to many people, and Redrum can do that as well. Also, with the Reason Sequencer, you can draw in your notes in Drum Edit Mode with the Pencil tool, which is another variety of workflow that you may find comfortable. In the following exercise, I am using a MIDI keyboard, but if you are advanced enough to have set up some trigger pads instead and it's all working for you, then that's great, too!

1 In an empty Reason rack, drag in a Mixer 14:2 and an instance of Redrum underneath. Click the Enable Pattern Section switch to turn it off. Now Redrum will not start its pattern section when you click Play on the Reason Transport.

2 In the Reason Sequencer, click the Edit/Arrange Mode selector button to change to Edit Mode. You will see the Drum Editor. Drag the Horizontal Zoom control almost all the way to the left, and then drag the horizontal scrollbar all the way to the left so that bar one fills up almost the entire window.

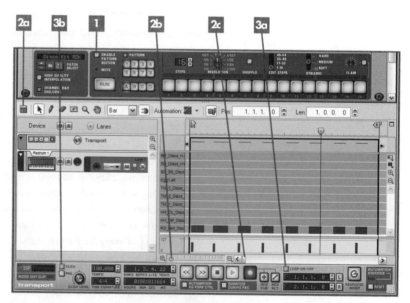

3 Turn looping on by clicking the Loop On/off button, and then make sure the Click button is on (lit green).

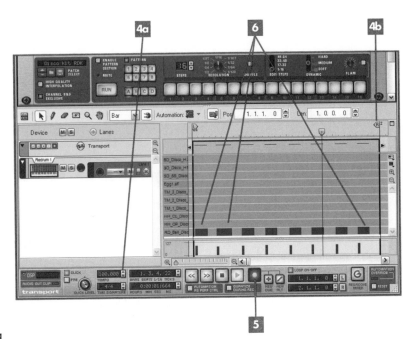

4 Turn Tempo down to 100 (so you won't feel rushed!). Then hold down the Alt key while you click on the bar 2 marker. This will set the right locator at bar 2.

5 Find and play the key C1 on your MIDI keyboard. You should hear the bass drum when you play it. Now move on up to key A1. This is a ride cymbal, and it's what you are going to record first. Click the Record button on the Reason Transport and listen to the groove of the click. It is playing quarter notes (1-2-3-4).

6 When you are ready, record an eighth note pattern with your ride cymbal (play 1 and 2 and 3 and 4) with your A1 key, twice as fast as the click.

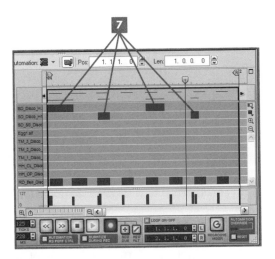

7 Once you have your ride cymbal recorded, record kick (C1) on beats one and three and record snare (C#1) on beats 2 and 4. As the click goes 1-2-3-4, you will play kick-snare-kick-snare. Your loop is only four beats long, so you will have just two kicks, snares, and eight ride cymbal hits when you are done.

8 Click Record again to stop recording, but play will continue. Double-click in the middle of your drum sequence so you can edit (your notes will turn from gray to red). Then click Ctrl+A to Select All (or choose Select All from the Edit menu). The notes in the sequencer will get darker, and black note-length adjustment arrows will appear to the right of each note.

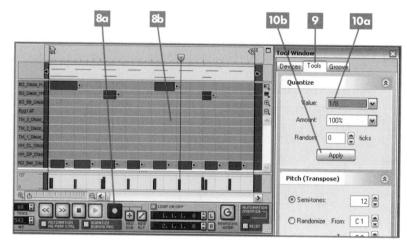

9 In your Tool window (F8 shows or hides the Tool window), click the Tools tab if it's not already highlighted.

10 Set the Quantize value to 1/8 (since that's the smallest time value you played). Quantize Amount should be set to 100% by default. Click Apply, and you will notice that all your beats are right on the money!

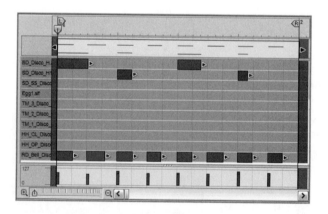

After quantizing, the start point of all the notes lines up perfectly on the grid. The timing is dead-on now!

So now you have a taste of the magic of quantize. If you wanted the beat to sound not quite so robotic, you could have set the Quantize Amount to 80% (or something like that—you can experiment) so that your notes are moved closer to the beat, but not perfectly right-on.

Now you may be saying to yourself, "He said my beats would be right on the money, but a few of them are totally off after quantizing!" Quantize moves the notes you played to the nearest eighth note (or whatever time division you have selected). If you were closer to the wrong beat than the right beat, Quantize will move the note to dead center of the wrong beat! Not to worry, you can just click on the note and drag it to the correct beat.

Digging into the Redrum Channels

For the last few sections of this chapter, we are going to take a look at some of the controls on Redrum's 10 channel strips. Unlike the Mixer 14:2 (reMix), where each channel is identical, you will notice that Redrum's channels are slightly different from one another. For a detailed, complete rundown of all the particulars, please see your Reason manual. For now, I am just going to highlight a few of the bits I think you will want to use the most.

Redrum Effects Sends (S1 and S2)

Redrum's Effects Sends are especially useful when you are connecting Redrum to the reMix Mixer on one stereo channel instead of routing each individual drum to a separate channel on reMix. On reMix (as well as on the smaller Micromix Line Mixer 6:2), each channel has its own effects sends. But when Redrum is connected to only one stereo channel of a mixer, using the effects sends on the mixer channel would apply the effects to all the drums simultaneously. Using Redrum's own effects sends allows you to send the audio signal from each individual drum to up to two separate effects at any level you want. If reMix is present at the top of the Reason Device Rack, when a new Redrum is created, Redrum's Send Out 1 and 2 outputs will be automatically routed to the first two available Chaining Aux inputs in the rear of reMix. These inputs bypass the red Auxiliary Send Level knobs on the front of reMix and send the signal directly to the effects device with no attenuation. That may have sounded more complicated than it actually is. Let's give this a spin!

1 Open the song you created earlier in this chapter, called Redrum-Ignite. Drag an RV7000 Advanced Reverb directly under the reMix Mixer, and then drag a DDL-1 Digital Delay directly under that. The effects will be "automagically" routed with the RV7000 on Effects Return 1 and the DDL-1 on Effects Return 2 of the reMix Mixer.

2 Flip your rack around (using the Tab key on your computer keyboard), and you will see that Send Outs 1 and 2 of Redrum have been automatically routed to Chaining Aux inputs 1 and 2 of reMix 14:2. This means that the signal from Redrum's Send 1 will be processed by the RV7000 Reverb, and the signal from Redrum's Send 2 will be processed by the DDL-1 Digital Delay. (If you are having trouble reading some of the labels because the cables are in the way, pressing L on your computer keyboard will show or hide the cables.)

3 Click Tab to flip the Reason Device Rack back around facing front. Click Play on the Reason Transport to hear that oh-so-familiar beat.

4 Turn up the Send 1 knob on Channel 2 halfway to send snare drum through the RV7000 Reverb.

5 Turn up the Send 2 knob on Channel 8 halfway to send some hi-hat through the DDL-1 Digital Delay.

6 Turn the Pan knob on the DDL-1 to about 3 o'clock. Now the delayed signal is panned right.

7 Turn the Send 2 knob on Channel 2 up halfway to send some snare drum signal through the DDL-1 Digital Delay.

8 Turn the Feedback knob on the DDL-1 up to 12 o'clock for some extra snare action. Turning up the Feedback knob causes the delay to repeat more times before fading out.

9 For a cool effect, click the solo button on the top of Channel 2. You will hear only the snare drum with its reverb and delay effects, while all the other drums will be muted.

10 Watch the progress marker in the Reason Sequencer as it travels from left to right within your loop. Just before bar 2 of the pattern finishes, click the Channel 2 solo button again to hear all the drums come in together.

Channel 8 & 9 Exclusive

When the Channel 8 & 9 Exclusive button is activated, the sounds on channels 8 and 9 will be exclusive of each other, meaning that when a sound is triggered on Channel 8, it will be cut off as soon as a sound is played on Channel 9, and vice versa. This is handy for adding realism to hi-hats, where a closed hi-hat is loaded into one channel, and an open hi-hat is loaded into the other channel. To get a feel for this, please try the following exercise.

1 Start with an empty rack. Create an instance of the Mixer 14:2 and then create an instance of Redrum. Then open Redrum's Patch Browser and select Reason Factory sound Bank > Redrum Drum Kits > Tight Kits > Dublab TightKit1.drp.

2 Click the Channel 8 Select button. This is a closed hi-hat. Click and drag your mouse across all 16 Step buttons so that they are all lit up yellow.

3 Click on Step buttons 1, 5, 9, and 13 to deactivate them.

4 Click the Channel 9 Select button. This is the open hi-hat. Click on Steps 1, 5, 9, and 13 so that they are lit up yellow.

5 Click the Run button. Now practice turning the Channel 8 & 9 Exclusive button on and off. When it is on, the open hi-hat will cease to ring out as soon as the closed hi-hat is played. If the Channel 8 & 9 Exclusive button is off, the open hi-hat will continue to ring out even when the closed hi-hat is played, which would be physically impossible for a real hi-hat!

Pan, Pitch, and Level

The Pan knob included on each channel determines the selected drum's position in the stereo image. Pan settings are very important for creating a realistic-sounding acoustic kit, as well as for creating ear-catching electronic kits. The little red LED above the Pan knob (between the Send knobs) lights up to indicate when a stereo sample is being used. Its little label looks like an infinity symbol or a bipolar microphone pattern, but of course it signifies stereo in this case. When it is not lit (as in the following exercise), this means a mono sample is being used, and the Pan knob will simply move the mono sample to the left or right of the stereo image. If the Stereo Sample LED is lit to indicate that a stereo sample is being used, then the Pan knob becomes a stereo balance control, emphasizing the left or right channel of the stereo sample. In the following exercise, you will try out the Pan knob, as well as the Pitch knob (which is used for tuning the sample) and the Level knob (which makes the sample louder or quieter).

1 Start with an empty rack. Create an instance of the Mixer 14:2 and then create an instance of Redrum. Click the Trigger Sample button on Channel 2 a few times to hear the snare drum.

2 Now turn the Channel 2 Pitch knob to the left and right. Each time you turn it to a new position, click the Trigger Sample button on Channel 2 a few times to hear the snare drum play back at a new pitch. When you are done experimenting, turn the Pitch knob back to 12 o'clock.

3 Turn the Channel 2 Pan knob to 9 o'clock. Now your snare drum sounds more or less as if it were in the same position as it would if you were sitting behind a right-handed drum kit (in front of you and to the left).

4 Turn the Channel 2 Level knob all the way up. Now when you trigger your snare sample, it is a bit louder.

✳ DON'T LOSE YOUR CHANNEL STRIP SETTINGS!

Loading a new individual sample into a Redrum channel (using the Browse Sample button) does not affect any of your other settings. However, when you load a new Redrum Patch (using the Browse Patch button), not only will new samples (drum sounds) be loaded into each of Redrum's 10 drum channels, but new channel strip settings will be loaded as well. This is important to keep in mind. If you are working with one patch (or kit), and you have all your pan, pitch, and tone settings perfectly the way you want them, you'd better save that as a new patch, or else when you load another kit, those settings will be lost forever! Patches (drum kits) are saved by clicking the diskette icon to the far right of the Patch Display window.

Now that you've spent some quality time with Dr.Rex in Chapter 2 and Redrum in this chapter, I hope you are already starting to feel pretty comfortable working with beats with Reason. Now it's time to move onto exploring the virtual synths Reason has to offer!

4 } Subtractor

Subtractor, modeled after classic analog synthesizers, was the first synthesizer ever developed for Reason. You might think that the name refers to bass (like sub-bass or subwoofer). Actually, although Subtractor does have some great bass sounds, the name comes from the fact that Subtractor uses what is known as *subtractive synthesis*. It's easy to remember that term when you keep in mind that with subtractive synthesis, you start with a basic tone and then shape that tone by filtering out (or subtracting) various frequencies. The three basic building blocks in subtractive synthesis are the oscillator (generates the basic tone), the filter (removes, or subtracts, frequencies from the basic tone generated by the oscillator), and the amplifier (amplifies the signal coming from the filter). We won't go much deeper into that subject for the moment, but you will notice oscillators, filters, and amplifiers on all of the Reason synths. For now, let's just dig in and have some fun with Subtractor.

In this chapter you will learn how to:

❋ Use the various synth parameter controls on Subtractor to make your own custom sounds

❋ Use all the features of the RPG-8 Monophonic Arpeggiator with Subtractor

❋ Use the Reason Sequencer with Subtractor

❋ Use effects devices such as the CF1 Chorus/Flanger to make your Subtractor patches sound even better

Subtractor Synth Parameters

Parameter is really a pretty generic word and in this case could be replaced with the word *setting*. The Pitch Bend Range is one parameter (or setting), the Filter Frequency is another parameter, and the Master Output Level is still another parameter. The purpose of this section of the chapter is to help you get your hands on a few of the most useful Subtractor parameters, so you can start getting a feel for what all those knobs, sliders, and buttons do. I'm into this sort of thing, so I think it will be fun, too!

Waveforms and Oscillators 1 and 2

Oscillators 1 and 2 are the basic tone generators for Subtractor. Each oscillator can generate any one of 32 waveforms. As you explore Subtractor's presets, you will find many skillfully programmed, rich, and elaborate sounds based on these basic waveforms. In this first exercise, however, you will hear what these waveforms sound like naked and unadulterated, prior to any filtering or modulation of any kind.

1 In a new, empty rack, create a Mixer 14:2, followed by Subtractor. Then right-click on the Subtractor and choose Initialize Patch. This will give you a very basic starting point.

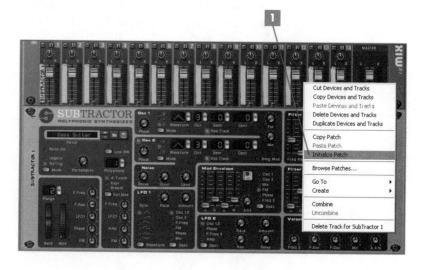

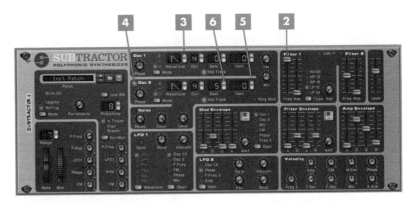

2 Turn up Filter 1 Frequency all the way. Now you can hear the sound of Oscillator 1 with no filtering or anything else between the oscillator and your ears!

3 As you play your MIDI keyboard, use the Osc 1 Waveform up-arrow to click one-by-one through the 32 waveforms and listen to each sound. When you are done, click and hold the down-arrow until you are back where you started (at the sawtooth wave).

4 Turn on Oscillator 2 by clicking the red (unlabeled) Osc 2 On/Off button.

5 While playing your MIDI keyboard, slowly turn the Oscillator 2 Cent parameter up to 10, and you will hear Oscillator 2 go just a bit out of tune with Oscillator 1. When you are done, turn the Oscillator 2 Cent parameter back down to 0. (A cent is 1/100 of a semitone, by the way.)

6 While playing your MIDI keyboard, turn the Oscillator 2 Semitone parameter up to 5. The musical interval you now have between the two oscillators is a fourth.

7 While playing your MIDI keyboard, turn the Oscillator 2 Semitone parameter up to 7 semitones. The musical interval you now have is a fifth, and I think you are ready to play the keyboard solo to "Abacab" by Genesis.

Waveforms and Low Frequency Oscillators

When used at audible frequencies (between 20Hz and 20,000Hz), the type of waveform used by a synthesizer's oscillator is the first determining factor in what the synthesizer patch (or program) will sound like. However, when used at a very low, inaudible frequency (like a few times per second) in an LFO (low frequency oscillator), these waveforms can control pitch, filter frequency, or any of a number of other parameters. The next exercise will allow you to hear the shape of a few waveforms, as they will be used at very low frequencies to modulate (change) the pitch of Subtractor's oscillators (sound generators).

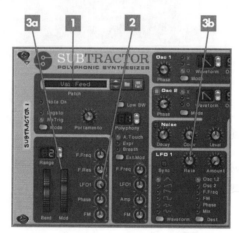

1 In a fresh rack containing Mixer 14:2 followed by Subtractor, select the following Subtractor patch: Reason Factory Sound Bank > Subtractor Patches > MonoSynths > Vai Feed.zyp.

2 Directly to the right of the mod wheel, turn the knob labeled LFO 1 all the way to the right. Now when you use the mod wheel on your MIDI keyboard, you will get a lot of LFO 1 instead of just a little.

3 Turn up the mod wheel on your MIDI keyboard (or use your mouse to move the mod wheel on Subtractor). You will hear the pitch of the sound (the pitch of Osc 1 and 2) going up and down, just as the shape of the currently selected triangle wave under LFO 1 goes up and then down. So you can hear this more clearly, turn the LFO 1 Rate knob down to a value of 60.

4 Click on the red LED next to the second waveform (an inverse sawtooth wave) to select it. Now you can hear the pitch of the sound ramp up over and over again, just like the shape of the waveform.

5 Click on the red LED next to the third waveform (a sawtooth wave). Now you can hear the pitch of the sound ramp down over and over again, just like the shape of the waveform.

6 Click on the red LED next to the fourth waveform (a square wave). Now you can hear the pitch switch sharply back and forth between two pitches, just like the shape of the waveform.

7 Select the fifth waveform (random). Now you can hear the pitch change sharply in a series of random steps like the sound of a computer in some ancient sci-fi movie.

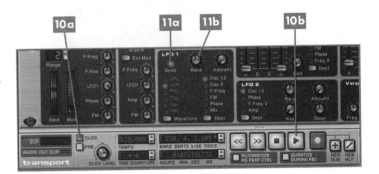

8 Select the sixth (bottom) waveform (soft random). Now the pitch changes more gradually (or softly) through a series of random steps.

9 Turn the LFO 1 Rate knob up and down, and hear the speed of the modulation (or change) go up and down.

10 Turn on the click, and press Play on the Reason Sequencer.

11 Turn on the LFO 1 Sync button. Now play with the LFO 1 Rate knob again, and you will hear that the modulation happens in time with the click. This is especially easy to hear at LFO 1 Rate settings of 2/4, 1/4, and 1/8.

In Step 11, feel free to experiment with the different waveforms as they play in time to the click. You will find that different waveforms have different characteristics when played in sync, especially at LFO 1 Rate settings of 2/4, 1/4, and 1/8. Please note that you can also use the Waveform button to click through the waveforms instead of directly clicking the LEDs to the left of the waveforms.

Portamento and Pitch Bend

Portamento is also called *glide* on some synthesizers. It controls the amount of time it takes for the pitch to rise or fall from one note you play to the next. When you switch from a low note to a high note on a piano, there is no portamento. When you switch from a low note to a high note on a trombone, there is plenty of portamento, depending on how quickly or slowly you move the slide. Portamento is good for emulating Theremin sounds and for classic analog synth lead sounds. The next short, easy exercise uses a Subtractor patch that already has some portamento built in. You will also try out Pitch Bend at the end of the exercise.

1 In a fresh rack containing Mixer 14:2 followed by Subtractor, select the following Subtractor patch: Reason Factory Sound Bank > Subtractor Patches > MonoSynths > Hip Hop Lead.zyp.

2 Play some low notes and high notes on your MIDI keyboard, and you will hear a little bit of portamento. As you play, slowly turn up the Portamento knob and hear that "glide" time increase. Then slowly turn down the portamento until the pitch changes sharply from note to note.

3 If this sound has too much treble for you, try moving your modulation wheel forward a bit. You can use the wheel on your MIDI keyboard or the one on the Subtractor. In this patch, it is set to lower the filter frequency, which will make a more mellow sound.

4 Turn the Pitch Bend Range down to 2. You can click on the arrows or click and drag in the Range window to do this. Now use the pitch bend wheel on your MIDI keyboard (or use the one on Subtractor), and the pitch will bend up or down two microtones, which is one full step.

5 Turn the Pitch Bend Range up to 12. Now use the pitch bend wheel on your MIDI keyboard (or use the one on Subtractor), and the pitch will bend up or down 12 microtones, which is one full octave.

6 Finally, turn the Pitch Bend Range up to 24. Now use the pitch bend wheel on your MIDI keyboard (or use the one on Subtractor), and the pitch will bend up or down 24 microtones, which is two full octaves!

If you used your modulation wheel to mellow out the sound in Step 3, you may have noticed something if you happened to use the Reason Transport controls afterward. When you press the Stop button on the Reason Transport, the mod wheel setting returns to zero automatically. If this is a problem for you, you could always adjust the filter frequency directly by using the Filter 1 Frequency slider, which will not reset when you stop playback.

Polyphony

In a synthesizer, *polyphony* refers to the number of independent voices that can be played simultaneously. If only one voice (one key) can be played at a time, the synthesizer (or synthesizer patch) is *monophonic*. The classic Minimoog is an example of a famous monophonic analog synth. Nearly all the patches (or programs) in the MonoSynths folder in Reason Factory Sound Bank > Subtractor Patches are monophonic. I'm not sure why a few of them (such as Chronic Lead) are actually *polyphonic* (as of version 4.0), but we'll skip that mystery for now. Let's play with Subtractor's Polyphony control and change a monophonic patch into a polyphonic patch.

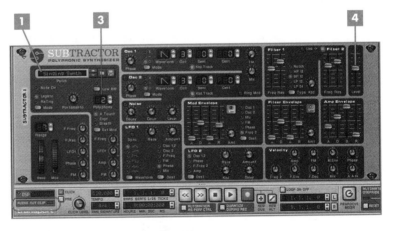

1. In a fresh rack containing Mixer 14:2 followed by Subtractor, select the following Subtractor patch: Reason Factory Sound Bank > Subtractor Patches > MonoSynths > Singing Synth.

2. Play around on your MIDI keyboard, and you will notice you can play only one key at a time (just like with Hip Hop Lead from the previous exercise).

3. Turn up the Polyphony control to 2. Now play around and notice that every time you try to play a third simultaneous voice, the first voice you played drops off.

4. You may notice your audio *clipping* (distorting because Subtractor's output is too much for Reason's audio output). This is because the patch you are using was designed to be loud with only one voice, and adding the extra voices is just too much signal, as evidenced by the Audio Output Clipping Indicator light. Turn down the (Master) Level slider on Subtractor to about 70 to avoid any further clipping.

✳ ✳ ✳

5 Turn up Polyphony to 10. Now you could make a chord with all 10 fingers if you wanted to. A whole choir of Singing Synths!

Subtractor's Polyphony control goes up to 99 voices. Some samplers or piano emulations go up to 150! Why would you need so many voices? Well, if you are playing piano and leave the sustain pedal down, you could easily rack up more than 50 voices (there are 88 keys after all!). Also, if you did an entire electronic orchestral arrangement and tried to play it through one synth, you could use quite a few voices.

Of course, simply using one voice (monophonic) is great for lead playing. When Polyphony is set to 1, the most recent note you touched will be the one you hear, even if you are holding down another note. This allows you to do some "hammer-on" or *pivot* effects. To hear what I'm talking about, set Polyphony to 1 and, while you are holding down one note, strike another key over and over again. Monophonic playing can also sound "cleaner" than higher Polyphony settings when playing fast, because you will hear only one note at a time, even if you accidentally hit two notes at the same time.

Modulation Wheel

You may have noticed that when you play with the modulation wheel on your MIDI keyboard, stuff happens. You may not have a clear rule in your brain for *which* "stuff" happens, since it seems like different things happen depending on which patch you are using. You are not imagining that! If you look to the right of the mod wheel, you'll see five different knobs. To *modulate* simply means (for our purposes) "to change." Each of those knobs to the right of the mod wheel determines to what extent a particular parameter (such as Filter Frequency or LFO 1 Amount) will be changed (or modulated) when you move the mod wheel. Let's take the mod wheel for a spin! (I couldn't resist.)

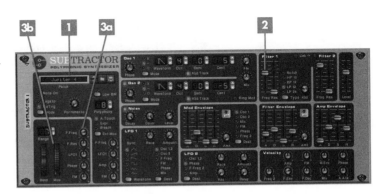

1 In a fresh rack containing Mixer 14:2 followed by Subtractor, select the following Subtractor patch: Reason Factory Sound Bank > Subtractor Patches > PolySynths > Jupiter 4.zyp.

2 While playing some notes on your MIDI keyboard, slowly turn the Filter 1 Freq slider all the way up and then back down to its default value of 80.

3 Look at the knob to the right of the mod wheel labeled F.Freq. This is the Filter Freq Mod Wheel Amount knob. As you can see, it is turned up to about 2 o'clock. Now play a few notes while you move the mod wheel on your MIDI keyboard or on Subtractor. You can hear the filter frequency being raised when you move the mod wheel, the same as you heard in Step 2!

4 Turn your mod wheel all the way back down, and turn the Filter Freq Mod Wheel Amount knob down to about 10 o'clock (a value of –20). Since you have set a negative value, when you turn the mod wheel, the filter frequency will go down instead of going up.

5 Set the Filter Freq Mod Wheel Amount knob to 12 o'clock. The little red light above it will turn off to show that filter frequency is not being affected by the mod wheel.

6 Hold down a note on your MIDI keyboard, and slowly turn up the LFO 1 Amount knob (turn clockwise). You will hear LFO 1 making the pitch of Oscillators 1 and 2 go up and down. When you are done, turn the LFO 1 Amount knob all the way back down again.

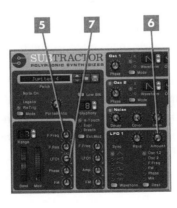

7 Turn the LFO 1 Mod Wheel Amount knob up to about 3 o'clock (a value of about +38). Now hold down a note on your MIDI keyboard and ease up the mod wheel. You will hear the pitch go up and down, the same way it sounded in Step 6.

95
❄❄❄

❄ **NOISE GENERATOR**

The Noise Generator does not react to pitch information, so it sounds the same no matter what key you press. It is also not controlled by the Amp Envelope (more on the Amp Envelope later). Instead, it has its own Decay knob, which determines how long the Noise Generator's sound will last when a note is played. Long decays can be used for wind noise or to fatten up a pad, and short decays can be used when you want the Noise Generator to provide a percussive attack. In fact, the Noise Generator can be used to create different electronic percussion patches, like snare drums and hi-hats. The Noise Generator can also be used to add "breath" to a flute patch.

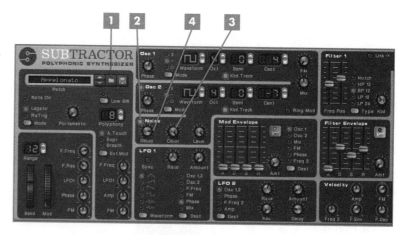

1 In a fresh rack containing Mixer 14:2 followed by Subtractor, select the following Subtractor patch: Reason Factory Sound Bank > Subtractor Patches > PolySynths > Appelonato.zyp. Play a bit on your MIDI keyboard to hear what this sounds like.

2 Turn on Noise, and you will hear an immediate effect.

3 While playing your MIDI keyboard, slowly turn the Noise Color knob all the way down and then back up again. Think of the Color control as a simple tone control, with brighter tone (more treble) as you turn toward the right and darker tone as you turn toward the left.

4 While playing your MIDI keyboard, slowly turn the Noise Decay knob down to 12 o'clock and then slowly back up to 3 o'clock, listening to the effect as you go.

By the way, the reason the sound sort of goes "owe, owe, owe" when you press new keys is because of the way the Filter Envelope is set. It's the sound of the Filter Frequency falling during the Decay portion of the Filter Envelope. Come back to this thought after you read the next section, and it might make more sense!

ADSR: Four Letters You Cannot Do Without

A-D-S-R. These four letters stand for Attack, Decay, Sustain, and Release. Please say the words to yourself a few times if this concept is new to you. From here on out, you will see these four parameters again and again throughout Reason and on just about any analog or emulated analog synthesizer you ever use in the future. It is with these four parameters that you will sculpt quite a bit of your sound. This is news you can use!

ADSR envelopes are used in Subtractor's Filter Envelope, the Modulation Envelope, and the Amp Envelope. In the exercise for this section, you will be applying ADSR to the Amp Envelope. Think of an envelope as the shape of an event over time. While Subtractor's Level control affects the overall volume (or amplification) of your sound, the Amp Envelope controls how the shape of that amplification is applied. Will the sound start sharply when you strike a key, or will it fade in slowly? Will it end abruptly when you let go of the key or fade out slowly? Is a short sound produced, like a drum hit, or is a long, sustained tone produced, like holding down a key on an organ?

Here is how ADSR relates to the Amp Envelope. You can refer to this when considering other ADSR envelopes as well.

Attack: The amount of time it takes the audio signal level to climb from 0 to its peak level.

Decay: The amount of time it takes for the audio signal to fall from its peak level to the level determined by the Sustain parameter, assuming you keep holding down the key(s).

Sustain: At the end of a note's decay, the Sustain value determines the level at which the audio signal rests as long as the note is being held. Note that Sustain is the only one of these four parameters that is not measured in time, but rather in signal level.

Release: The amount of time it takes for the level of a sound to drop to 0 from whatever level it was when you let go of a note.

If all of the above seems a little confusing, don't worry. The following exercise should make this all quite clear.

1 Start with an empty rack. Create an instance of Mixer 14:2 from the Create menu at the top of the Reason window, and then create an instance of Subtractor. In Subtractor's Patch Browser window, it should say Bass Guitar. Let's use this patch.

2 By default, the Attack setting on the Amp Envelope is all the way down at 0 (fastest/shortest attack possible). So when you hit a key, you hear sound instantaneously. Please move the Attack slider up to a value of about 69 (a little over half way). Depress a key on your MIDI keyboard, and you will now hear that the note fades in slowly. Feel free to experiment with different Attack values to get a feel for this.

3 Turn Attack back down to 0, then turn Sustain down to 0 and play a few keys. Not such a long note anymore!

4 While playing notes on your MIDI keyboard, slowly turn Decay up to a value of about 70. If you turned it all the way up, your note would sound for as long as you held the key down.

5 Now turn Decay down to a value of about 20. You have a very short note now!

6 With Attack still at 0, and Decay set at 20, turn up your Sustain level to about 70. Hold down a key. You will hear the sharp attack and the quick decay, but the decay will no longer fall down all the way to silence. It stops and holds at an intermediate level (the Sustain level).

7 Now turn up Sustain all the way. When you hold down a key, the sound stays at its maximum level until you let go. Theoretically, the Decay setting would still allow the level to fall to the value designated by the Sustain slider, but since the Sustain value is set at maximum, there is no place to fall!

8 With Attack still at 0, Decay at 20, and Sustain at maximum, move the Release slider up to a value of 64. Now strike a key and let go. Notice how the note continues to fade out after you release it.

9 Move the Release slider up to maximum. Now hit a note, and after you let go of the note, it will hang on for quite a long time before it finally fades out.

If that last section had you saying, "Hey, I thought this book was for beginners," then I hope you'll take the time to go over it again. ADSR is a really fundamental concept that is important to understand when producing electronic music. Anyway, if any of that last section tasted like medicine, this next section will taste like candy! You are about to have fun playing with the RPG-8 Monophonic Arpeggiator!

Subtractor, Meet the RPG-8 Monophonic Arpeggiator!

According to the *American Heritage Dictionary of the English Language*, an arpeggio is "the sounding of the tones of a chord in rapid succession rather than simultaneously." RPG-8 does exactly that, automatically. You play a chord, and it plays back the notes separately in perfect time, in a variety of different user-definable patterns, at any speed you wish, using any Reason synth that you wish. This feature is one I have wanted in Reason for a long, long time, and bless those Propellerheads, they finally gave it to me!

RPG-8 Octave, Mode, Insert, and Hold

Once you start playing with RPG-8, you may find it to be one of the most fun new features in Reason 4. The following exercise will help you become familiar with some of its key features.

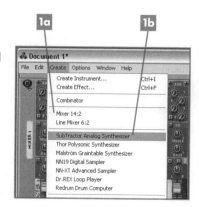

1 Open a new Reason rack, and use the Create menu to add an instance of Mixer 14:2. Then use the Create menu again to add a Subtractor.

2 Now, add an RPG-8 directly under Subtractor. Play a four-note chord (spanning less than one octave), and you will hear the notes in the chord separated and played in an upward repeating pattern. Click the 2 Oct button, and now those notes will play in both the original octave and one octave above.

3 While still holding down the chord, click the Hold button, and let go of the chord. It will keep playing.

4 You are currently using the Up mode. Try the Up + Down mode, the Down mode, and the Random mode. When you are done, switch back to the Up mode.

5 Click the Low Insert button, and you will hear the lowest note in your chord pivot with each of the remaining notes in the chord.

6 Click the Hi Insert button, and you will hear the highest note in your chord pivot with each of the remaining notes in the chord.

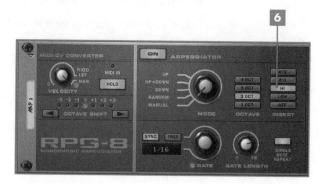

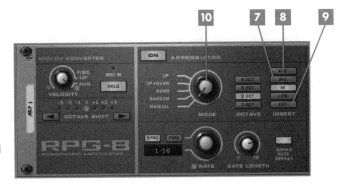

7 Click the 3-1 Insert button, and you will hear an ascending triplet pattern (ascending because you are in the Up mode).

8 Click the 4-2 Insert button, and you will hear an ascending four-note pattern.

9 Turn Insert off.

10 Switch the mode to Manual. Now play a chord, laying down the notes one finger at a time from high to low. The Arpeggiator will play the notes in that order. If you play another chord laying down the notes one finger at a time from low to high, the Arpeggiator will play them back in that order. In Manual mode, the RPG-8 plays back the notes in whatever order you played them.

RPG-8 Rate Control Video Game Trick

The next exercise uses the Rate control, which is pretty self explanatory, but I think when used in the extreme, the sound will remind you of *Pac-Man*.

1 Open a new song and add Mixer 14:2, followed by Subtractor and RPG-8. Click the 3 Oct button.

2 Click the Hold button. Then hold down all five notes from C3 to G3 on your MIDI keyboard. The first note will line up with the C3 mark on the far right of the RPG-8.

3 Turn the Rate knob all the way to the right so it reads 1/128. This sound may annoy spouses or roommates.

4 Switch back and forth between the following modes: Up, Up + Down, and Down. The Up + Down mode and the Down mode both sound like *Pac-Man* to me. Then try Random. It's pretty weird.

5 Click the Hold button again to stop the madness.

RPG-8 Pattern Section

Wow, I swear, with the RPG-8 on, I can play the keyboard with my forehead and it sounds good! But wait, there's more! The RPG-8 has a Pattern section that allows you to silence certain steps in the arpeggio. To try this out, you can leave your rack "as is" from the preceding exercise, with Mixer 14:2 followed by Subtractor and RPG-8 in your rack.

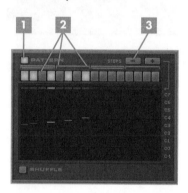

1 Click the Pattern button to turn on the RPG-8's Pattern section.

2 Hold down a chord with your left hand or use the Hold button, and then click on a few of the Step buttons. You will hear silence whenever one of the deactivated steps is (not) played.

3 As you listen to this, click the Remove Step button until only eight steps are in use.

4 Drag your mouse across those first eight steps twice, so that all eight steps are lit.

5 Click Play, and turn on the Click.

6 With your arpeggio still playing, on the RPG-8, click Shuffle.

7 Click the ReGroove Mixer button, and turn the Global Shuffle knob all the way to the right so you can hear the maximum shuffle amount. This works the same as it did with Redrum.

Arpeggio Notes to Track

It is possible to export the fancy fingerwork that RPG-8 creates as MIDI notes to be played by any of the Reason synths. It does take a couple of steps to do this, but it is similar to Redrum's Copy Pattern to Track function, as well as Dr.Rex's Copy REX Loop to Track function. It requires that you first record some MIDI data on the RPG-8 Sequencer track.

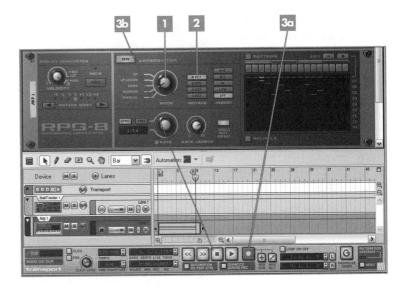

1 Open a new song and add Mixer 14:2, followed by Subtractor and RPG-8. Switch the RPG-8 mode to Random.

2 Click the 4 Oct button.

3 Click Record and immediately play and hold any chord on your MIDI keyboard. Keep holding the chord until the progress bar passes the right locator at bar 9. Then click Stop. You should have a short recording on the Arp 1 track in the Reason Sequencer.

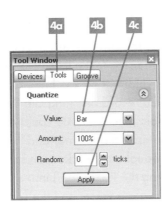

4 In the Tool window, click the Tools tab, choose Bar for the Quantize Value, then click Apply.

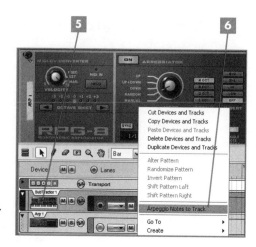

5 Click on the little Subtractor icon on the Subtractor 1 Sequencer track to select that track.

6 Right-click on RPG-8, and choose Arpeggio Notes to Track from the context menu. You will see a mess of notes appear on the Subtractor track.

7 Click on the RPG-8. Then click Ctrl+Delete. The RPG-8 and its corresponding Sequencer track should disappear. (This step is not pictured.)

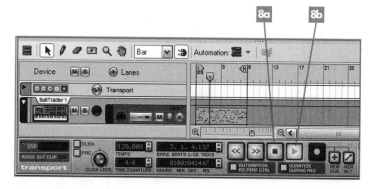

8 Click Stop, and then click Play. You should hear your arpeggiated sequence, even though the RPG-8 has been deleted from the rack.

Sequencing with Subtractor

As we go forward, please remember that when I refer to clips, I am simply referring to the little colored rectangles that contain the notes or other information you have recorded into the Reason Sequencer. You could record one long clip that lasts three minutes (perhaps a piano solo piece), or you could record one short clip (maybe only eight notes of a bass line) and then copy and paste that clip several times throughout your Reason song. You could also cut up a long clip (using the Razor tool) into shorter clips. Perhaps the first part of a long clip is a verse, and the second part is a chorus. You can cut those into their own separate clips to help you organize your song and to facilitate copying and pasting certain defined sections into other parts of the song, perhaps onto other tracks with other instruments playing the MIDI data. OK, time to practice some sequencing!

Using the Razor Tool

This exercise is a bit long, but not too difficult. The idea is to get used to cutting up clips into smaller clips with the Razor tool, copying and pasting those clips, and then joining them into one clip when you are done.

1 In a fresh rack containing Mixer 14:2 followed by Subtractor, click directly on the Patch window and choose WarmPad.zyp.

2 Turn on the Click.

3 Turn Precount on. This will give you a one-bar (four clicks) count-in from the time you press Record.

4 Click Record, and after the four-beat count-in, play four whole notes. These could be chords or single notes. Let each note or chord hang on four beats before moving on to the next. When you are done, you should have just passed bar 5. Click Stop.

5 Switch to Edit mode by clicking the Arrange/Edit Mode button.

6 Drag the right clip handle to the left so the clip ends at bar 5.

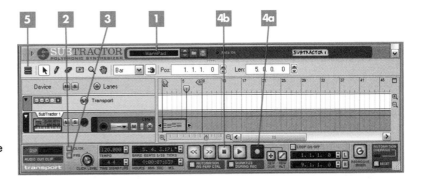

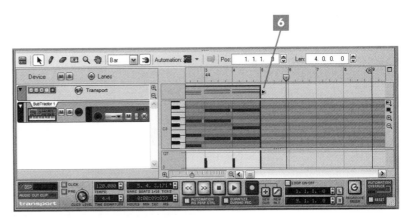

7 Double-click **inside the** Key Edit window. **Then** press Ctrl+A **to select all.**

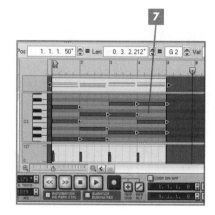

8 In the Tools tab of the Tool window, set the Quantize Value **to Bar, and** click Apply.

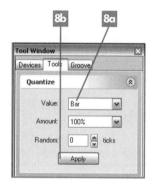

9 Click **directly to the right of the** clip.

10 Select **the** Razor tool. **Then** click **on the** clip **at each bar line. Now you have four clips.**

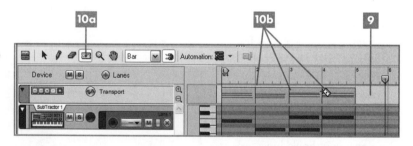

11 Choose **your** Selection tool. Ctrl+click **on the** clip **at bar 3 and** drag **it to bar 5; then** release **the** mouse **button followed by the** Ctrl **key. Now you have five one-bar clips.**

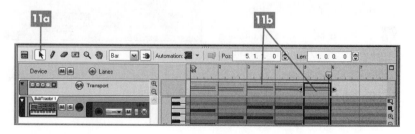

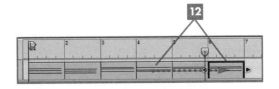

12 Ctrl+click on the clip at bar 4 and drag it to bar 6; then release the mouse button followed by the Ctrl key. Now you have six one-bar clips.

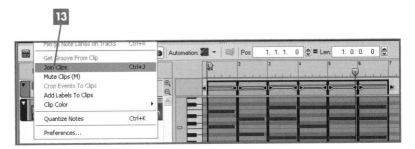

13 Press Ctrl+A to select all the clips. Then choose Join Clips from the Edit menu. (Note that you can also use Ctrl+J to join the clips.) Now you have one six-bar clip.

Of course, there are no real rules regarding when you should join your clips, when you should leave them split, or when you should cut a larger clip into smaller clips. This will depend on your own logical sense, style, and workflow and on the nature of the song you happen to be working on at a given time. I'm just trying to help you get a comfortable grip on the tools and techniques. It's up to you to decide how they best work for you!

Making a Velocity Ramp

Although you may choose to use Subtractor primarily for bass lines, lead lines, and other keyboard-oriented sounds, it also can produce some nice electronic percussion sounds. The next exercise could have easily been included in the "Using the Reason Sequencer with Redrum" section of Chapter 3, but it works just as well here.

1. In a fresh rack containing Mixer 14:2 followed by Subtractor, select the following Subtractor patch: Reason Factory Sound Bank > Subtractor Patches > Percussion > Snare Drums > Tribe Snare.

2. In the Reason Sequencer, switch to Edit mode.

3. Alt+click at the end of bar 2 to set the right locator there.

4. Turn the Loop button on.

5. Set Grid to 1/16.

6. Click the Horizontal Zoom button until two bars take up almost the entire Sequencer window, and then drag the horizontal scrollbar all the way to the left so you can see bars 1 and 2.

7. Select your Pencil tool, then draw in a clip by dragging your cursor from left to right across the top of the Sequencer window between the left and right locators.

8. Pick any note. The snare sound is not pitched, so it sounds the same on any note. Click in each grid box on one note between the left and right locators. That's 32 little notes. It'll take about a minute or less.

9. Click Play and you will hear that all the notes are at the same volume.

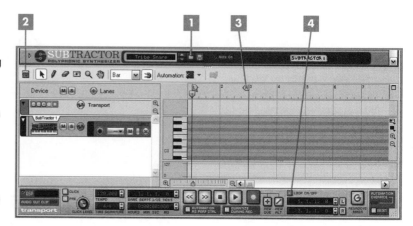

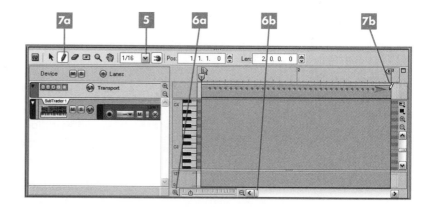

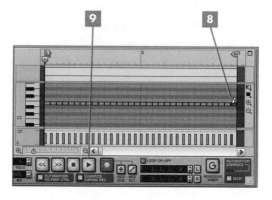

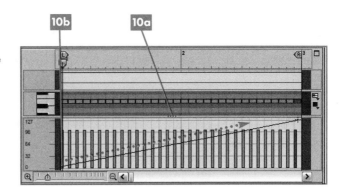

10 Drag up the top handle of the Velocity Editor so you have more room to work. Then Ctrl+click (and hold) in the bottom left of the Velocity Editor, and your Pencil tool will become a Line tool (the pencil icon will turn into crosshairs). Drag upward diagonally from left to right to draw a velocity ramp up from 0 to 127.

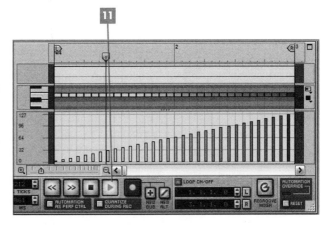

11 Click Play to hear the result! Notice that the higher a note's velocity is, the darker the shade of red used for the note. This is true in all the edit modes: Note, Drum, REX, and Velocity.

Quantize During Record

Quantize During Record is a great feature for people whose timing when playing into the sequencer is less than perfect (which would be many or most of us!). It's especially good for any style of electronic music where a "computer" feel is favored over a "human" feel. The danger is that if you have the Quantize Amount set at 100%, you will remove 100% of the human feel in timing, so you might not want this feature on when you record your piano concerto! Let's give it a try.

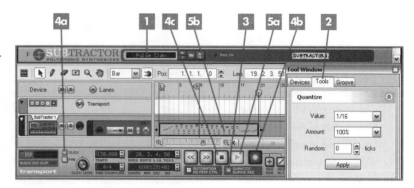

1 In a fresh rack containing Mixer 14:2 followed by Subtractor, select the following Subtractor patch: Reason Factory Sound Bank > Subtractor Patches > PolySynths > Pulse Clav.zyp.

2 Look on the Tools page of the Tools window, and make sure the Quantize Value is set at its default value of 1/16. The Quantize Amount should be at 100%, and the Random value should be 0.

3 Click on the Quantize During Record button, and it will light up green. Now anything you play into the Reason Sequencer will be automatically quantized to the nearest 1/16 note.

4 Turn on the Click, and press Record. Then play whatever feels good into the sequencer for a minute or two, and click Stop when you're done.

5 Click Play, and double-click on the clip you recorded.

6 Zoom way in on the Horizontal Zoom, and you will see that every note starts dead-on at a 1/16-note division on the grid.

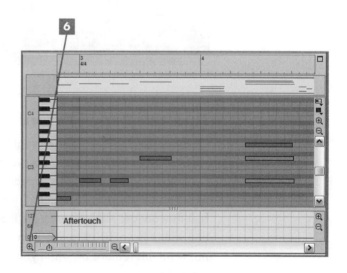

Now, if you really freaked out with reckless abandon while you recorded that last bit, some stuff may still sound off because you played the note closer to the *wrong* 1/16 note than to the *right* 1/16 note. You can move those notes to the right place in Edit mode as needed. Also, if you know you are going to record a simple 1/8-note bass part, set the Quantize value to 1/8. Or if you are playing a 1/4 note snare drum part, set the Quantize value to 1/4. You are more likely to be closer to your intended 1/4 note than to the correct 1/16 note or 1/32 note. It makes things easier. Finally, if you want to quantize as you record, but you don't want to entirely lose the human feel, set the Quantize Amount to 80% or 90% instead of to 100%.

New Dub/New Alt

New Dub and New Alt are used when recording a new take in the Reason Sequencer. When you think of New Dub, think "new over-dub." If you are going to play a synthesizer melody that harmonizes with a synthesizer melody you just recorded with the same synth, use New Dub so that you can hear the older part you are harmonizing with. When you think of New Alt, think of "new alternative take." If you are playing a keyboard solo, and you want to take several passes of the same solo section and then choose the best take, then use New Alt. This will mute the previous solo takes so that you won't hear them while you play the new one.

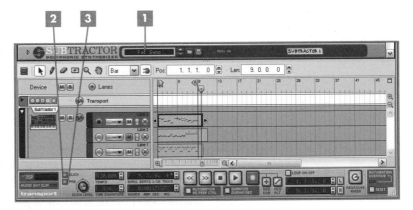

1 In a fresh rack containing Mixer 14:2 followed by Subtractor, select the following Subtractor patch: Reason Factory Sound Bank > Subtractor Patches > PolySynths > Fat Sync.zyp.

2 Turn on the Click. Make sure Loop is off.

3 Turn Precount on so that you will get a one-bar click lead-in before recording commences after you click Record.

III

❋ ❋ ❋

4 Click Record, and after the one-bar count-in, record a very basic chord rhythm part (or bass part if you prefer).

5 After bar 9, click Stop. Then click the Go to Left Locator button to return the song position marker to bar 1.

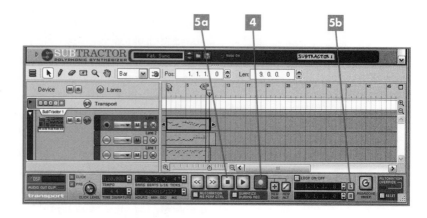

6 Click the New Dub button. A new lane (Lane 2) will be created above the old one, but Lane 1 will not be muted.

7 Click Record again and record a melody.

8 After bar 9, click Stop. Then click the Go to Left Locator button to return the song position marker to bar 1.

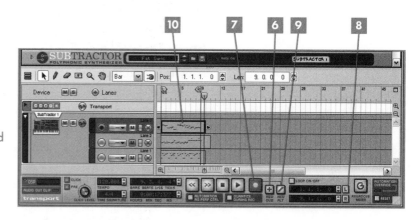

9 Click the New Alt button. A new lane (Lane 3) will be created above Lane 2, and Lane 2 will be muted (the little button marked "M" will be red).

10 Record a different melody. You will hear Lane 1 play back as you record, but you will not hear Lane 2.

Even when overdubbing, it's great to create these new lanes each time so that it remains easy to edit the separate performances. Also, New Alt is not only great for recording a bunch of takes and picking the best one. You can pick the best parts from several takes and edit them together into one dazzling, perfect solo using the Razor tool and cut, copy, and paste!

Subtractor, Meet Effects!

Subtractor is the only Reason synth that has a mono (instead of stereo) output. For bass sounds, as well as lead sounds, this may not be an issue for you. But if you want a fat pad to sound fatter, you might want it to be in stereo. This is easily done by adding effects.

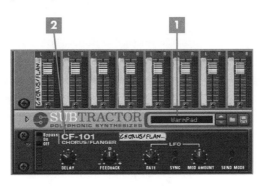

1. Create fresh rack containing Mixer 14:2 followed by a Subtractor. Click directly on the Patch window and choose WarmPad.zyp. Now play a chord on your MIDI keyboard to hear this sound.

2. Create a CF-101 Chorus/Flanger directly under Subtractor. Now play the chord again. The basic feeling of the sound is the same, but now it is spread out nicely across the stereo image.

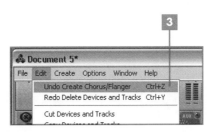

3. From the Edit menu, choose Undo Create Chorus/Flanger. (You can also press Ctrl+Z to undo.)

4. For a more dramatic sound, create a PH-90 Phaser directly under Subtractor. Play a chord and listen to the sound swim around between your ears.

Subtractor and Control Voltage

All of the devices in Reason have control voltage inputs and outputs on the rear of the devices. You will remember that in the waveforms exercise LFO 1 made the sound go "wah wah wah wah" (or something like that!). In slightly more scientific terms, LFO 1 modulated a parameter of the patch. You could do something similar by turning the volume or tone control up and down on a guitar or stereo system or by turning a dimmer switch up and down for a light in a room. The "virtual voltage" that LFO 1 is using to make those weird sounds can be sent to control other things as well—things outside of Subtractor! It won't make the light in your room get brighter and dimmer, but in the next exercise, it will make the sound of your Subtractor patch go back and forth from left to right in the stereo image.

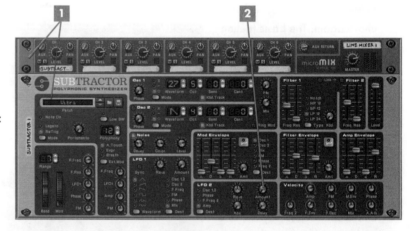

1 Open a new empty rack. Instead of Mixer 14:2, create a Line Mixer 6:2. Under that, create a Subtractor and select the following Subtractor patch: Reason Factory Sound Bank > Subtractor Patches > PolySynths > Vibra.zyp.

2 Play a few keys on your MIDI keyboard. You will find that this sound has some "wah wah wah wah" (it has some tremolo/vibrato), but it is still mono in the center of the stereo image. Turn the LFO 2 Amount knob all the way down, and the tremolo will stop.

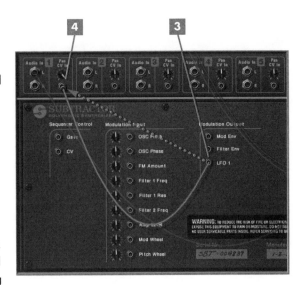

3 Press the Tab key to flip the Reason rack around. Click and hold on LFO 1 Modulation Output, and drag a cable to connect to Pan CV In on Channel 1 of the Line Mixer. Of course, Pan controls left or right in the stereo image, and CV stands for control voltage.

4 Turn the Channel 1 Pan CV In knob up all the way to the right. Play your MIDI keyboard, and you will hear the sound moving from left to right and back as you play.

If you have any trouble hearing the stereo effect, perhaps you need to move your speakers farther apart from each other, or you might want to put on some stereo headphones.

There are all kinds of deeply crazy things you can do with control voltage in Reason, but that's another book! Seriously, the way Reason uses control voltage is one of the most fun things about the program for synth geeks like me, and it's a great link between the Reason software and the vintage synth hardware that inspired it. If you flip your Reason rack around when you are using the RPG-8 Arpeggiator or the Matrix Pattern Sequencer, you will see that they output their note, velocity, and other information to the Reason synths using control voltage connections.

Alright! Now that you've gotten a good handle on Subtractor, it's time to dig into the next synth in Reason's virtual instrument line-up: Malström!

5 } Malström

The Malström Graintable synthesizer offers a whole new range of sounds distinct from what you experienced with Subtractor in Chapter 4, "Subtractor." Rather than producing sound by emulating analog oscillators (as is the case with Subtractor), the Malström uses Graintable synthesis, which is Propellerhead's hybrid of *granular* and *wavetable* synthesis. You will hear the difference because many of the sounds really sound like a human voice, or thunder, or some other real sound. It's not a sampler, however. The Malström Graintable designers start with a sample, chop it up, detonate it into a zillion grains, and slap it back together (as a Graintable) so that sound can be manipulated and warped in ways a simple sample might run and hide from.

In this chapter you will learn how to:

❋ Build a song in the Reason Sequencer using multiple Malströms

❋ Understand and use all the synth parameters unique to the Malström

❋ Use the Matrix Pattern Sequencer to control the Malström

❋ Use the Malström as an effects processor, playing Dr.Rex through the Malström's filters and shaper section

Building a Song with the Malström

Before we start tinkering under the hood, let's just have some fun seeing what the Malström can do. In the Reason Factory sound bank > Malström > Rhythmic folder, there are all kinds of sounds that play a rhythm all by themselves if you just hold down one note. This can help you build a track in a hurry. This exercise is a bit longer than average (20 steps), but it's pretty easy and really super cool.

1 In an empty rack, create a Mixer 14:2, followed by three Malströms. In the first Malström, load the patch Reason Factory Soundbank > Malström > Rhythmic > Sound On Sound.xwv.

2 In the second Malström, load the patch Reason Factory Soundbank > Malstrom > Rhythmic > 8bitLead.xwv.

3 In the third Malström, load the patch Reason Factory Soundbank > Malström > Rhythmic > Gated Pads.

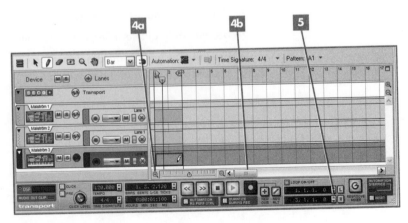

4 In the Reason Sequencer, increase the horizontal zoom so that you can see the individual bars clearly, and drag the horizontal scrollbar all the way to the left.

5 Click the right locator position down arrow until the right locator is at bar 3.

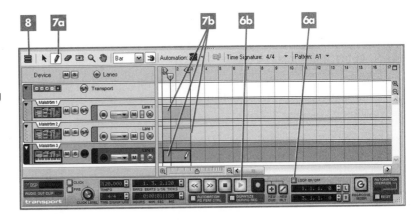

6. Click the Loop On/Off button to activate looping, and click Play (you won't hear anything yet).

7. Select the Pencil tool and draw a two-bar clip into each Malström track.

8. Click the Edit/Arrange Mode switch to get into Edit mode.

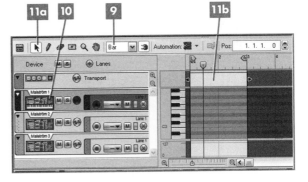

9. Make sure the grid mode is set to Bar.

10. Click the keyboard icon under Malström 1 to select the track.

11. Choose the Selection tool, and double-click on the clip so that you can edit it.

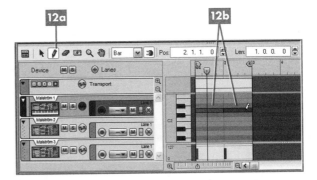

12. Choose the Pencil tool, and draw in a note at D2 on bar 1 and bar 2. You only need to click in each grid square; the note will fill up the whole bar. You should hear something now.

13 Click the keyboard icon under Malström 2 to select the track.

14 Choose the Selection tool, and double-click on the clip so you can edit it.

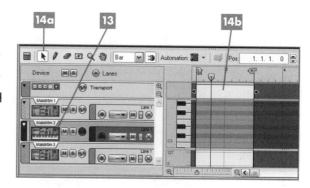

15 Choose the Pencil tool, and draw in a note at F1 on bar 1, and then draw in a note at D1 on bar 2.

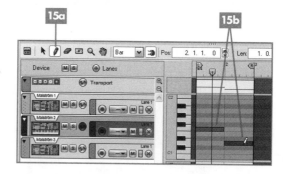

16 Click the keyboard icon under Malström 3 to select the track.

17 Choose the Selection tool, and double-click on the clip so you can edit it.

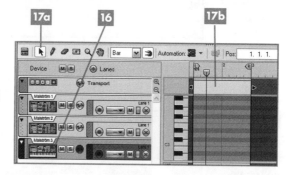

18 Choose the Pencil tool, draw in a note at C5 on bar 1, and then draw in a note at A4 on bar 2.

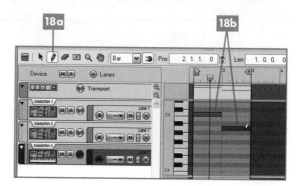

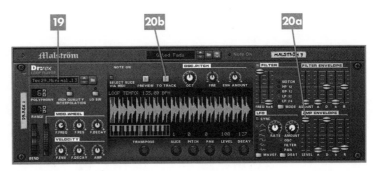

19 Create a Dr.Rex directly below the third Malström, and load the patch Reason Factory Sound Bank > Dr Rex Drum Loops > Techno > Tec29_Minimal_135_eLab.rx2.

20 Turn Dr.Rex's Amp Level slider up all the way, and click the To Track button.

You did a lot of work on that exercise, so save it when you're done. Also, we're going to use it again in a moment, so please, really save it.

For extra fun and creativity, I suggest that while this song plays, you click in the patch display window of Malström 1 and try some other rhythmic patches. You might find that some of the other patches fit nicely also.

❄ **SCROLLING IN THE KEY EDITOR**

If you have a mouse with a wheel on it, you may have noticed that you can use it to scroll up and down inside the Key Editor, so you can get to the higher or lower octaves of the keyboard. If you do not have a wheel, and you have your Sequencer window really short, you may freak out wondering how to scroll. Calm down, everything is OK. Drag the top of the Sequencer window upward until you see a vertical scrollbar appear on the right side of the Key Editor.

Stereo-ize That Sequence

By the way, here is a bonus trick that you can add on to the end of the last exercise if you want to. It'll make everything in trippy super-stereo.

1 Starting at the end of the previous exercise (or with the file you saved after completing the previous exercise), create a new Malström under Dr.Rex, and right-click and select Initialize Patch.

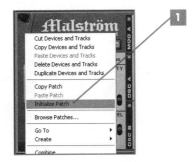

2 Click the Sync buttons on both MODs A and B.

3 Turn down the MOD A Rate knob to a value of 8/4.

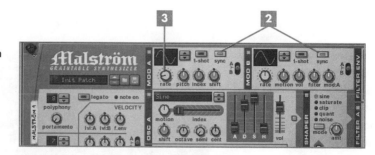

4 Press the Tab key on your computer keyboard to flip your rack around and click Play.

5 On the bottom Malström, right-click on the MOD A Output jack, mouse over Mixer 1 in the context menu, and select Channel 2 Pan CV.

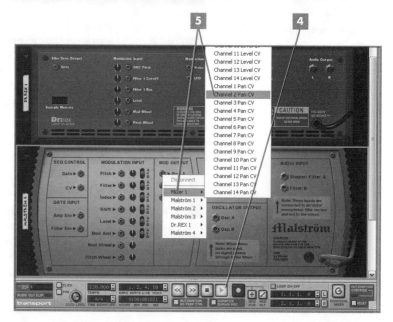

6 Right-click on the MOD B Output jack, mouse over Mixer 1 in the context menu, and select Channel 3 Pan CV.

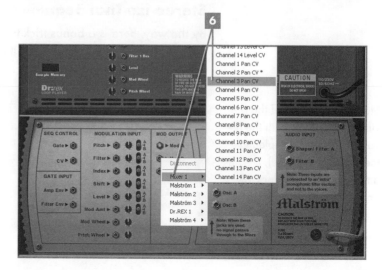

The sounds from Malströms 2 and 3 should be swimming through the stereo field now. If you have any trouble hearing this, you might want to put on some headphones. There is no sound coming out of that last Malström you created. It's just controlling the stereo pans on Channels 2 and 3 of the Mixer 14:2.

Turn That Loop into a Song

I find it can be a cool creative process to start with a short loop (maybe only two bars as we've done here) and fill it up with a lot of layers (clips) that all fit together. Then I can spread those puzzle pieces throughout an entire song, leaving some space and bringing the parts in and out. I hope you'll see what I mean after you complete the next exercise.

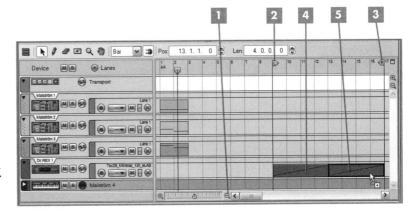

1 Reduce the horizontal zoom so that the hash marks between bars disappear and you can see 16 bars at a time in the Arrange window.

2 Drag the left locator to bar 9.

3 Drag the right locator to bar 17.

4 Drag the Dr.Rex 1 clip over so that it starts at bar 9 (at the left locator).

5 Ctrl+click on the Dr.Rex 1 clip and drag it over so that it starts on bar 13, then let go of the Ctrl key first and let go of your mouse button second.

6 Drag the Malström 1 clip over so that it starts at bar 3, then Ctrl+click on it and place copies at bar 7, bar 11, and bar 15.

7 Ctrl+click on the Malström 2 clip and drop the copy at bar 5.

8 Drag the Malström 3 clip to bar 5.

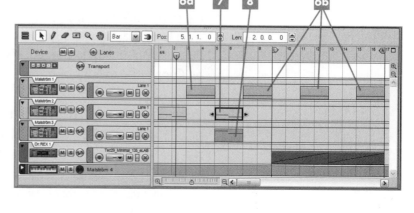

9 Select the Malström 2 and Malström 3 clips at bar 5 by clicking and dragging a rectangle around them or by Ctrl+clicking on each one.

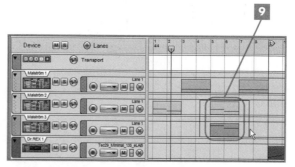

10 Ctrl+click (and hold) on the Malström 2 clip, and you will be able to drag and drop copies of both Malström 2 and Malström 3 clips simultaneously at bar 9 and then at bar 13.

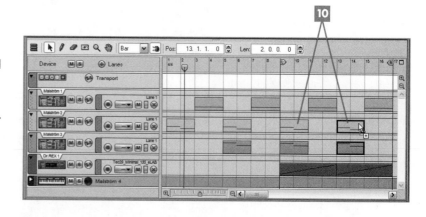

Now you can click Play and hear your little arrangement. You should still have Loop active on the Transport panel, so the song should loop between bars 9 and 17. Of course, you can turn the tempo up a little bit if 120 bpm is too slow for you.

Exporting the Song as an Audio File

Now that you've finished your mini-song, you will need to export it as an audio file before it can be burned onto a CD or converted to MP3. This next tutorial will show you how to do that and will also give you a sneak peak at the Combinator. Why would I suddenly bring the Combinator into this exercise? Because you are going to use the MClass Mastering Suite (a Combinator preset) to give your mix a little extra oomph.

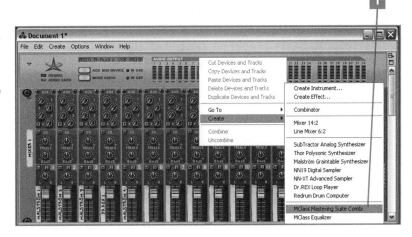

1 Right-click on the Reason hardware device (the one that says Audio Output) at the very top of the rack, and choose Create > MClass Mastering Suite Combi from the context menu.

2 Move the Combinator's On/Off/Bypass switch to the Bypass position. This will make the audio signal pass around the Mastering Suite's electronics so that the signal is not processed.

3 Click Show Devices on the Combinator.

4 Turn up the Input Gain knob on the MClass Maximizer to a value of 6 dB (a little past 2 o'clock).

5 Click Play to hear your sequence without the Mastering Suite (which is bypassed).

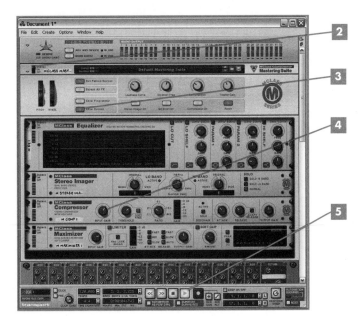

6 Move the Combinator's On/Off/Bypass switch to the On position. Now your mix sounds much louder but is not overloading anything.

7 Click Stop in the Reason Transport.

8 In the Reason Sequencer, drag the horizontal scrollbar so you can see the end marker.

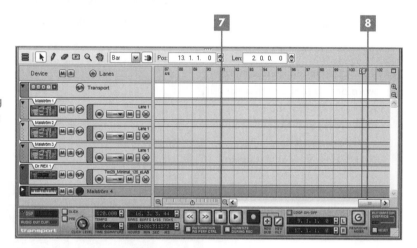

9 Drag the end marker to bar 18.

10 Deactivate the Loop On/Off button. Then listen to your 30-second song one more time to be sure that all the echoes and sounds stop completely before the end marker, so you will not cut off the end of your sound when you export.

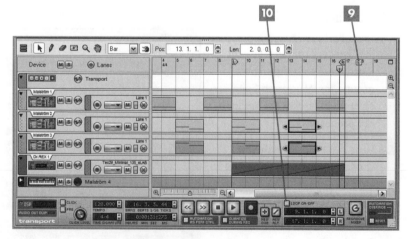

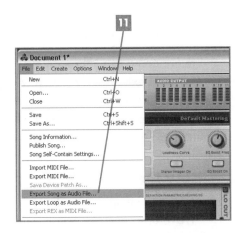

11 From the File menu, select Export Song as Audio File.

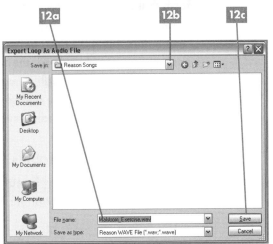

12 In the Export Song as Audio File window, choose a filename and a location to save in, and click the Save button.

13 Choose your desired sample rate and bit depth in the Export Audio Settings window. The default of 44,100Hz 16-bit is perfect for CD or MP3, so you can choose that unless you are planning to master and dither in another application. You can leave the Dither box checked as well. Then click OK.

Now you should find a 16-bit 44.1kHz wave file in the folder you saved to. If you want to turn it into an MP3, one easy and free way to do that is to import it into iTunes using the iTunes MP3 encoder.

Malström Synth Parameters

I'm not going to go through every single parameter on the Malström exhaustively (you have the Reason Operation Manual PDF for further reference), but I would like to point out some of the bits that make it unique, which also happen to be some of the bits that make it such a cool and fun synth to make music with.

How the Malström Produces Its Sound

At the beginning of Chapter 4, in the first exercise (in the section "Waveforms and Oscillators 1 and 2"), you listened to each waveform that Subtractor's oscillators could produce. These oscillators work like standard analog oscillators, producing a steady tone. The only noticeable difference between the waveforms is the harmonic content (how bright or dark the sound is, etc.). The Malström is entirely different. Although a few of its Graintables are based on basic waveforms like sine and sawtooth, you will find all kinds of craziness not found in analog synthesizers.

Trying Out the Graintables

The simple exercise below is really a good way to start getting a handle on the personality of the Malström.

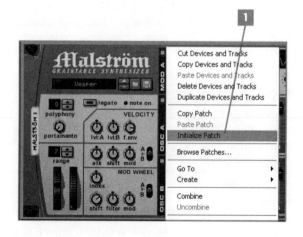

1. Open a new rack and create a Mixer 14:2 followed by a Malström. Then right-click on the Malström and choose Initialize Patch.

2 In order to start from the top of the list of Graintables, click once in the OSC A Graintable display window, and click on Bass: AcidBass at the top of the enormous context menu. By the way, I counted 82 Graintables in that list.

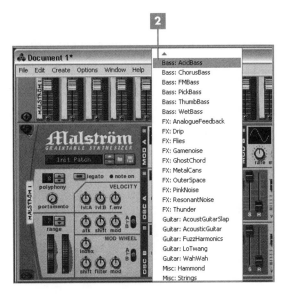

3 Play your MIDI keyboard to hear the sound. After you are done checking out the AcidBass Graintable, use the down arrow in the OSC A Graintable selector to try each Graintable one at a time.

It should really only take a couple of minutes to try all the Graintables, even though there are 82 of them. Some of the weirder sounds go on for a few seconds before repeating, so you might want to hold the key down for a few seconds to hear the whole story. Several of those sounds are really interesting (and often a bit crazy), and yet you haven't even applied any filters or other tricks, and you are only using one of the two oscillators. Just the naked Graintables sound great.

Motion, Shift, and Index

These three controls have a dramatic affect on the sound and are pretty easy to understand. The Motion knob controls how fast the Graintable is played back by the oscillator, Index determines the starting point for playback of the Graintable (the Index slider represents the Graintable from left to right with the start being at the far left and the end being at the far right), and Shift "shifts" the harmonic content of the Graintable (generally messes with the sound).

1. In a rack containing Mixer 14:2 followed by a Malström, right-click on the Malström and choose Initialize Patch.

2. Click in the OSC A Graintable display window and choose Wind: Trumpet from the bottom of the context menu. You will probably have to use the arrow at the bottom of the context menu to get all the way down there.

3. Find a note on your MIDI keyboard where the trumpet sounds realistic. Move the Index slider to the middle, and you will hear that trumpet line start at a different point in its phrase. Experiment with different positions, and when you are done, move the Index slider back to the far left (start) position.

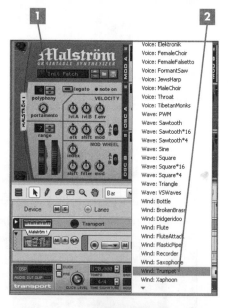

4. Hold down a key on your MIDI keyboard and slowly turn the OSC A Motion knob all the way to the left (you will hear the trumpet speed up, but the pitch will remain the same), then turn the knob slowly all the way to the right. When you are done, return the Motion knob to its middle position.

5. Hold down a key on your MIDI keyboard and slowly turn the OSC A Shift knob all the way to the left, and then all the way to the right. The trumpet gets a lot weirder.

The Malström isn't really that complicated when you look at it in bite-size pieces. The stuff all makes sense. You can plainly see that each oscillator has an ADSR amplifier envelope (just like the Amp Envelope on Subtractor) as well as its own volume control. You will also recognize the tuning knobs (Octave, Semi, and Cent) just like the ones you learned about in the Subtractor and Dr.Rex chapters.

Malström Filters

The Malström has two filters (Filter A and Filter B) that are identical. Each of them has a low-pass (labeled *lp*) filter and a band-pass filter (labeled *bp*) just like on Subtractor and Dr.Rex. In addition to these familiar offerings, the Malström also includes a comb filter (with two variations) as well as ring modulation in both Filter A and Filter B.

Comb Filter

The first new type of filter I think you would enjoy getting familiar with is a comb filter. The Malström has this feature, so let's take it for a test drive.

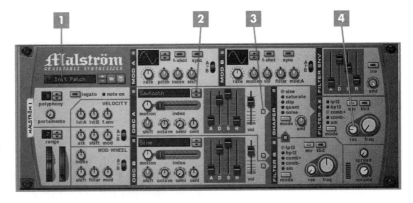

1 In an empty rack, create a Mixer 14:2, followed by a Malström. Then right-click on the Malström and choose Initialize Patch. This will give you a very basic starting point.

2 Right now, OSC A is the only oscillator active (indicated by the amber light above OSC A). The currently selected Graintable is Sine. Click the up arrow three times to select the Sawtooth Graintable (not Sawtooth*4 or Sawtooth*16, just plain Sawtooth). Play a chord on your MIDI keyboard to hear this raw, basic sound.

3 Click on the (unlabeled) Route OSC A to Shaper button. The signal from OSC A has to pass through the Shaper (which is turned off right now) on its way to Filter A (see the arrows pointing the way?).

4 Look at Filter A and play a chord on your MIDI keyboard, and you will hear that the lp12 (low-pass filter) is filtering out a bunch of high frequencies. Turn up Filter A Resonance to about 9 o'clock (a value of 26).

5 Click on comb+ to activate the comb filter.

6 Turn the Filter A Frequency knob down all the way to the left. Now hold down a chord on your MIDI keyboard, and slowly turn the Filter A Frequency knob all the way up and all the way down a few times to hear the comb filter doing what it's good at. When you're done, turn the Filter A Frequency knob down all the way to the left again.

7 Turn the Filter Envelope Amount knob all the way to the right. Now play a chord, and you will hear the Filter Envelope effectively turn the Filter A Frequency knob for you.

In Step 7 above, that's the decay portion of the Filter Envelope you are hearing. The very short attack instantly turns the filter frequency up to maximum, and then the very high (very slow) decay setting slowly brings the frequency back down again.

Just to be clear: Although I am using the terms "filter frequency" and "resonance" (because that is how the knobs are labeled), on Malström, when you select a comb filter, the Filter Frequency knob becomes a delay time knob, and the Resonance knob becomes a delay feedback (number of repeats) knob, just like on a flanger. A flanger is a comb filter with a delay time control, a delay feedback control, and a low frequency oscillator (with rate and amount controls) to regularly modulate (change) the delay time. You don't really hear the delay distinctly because the delay time is so short.

Amplitude Modulation (Ring Modulation)

Although it is perhaps an odd thing to include in a filter section, the Malström has an AM selection in each of its filters. The AM stands for *amplitude modulation*. The specific application of amplitude modulation here is actually more commonly referred to as *ring modulation*. You may be familiar with the Mooger Fooger Ring Modulator pedal (or the plug-in version that looks like it). This will sound a lot like that.

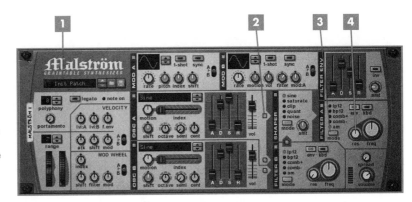

1 In a rack containing Mixer 14:2 followed by a Malström, right-click on the Malström and choose Initialize Patch so that we can start from scratch.

2 Click on the (unlabeled) Route OSC A to Shaper button so that the signal from OSC A can pass on through the Shaper and into Filter A.

3 Click the Filter A Mode button until the amber LED next to AM is lit.

4 The Filter A Resonance knob becomes a "mix" knob when AM is selected. It mixes between the dry signal and the ring modulator signal. Play around on your MIDI keyboard as you turn the Filter A Resonance knob up halfway.

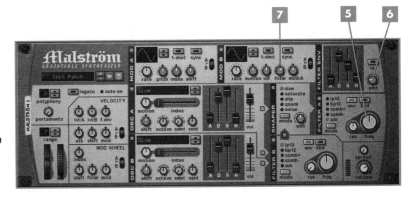

5 The Filter A Frequency knob controls the frequency of the inaudible carrier signal that the ring modulator uses to work its magic. Play around on your MIDI keyboard as you turn this knob back and forth. Turn it back to 12 o'clock when you're done.

6 Turn the Filter Envelope Amount knob up to 9 o'clock (a value of 26). Now play a bit on your MIDI keyboard, and hear the Filter Envelope modulate the Filter A Frequency (ring modulator frequency).

7 To get even weirder, turn the MOD B to Filter knob up to a value of 16 (about 1 o'clock). MOD B is an LFO (low frequency oscillator), and you just routed it to control the ring modulator frequency.

Now the Filter Envelope makes the ring modulator frequency go slowly downward every time you play a note, at the same time MOD B makes the frequency rock back and forth in a sine wave pattern. Sounds like lo-fi sci-fi. By the way, Subtractor has a ring modulator, too.

Filter Envelope

You already have experience using the Filter Envelopes in Subtractor and Dr.Rex. Like Subtractor and Dr.Rex, the Malström's Filter Envelope has sliders for Attack, Decay, Sustain, and Release, as well as a Filter Envelope Amount control.

A feature that has not been covered yet in this book is Filter Envelope Invert. Dr.Rex does not have this feature. Both the Malström and Subtractor do have the feature (as do the NN-19 and Thor), and you are about to learn how to use it. Of course, one simple definition of the word "invert" is simply to "turn something upside down." And that's exactly what Filter Envelope Invert does. It turns the shape of the Filter Envelope upside down. You can hear this in the next exercise.

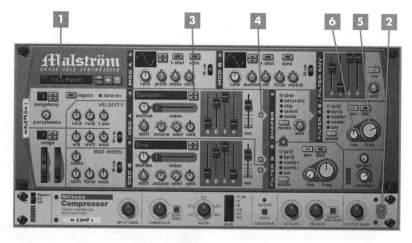

1 In a rack containing Mixer 14:2 followed by a Malström, right-click on the Malström and choose Initialize Patch.

2 Create an MClass Compressor directly under the Malström.

3 Click the up arrow three times on the OSC A Graintable selector to choose the Sawtooth Graintable. (Its full name with classification if you clicked in the Graintable display window is Wave: Sawtooth.)

4 Play a note on your MIDI keyboard. Then click the Route OSC A to Shaper button. Now play a key, and you will hear the lp12 low-pass filter in Filter A cutting off some high-end.

5 Turn up the Filter A Frequency knob to a value of 94. Play a key on your MIDI keyboard and you will hear that some of the highs are back because you turned up the cut-off frequency.

6 Turn the Filter A Resonance knob up about halfway to a value of 62.

7 Turn the Filter Envelope Amount knob up about halfway, to a value of 62.

8 Turn the Filter Envelope Attack slider up to a value of 84.

9 Turn the Filter Envelope Decay slider all the way down to 0.

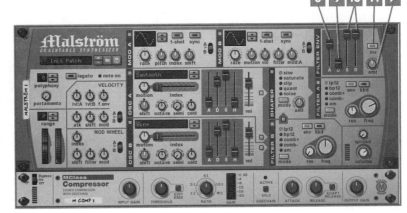

10 Turn the Filter Envelope Sustain and Release sliders all the way up to the top, and play your MIDI keyboard. Do you hear the upward filter sweep as the attack rises?

11 Click on the Filter Envelope Invert button to activate it. Now play your MIDI keyboard and hear the filter start up at a high cut-off frequency and then fall down with the Attack portion of the envelope.

Once you have the exercise above set up, switching the Filter Envelope Invert button on and off while playing your MIDI keyboard is a great way to hear the Invert button turning the Filter Envelope upside down. Normally, pitch, filter cut-off frequency, or whatever is being modulated by an envelope will start at a low or zero level and then rise during the attack portion of the envelope. When you activate Filter Envelope Invert, exactly the opposite happens.

Velocity

You've already played with velocity, so you know that it is a MIDI value that refers to how hard a note or pad is struck. All the Reason synthesizers have velocity controls, which allow you to decide what will happen when you hit a key with more or less force. The most common use is to set the velocity controls so that when you play a key harder, the note sounds louder (like a piano) instead of having all the notes play at the same volume no matter how hard you play (like an organ). But you can choose to make that velocity information control other things as well.

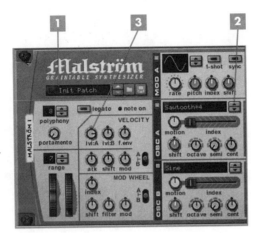

1. In a rack containing Mixer 14:2 followed by a Malström, right-click on the Malström and choose Initialize Patch.

2. Click once on the up arrow in the OSC A Graintable selector to choose Sawtooth*4 and play your MIDI keyboard to hear what this sounds like.

3. Turn up the Velocity to Level A knob (labeled lvl:A) to 3 o'clock. Now play your MIDI keyboard, and you will find that the harder you play, the louder the sound is. It sounds quieter than before because it used to be playing at full volume even when you played softly.

4. Turn the Velocity to Level A knob back to 12 o'clock.

5. Click the Route OSC A to Shaper button, and play your MIDI keyboard to hear what this sounds like. The sound is filtered now, so there is less treble.

6. Turn the Velocity to Filter Env (f.env) knob all the way to the right. Play your MIDI keyboard, and you will hear that the harder you play, the more the Filter Envelope is turned up, which raises the cut-off frequency of Filter A, resulting in more treble in your sound. It sounds the same as if you used your mouse to turn up the Filter Envelope Amount knob.

7. Turn the Velocity to Shift knob all the way to the right. Play your MIDI keyboard, and listen as the harmonic content of your sound is "shifted" the harder you play. Kind of a cool effect.

Just think of everything in terms of control voltage. Here's what I mean: The same way you connected a cable on the back of the Malström to the Stereo Pan control on the 14:2 Mixer in the "Stereo-ize That Sequence" exercise, virtual control voltage is always available to do what you want it to, even when you do not connect cables. Do you want to send control voltage from Velocity to control the Filter Envelope or the Shift amount? Would you like the Mod wheel to control the Filter Frequency? In all these cases, you are routing voltage created by one part of the Malström to control another part of the Malström. So it is with all the Reason instruments.

LFOs (MOD A and MOD B)

To further enjoy controlling bits of the Malström with other bits of the Malström, there's no better place to go next than the Malström's two low frequency oscillators: MODs A and B. Of course, the word "modulator" could be exchanged with the phrase "automatic parameter adjuster." This next exercise will probably remind you of when you explored the Subtractor LFOs.

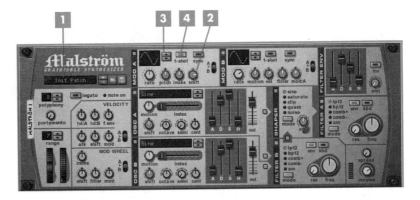

1 In a rack containing Mixer 14:2 followed by a Malström, right-click on the Malström and choose Initialize Patch. Play a note or chord on your MIDI keyboard to hear this plain sine wave.

2 Turn the MOD A Shift knob to 3 o'clock and play. Now the OSC A Shift value is being modulated by MOD A's low frequency sine wave. Sounds pretty, don't you think?

3 Use the up arrow on the MOD A waveform selector to go one by one through each available waveform as you hold down a chord on your MIDI keyboard.

4 Click the MOD A 1-shot button and play your MIDI keyboard some more. Now MOD A only plays its waveform once each time you strike a note, instead of cycling over and over again.

5 Turn off MOD A by clicking the MOD A on/off button.

6 Turn up the MOD B to Volume knob a bit past 2 o'clock (a value of 25). Play your MIDI keyboard to hear the slow vibrato (tremolo).

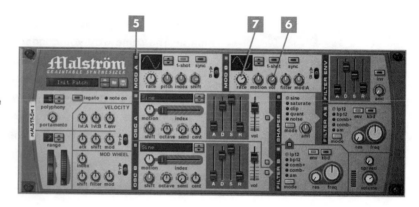

7 Hold down a chord on your MIDI keyboard, and slowly turn the MOD B Rate knob up to a value of 90 (just past 2 o'clock), and it will sound kind of like turning up the vibrato speed on an organ.

As you probably figured out, all the blue knobs in each Modulator section are parameters that can be modulated by the MOD A or MOD B LFO waveform. MOD A can modulate the Pitch, Index, and Shift parameters of either or both OSC A and B, while MOD B can modulate the Motion and Volume parameters of either or both of the oscillators, as well as either or both of the Maström's filters, and can even modulate MOD A for some weird effects. Finally, you should know that the A/B target switch found on each modulator (as well as in the Velocity and Mod wheel sections) routes the modulator to either OSCA/Filter A (top position), OSC B/Filter B (bottom position), or both (middle position).

Modulation Wheel

In the "Modulation Wheel" section of Chapter 4, you learned how to route the modulation wheel to control LFO amount and filter frequency. You can do that with the Malström's Mod wheel as well (except that LFO is labeled "Mod" on the Malström). But since you already learned how to do that in the last chapter, let's do something now that only the Malström can do. In the next exercise, you will use the Malström's modulation wheel to control the Index and Shift parameters of the Malström's oscillators.

1 In a rack containing Mixer 14:2 followed by a Malström, right-click on the Malström and choose Initialize Patch.

2 Click in the OSC A Graintable display window and select Perc: Anvil Hammer.

3 Turn the Mod Wheel to Index knob (labeled Index) all the way to the right. Then hold down some keys on your MIDI keyboard and move your Mod wheel up and down to hear the Graintable play forward and backward.

4 Click the OSC B On/Off button to turn on OSC B.

5 Click in the OSC B Graintable display window and choose Voice: Throat from the bottom of the menu. You will probably have to use the scroll arrow at the bottom of the menu to get down that low in the list.

6 Hold down one or more keys on your MIDI keyboard, and move your Mod wheel (on your keyboard or the Malström) up and down. You will hear the index of both oscillators being adjusted, because the Mod wheel target switch is in the middle position.

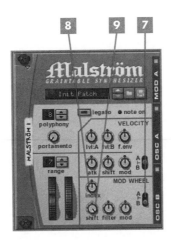

7 Move the Mod Wheel target switch into the lower, B position. Play your MIDI keyboard while moving your Mod wheel back and forth, and only the index of OSC B will be affected.

8 Turn the Mod Wheel to Index knob back to the 12 o'clock position.

9 Turn the Mod Wheel to Shift knob all the way to the right. Play your MIDI keyboard while moving your Mod wheel forward, and you will hear the Shift parameter turned up for only OSC B, since the Mod wheel target switch is still in the lower, B position.

10 Move the Mod Wheel target switch into the upper, A position. Play your MIDI keyboard while moving your Mod wheel forward, and you will hear the Shift value turned up for only OSC A.

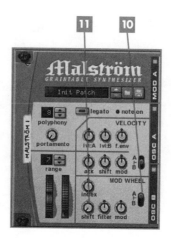

11 Turn the Mod Wheel to Shift knob all the way to the left. Now play your MIDI keyboard while moving your Mod wheel forward. Since you have the Mod Wheel to Shift knob turned all the way down, moving your Mod wheel forward actually turns down the OSC A Shift value.

Malström, Meet the Matrix Analog Pattern Sequencer

In Chapter 4, you were introduced to the RPG-8 Arpeggiator. The RPG-8, of course, can be used with any of the Reason synths. Its use is not limited to the Subtractor. In the same way, the Matrix Analog Pattern Sequencer can be used with any of the Reason synths. The Matrix is modeled after very old sequencers that actually required plugging in a separate patch cable for each note that was to be triggered. While the Matrix is great for sequencing notes, it also can control other things, such as filters, making it useful in conjunction with almost every device in Reason.

Key Mode

Key mode is what you will use to control what notes are played by the Malström. By default, the Keys/Curve switch is in the Keys position. Just to the left of this switch, you will see a Pattern section that works the same way as Redrum's Pattern section, with four banks of eight patterns, a Run button, and a Pattern Enable button. Let's give it a try.

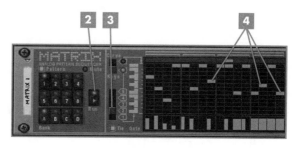

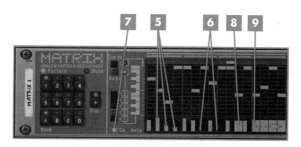

1 In an empty rack, create a Mixer 14:2, followed by a Malström and a Matrix Pattern Sequencer underneath the Malström. Load the following patch into the Malström: Reason Factory Sound Bank > Malstrom Patches > Bass > Bassic.xwv.

2 Click Run on the Matrix and you will hear the default pattern.

3 Move the Octave switch down from 3 to 2. This determines which octave you will be editing but does not change the octave of the existing notes.

4 Click around in the left half of the upper grid section of the Pattern window to change some notes. By default, you are dealing with only those first 16 steps.

5 Make a few of the notes quieter or louder by dragging their velocity down or up in the lower Gate section of the Pattern window.

6 Take out a few of the notes completely by dragging their velocity all the way down.

7 Click on the Tie button.

8 Double the length of a few notes by clicking on their Gate value in the lower Gate section of the Edit window.

9 If you have a few of the same note in a row, click and drag across their Gate values in the lower Gate section of the Edit window. They will then all be tied together as one continuous note.

Curve Mode

Curve mode is used for controlling filters and other parameters on Reason devices. Editing in Curve mode does not change anything you did in Key mode, so you can send distinct key and curve information on the same pattern. For this exercise, you can use the same rack as the last one, with Mixer 14:2 followed by a Malström (with the bass patch Bassic.xwv loaded) and a Matrix Pattern Sequencer underneath the Malström.

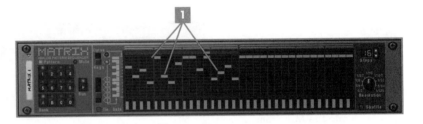

1 While still in Key mode, draw in some notes in the left portion of the Matrix grid. Use any octave you like (I like Octave 2 for this sound).

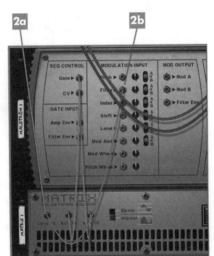

2 Press Tab to flip your rack around. Then click and drag a cable connecting the Matrix's Curve CV output to the Malström's Filter Modulation input.

3 Flip your rack back around facing front, and move the Key/Curve switch to the Curve position.

4 Draw in some curve information in the left half of the upper portion of the grid. You will hear the Malström's filter frequency changing (the sound will get brighter and darker).

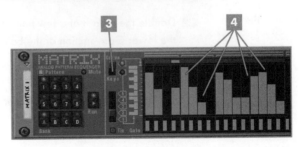

5 Right-click on the Matrix and click Randomize Pattern. You will hear that the pitch has been randomized, and you will see that the Curve has been randomized at the same time.

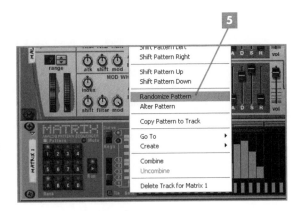

6 Press Tab to flip your rack around. For a different effect, move the end of the cable that is in the Malström's Filter Modulation input so that it is plugged into the Shift Modulation input.

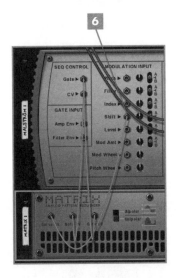

7 Finally, move the end of the cable that is in the Malström's Shift Modulation input so that it is plugged into the Pitch Modulation input. Now you are controlling the Malström's pitch with the Matrix's Curve output and its Note CV output at the same time.

Randomize Pattern in Step 5 probably reminded you of Redrum. There are also other selections from the Matrix's context menu that work the same as Redrum: Copy/Paste Pattern, Shift Pattern Left/Right, and Copy Pattern to Track. There is also a Shuffle button and Resolution knob, which also work the same as on Redrum and the RPG-9 Arpeggiator.

> ❄ **WHEN THE CABLES GET IN THE WAY**
>
> Always remember that when you are plugging and unplugging cables on the back of your Reason Rack, if you have trouble reading something because a cable is in the way, you can press the L key on your computer keyboard to hide the cables. If you want to see them again, just press L again, and they will reappear.

Using the Malström as an Effects Processor

This next bit is pretty cool. The Malström actually has audio inputs. This is so you can connect the outputs of another Reason device (such as Dr.Rex or Redrum) to those inputs and use the Malström's filters and Shaper to process the sound from the other device. I hope you will enjoy trying this in the following exercise.

Playing Dr.Rex Through the Malström's Filters

 In a brand spankin' new rack, create a Mixer 14:2, followed by a Malström, and then Dr.Rex under that. Then press the Tab key to flip your rack around.

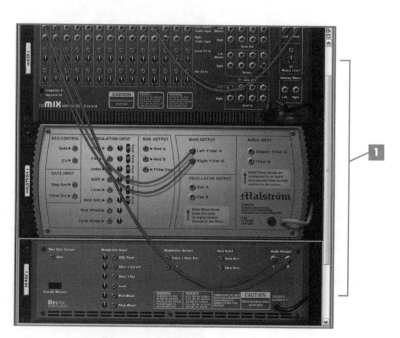

2 Click, drag, and release the cable out of Dr.Rex's left Audio Output. This will actually disconnect both left and right Audio Outputs.

3 Click and drag a cable connection from Dr.Rex's left Audio Output to the Malström's Shaper/Filter: A Audio Input.

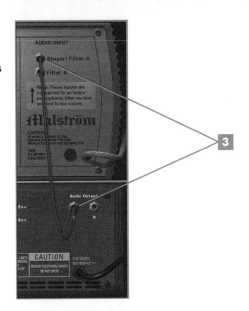

4 Click and drag a cable connection from Dr.Rex's right Audio Output to the Malström's Filter: B Audio Input.

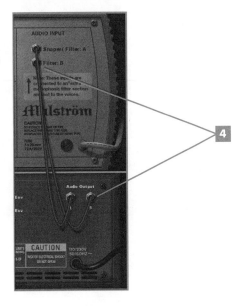

5 Press the Tab key to flip your rack around facing front. Then click directly in Dr.Rex's Loop Name display window and choose Hse40_RideBeat_130 _eLAB.rx2.

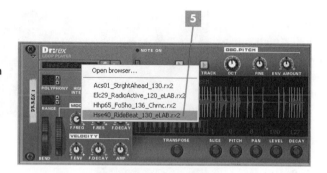

6 Right-click on the Malström and choose Initialize Patch.

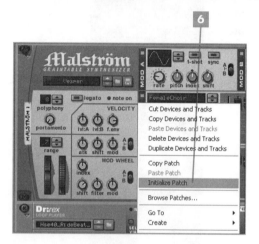

7 Turn up the tempo to 133 bpm in the Reason Transport panel.

8 Click the Preview button in Dr.Rex.

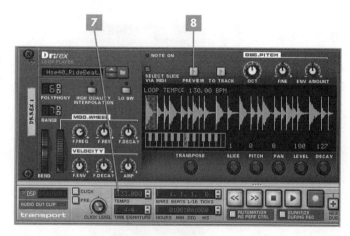

9 Click the Sync button on MOD B and turn the MOD B Rate knob down a notch to 4/4.

10 Turn the MOD B to Filter knob up all the way to the right.

11 Turn the Spread knob all the way to the right (to make maximum stereo separation with the output from Filter A/Shaper on the left and the output from Filter B on the right).

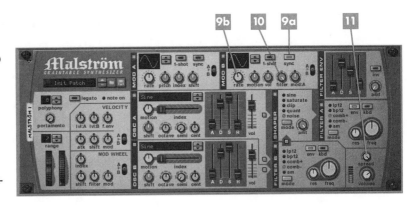

12 Choose comb+ for the filter type on Filter A, and turn the Filter A Resonance knob up halfway to a value of 65.

13 Choose comb– for the filter type on Filter B, and turn the Filter B Resonance knob up halfway to a value of 65.

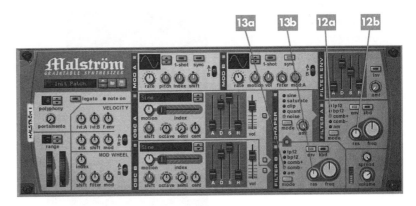

14 Use the up arrow on the MOD B Waveform selector to try all the different waveforms. When you are done, go back down to the first waveform (sine wave).

15 Turn on the Shaper and listen for a moment. Then turn the Shaper Amount knob all the way up and try each Shaper mode. The Noise mode is the freakiest!

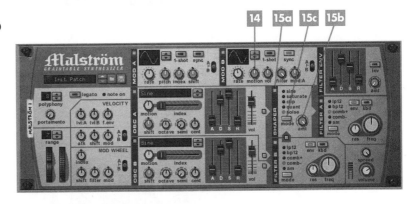

Please feel encouraged to try different settings on the MOD B Rate knob, as well as different combinations of Shaper modes and MOD B waveforms.

Playing Dr.Rex Through the Shaper

Although you tried playing Dr.Rex through the Shaper in Step 15 of the preceding exercise, there was so much other insanity going on that you may still not have a clear picture of the character of the Shaper. The Shaper uses a process called *waveshaping* to distort incoming signals. A good way to get a feel for what effect the Shaper has is to run a drum loop through it, with no other filtering or modulation applied to the signal.

1 In a new rack, create in this order: Mixer 14:2, Malström, Dr.Rex. Then press Tab to flip the rack around.

2 Right-click on Dr.Rex's left audio output and select Disconnect from the context menu.

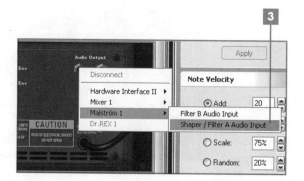

3 Right-click on Dr.Rex's left audio output and select Malström 1 > Shaper/Filter A Audio Input from the context menu.

4 Flip the rack back around facing front, and load the following REX file into Dr.Rex: Reason Factory Sound Bank > Dr Rex Drum Loops > Abstract HipHop > Trh11_Dopest_090eLAB.rx2.

5 Click the Malström's Filter A On/Off button to turn the filter off.

6 Click the Preview button on Dr.Rex. Since neither Filter A or the Shaper is on, you are hearing the natural, unaffected drum loop (at 30 bpm faster than the loop was originally recorded).

7 Turn the Shaper Amount knob up to 3 o'clock (a value of about 104).

8 Hang onto your hat and click the Shaper On/Off button to activate the Shaper.

9 Click on each Shaper mode to hear what it sounds like.

By now I hope you can see what a unique synth the Malström is. I find new ways to have fun with this thing every time I play with it. I invariably end up designing a new patch or becoming inspired to work on a new piece of music thanks to some interesting sound that comes out of the Malström. The logical, easily useable design with its simple yet powerful controls helps make the Malström a true classic. As you put to use what you've learned in this book and consult the Reason Operation Manual when you have questions, you will master the Malström in no time, and it will become yet another useful tool for making great-sounding music with Reason.

6 } Thor Polysonic Synthesizer

Thor is an amazing new addition to Reason, capable of very warm analog sounds, complex, deeply weird, and exciting textures and effects, lead sounds that really cut through, and tons of groove. Thor offers significant new features not found on Subtractor or the Malström. It features a very cool Step Sequencer that opens up whole new areas of inspiration and rhythmic possibilities. Its oscillators and filters are modular: When you change oscillator type (analog, wavetable, phase modulation, FM pair, multi oscillator, or noise) or filter type (including new Formant and State Variable filter types), you are presented with a completely different user interface for that oscillator or filter. Finally, Thor's Modulation Bus Routing section allows you to easily connect just about any part of Thor to any other part of Thor.

Go ahead and stick Thor in a rack and click the Show Programmer button in the lower left corner of Thor. Now you can see Thor in all its glory. Look at the size of that thing. As you can see, Thor is a big synth with quite a lot going on. You may have been a beginner at the start of this book, but now that you're becoming something of an expert on Reason 4, you are ready to learn how to use Thor's exciting and unique new features. I wouldn't be giving you your money's worth if I didn't dig into this beautiful new synth and show you what it has to offer.

In this chapter you will learn how to:

❋ Use Thor's Step Sequencer

❋ Make your own sounds using each of Thor's six oscillator types

❋ Use Thor's unique new Formant filter

❋ Become a master of Thor's very useful Modulation Bus Routing section

❋ Use the BV512 Digital Vocoder with Thor to vocode beats instead of voice

Using Thor's Step Sequencer

One thing that makes Thor such a powerful new addition to Reason is its Step Sequencer. What can you do with it? Well, there are plenty of patches in the Rhythmic and Percussion folders that use the Step Sequencer. But you can also use the Step Sequencer with any sound you like, even if the patch wasn't originally programmed that way.

All the exercises in this section are connected to each other. When you are done with one, don't close the window, because the next exercise will pick up where the last one left off. You may even want to save between exercises. I promise some cool payoffs as you work through these Step Sequencer tutorials. Let's go.

Using the Step Knobs to Control Pitch

Each step in Thor's Step Sequencer has a step knob that can be used to set the note value, velocity, gate length, and step duration for each step. Which value you are editing with a step knob at any given time is determined by the position of the Edit knob. In addition to note value, velocity, and so on, you can also program a step to send modulation information to just about any other part of Thor you want using the Curve 1 and Curve 2 positions on the Edit knob. In this first exercise, you will use the step knobs to edit pitch (note value). The Edit knob is already set to the Note position by default.

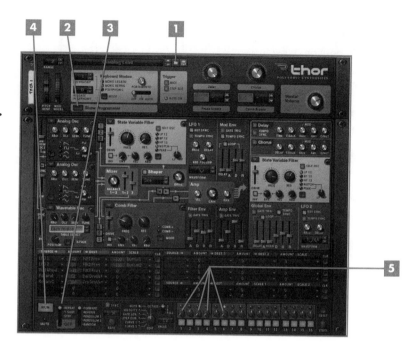

1 In a rack containing Mixer 14:2, followed by Thor, load the following patch into Thor: Reason Factory Sound Bank > Thor Patches > Lead Synths > Combing Lead.thor.

2 Click the Show Programmer button.

3 Set Sequencer Run Mode to Repeat.

4 Click Run.

5 Turn the step knobs all the way down for steps 1, 3, 4, and 6.

6 The Octave switch is currently set for two octaves. Switch it to four octaves.

7 Turn the step knobs all the way down for steps 9, 11, 12, and 14.

8 Turn the step knob on step 13 down a hair to a MIDI note value of A#2.

Please note that the Octave switch only affects note information. It has no effect for editing done in the Velocity, Gate Length, Step Duration, Curve 1, or Curve 2 Edit knob positions.

Using the Step Knobs to Control Gate Length

Gate Length controls the length of the note played for a given step. The step still lasts for the same duration no matter what the Gate Length value is (by default, each step lasts for a single 1/16 note). Gate Length determines what percentage of the step will actually have a note playing in it. The default value is 75%.

153

❊ ❊ ❊

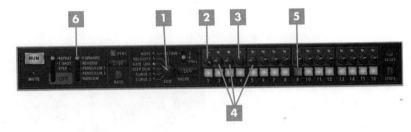

1. Turn the Edit knob to the Gate Length position. Now the control knobs will control gate length instead of note value.

2. Turn the step 1 knob all the way up.

3. Turn the step 4 knob down to 12 o'clock.

4. Turn the step knobs on steps 2, 3, and 5 down to 9 o'clock.

5. Click on the step 9 button to turn that step off.

6. Try all five Sequencer Direction switch positions: Forward, Reverse, Pendulum 1, Pendulum 2, and Random. When you are done, switch it back to Forward.

Controlling the Step Sequencer with Your MIDI Keyboard

So far, the Step Sequencer starts when you click the Run button and stops when you click the Run button again. By the end of the next exercise, not only will the Step Sequencer start when you play a note on your MIDI keyboard and stop when you let go, but it will also transpose the sequence according to which note you play on your MIDI keyboard. This exercise starts where the last exercise left off.

1. Click the Note Trigger MIDI button to turn it off.

2. In the Step Sequencer, click the Run button to stop the sequence.

3. Set Modulation Bus 6 Source for MIDI Key > Gate by clicking in the first empty space in the Source column on the left side of the Modulation Bus Routing section of Thor and selecting MIDI Key > Gate from the pop-up menu and sub-menu.

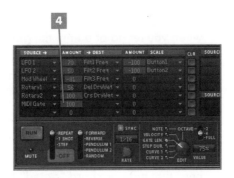

4 Set Modulation Bus 6 Destination Amount to 100. Do this by clicking in the Amount cell and dragging upward while you hold your mouse button down.

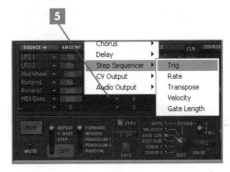

5 Set the Modulation Bus 6 Destination to Step Sequencer > Trig. Now the sequencer will play when you are holding down a key on your MIDI keyboard, and it will stop when you let go. The same notes are played no matter which key you play.

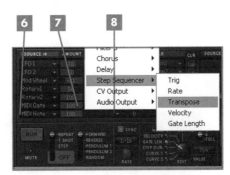

6 Set Modulation Bus 7 Source for MIDI Key > Note.

7 Set Modulation Bus 7 Destination Amount to 100.

8 Set Modulation Bus 7 Destination to Step Sequencer > Transpose. Now the sequence will be transposed according to what note you play on your MIDI keyboard.

Using the Step Sequencer to Gate Thor's Amplifier

In analog synths and sequencers, gate inputs and outputs transmit note on/off but do not transmit note values (such as A#1 or D2). A gate is either open or closed, on or off. Reason departs from this a bit in that Reason also transmits velocity information via its gate I/O.

Normally, when you play a note, the gate is opened (note on), and when you let go of a note the gate closes (note off). In the next exercise, when you play a note, it triggers the Step Sequencer, and the Step Sequencer opens and closes the gate with each step of the sequence.

At the end of this exercise, you won't hear the notes you sequenced anymore (since note value is not transmitted via gate CV). Instead, when you play a note or chord on your MIDI keyboard, you will hear that note or chord "gated" (or triggered) to the rhythm of the Step Sequencer. This is a pretty neat trick, lending itself to some nice locked rhythmic effects. This exercise picks up at the point where the last exercise left off.

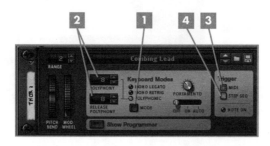

1 Set Keyboard Mode to Polyphonic.

2 Turn Polyphony and Release Polyphony up to 8.

3 Turn on the Note Trigger MIDI button.

4 Turn off the Note Trigger Step Sequencer button.

5 Turn the Amp Gain knob all the way down.

6 Set Modulation Bus 8 Source to Step Sequencer > Gate.

7 Set Modulation Bus 8 Destination Amount to 60.

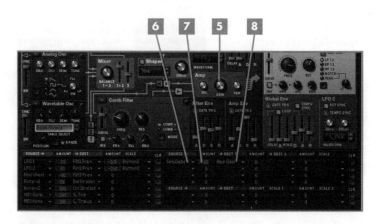

8 Set Modulation Bus 8 Destination to Amp > Gain. Play some chords on your MIDI keyboard, and you will hear your chords played with the rhythm from the Step Sequencer.

Using the Step Knobs to Control Curve Values

In analog hardware (and in Reason), gate information is transmitted via control voltage (CV). Curve CV (as opposed to gate CV) can transmit note value information and can be used to modulate other parameters as well.

The last two positions for the Edit knob (Curve 1 and Curve 2) are generic in nature and can be assigned in the Modulation Bus Routing section to control whatever you want. Since Thor's Edit knob already has a Note position, we will use Curve 1 to control the frequency of Filter 3. Again, we are picking up where the last exercise left off.

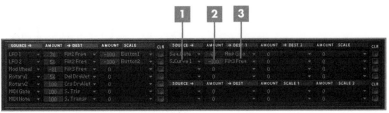

1 Set Modulation Bus 9 Source for Step Sequencer > Curve 1.

2 Turn Modulation Bus 9 Destination Amount all the way down to –100.

3 Set Modulation Bus 9 Destination to Filter 3 > Frequency.

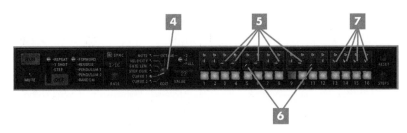

4 Move the Edit knob to the Curve 1 position (or click directly on the green LED next to Curve 1).

5 Turn down step knobs 3, 4, 6, 8, and 10 to about 9 o'clock (a curve value of about 1:22).

6 Turn step knobs 5 and 11 all the way down (all the way to the left).

7 Turn step knobs 13, 14, 15, and 16 down to about 11 o'clock (a curve value of about 1:46). Then hold down some chords on your MIDI keyboard to hear the effect.

Here is one last trick (the cherry on top).

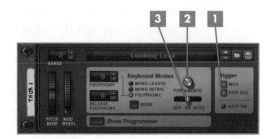

1. Turn the Note Trigger Step Sequencer button back on.

2. Turn the Portamento knob down to a value of 35.

3. Turn the Portamento switch to the on position. Then hold a note on your MIDI keyboard to hear the effect.

While you're at it, try some modulation wheel. It's mapped to modulate the Filter 3 frequency on this patch. OK, that's the end of the "connected" Step Sequencer exercises. The following Step Duration exercise starts fresh and does not reference the preceding exercises.

Using the Step Knobs to Control Step Duration

If you increase the step duration, the Step Sequencer will stay on that step longer before moving on to the next step. If the gate length is short but the step duration is long, the Step Sequencer will still stay on the step for the entire designated step duration, and you will hear silence from the time the note ends until the next step is played. However, if you set a very short step duration, the note will be short no matter what, since the gate length is a percentage of the step duration, and even 100% of "short" is still short.

A great example of step duration in action can be found in the patch I Am Thor. This is an interesting patch to study, not only for the use of step duration, but for the way Curve 1 and Curve 2 are used to modulate the Formant Filter X and Y sliders, which control the vowel sound.

1 In a fresh rack with Mixer 14:2 followed by Thor, click in Thor's Patch Display window and choose I Am Thor from the pop-up menu.

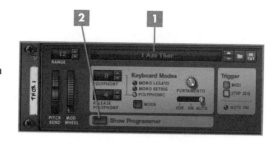

2 Click the Show Programmer button.

3 In Thor's Step Sequencer, move the Edit knob to the Step Duration position.

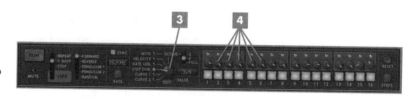

4 Play a note on your MIDI keyboard, and watch how the lights above the steps move very quickly through the first few beats. Now turn up step knobs 2, 3, 4, 5, and 6 all the way to the right and play your MIDI keyboard again.

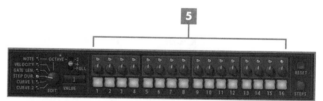

5 Ctrl+click on each of the 16 step knobs to return them to their default position of 1. Play your MIDI keyboard, and all steps will have an equal duration.

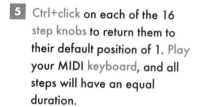

The potential drawback to messing with step duration is that you can end up with step sequences that do not line up with the rest of the track when looped. If your track is in 4/4 time, you would have to make sure your step sequence still adds up to four beats (or a multiple thereof), or else the downbeat on Thor's step sequence will not line up with the "ones" in the rest of your Reason song. This is not a problem with a one-shot, arrhythmic patch like I Am Thor.

Sequencer

Building Sounds in Thor

I will not lie to you: Thor is a beast of a synth. But I mean that in a good way. You can do lots and lots with just one Thor. It's amazing how much good stuff Propellerhead built into Thor. And it all makes sense. Here it comes in bite-size pieces: making your own sounds with Thor.

Thor's Oscillators

"Polysonic" is probably not a word you need to learn for the Basic Synthesis 101 exam. I mean, don't most synthesizers make more than one sound, thus making them polysonic? Most likely what Propellerhead is referring to with that name is the choice of oscillator types. Each of Thor's three oscillator slots offers a choice of six completely different types of oscillators, each with its own very specific character. To give you a feel for what each oscillator type can do, I will introduce key features of each oscillator in the exercises that follow.

Each oscillator type shares one thing in common: a group of four knobs across the top of the oscillator. The Octave, Semi, and Tune knobs should be familiar to you from your experience with other Reason synths. But what's that knob labeled "KBD" in the upper left corner? You will try that knob as you study the first oscillator type on your tour: Thor's analog oscillator.

Analog Oscillator

The analog oscillator will probably be the most immediately familiar to you. But it still has a couple of tricks worth mentioning. From top to bottom, you can see four familiar basic waveforms: sawtooth, square, triangle, and sine. But wait—the Reason Operation Manual does not refer to that second wave as a square wave. They call it a *pulse wave*. That's fine, because there is a Pulse Width knob, and as you can (sort of) see from the marks around the PW knob, it is only a perfect square wave when the knob is set at 12 o'clock. Otherwise, you can just think of a pulse wave as a rectangular wave, which is the way it is sometimes referred to. Let's give this a try.

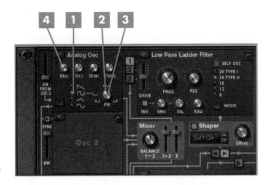

1 In a freshly initialized Thor, select **Oscillator 1's** pulse wave. Play a few notes to hear this.

2 Move the **Pulse Width** knob to 12 o'clock (a value of 64), and you will hear the classic square wave sound, with some highs rolled off thanks to the Low Pass Ladder filter it's going through.

3 Turn up the Pulse Width knob to a value of 124 and hear how thin the sound becomes. Then play your MIDI keyboard with one hand as you slowly turn the Pulse Width knob all the way to the left and then back to center. You just did pulse width modulation.

4 Turn the Keyboard Tracking knob down to about 3 o'clock. Play your MIDI keyboard, and you will find that the difference between two octaves is less than 12 semitones now.

5 Turn the Keyboard Tracking knob all the way to the left, and you will find that any key you play will play the same note.

Changing the Keyboard Tracking knob to intermediate values could be useful when dealing with non-pitched sounds (like percussion, noise-based effects, or other sound effects). It is also useful for exotically pitched sounds, horror suspense, or general weirdness.

Wavetable Oscillator

As you know, Propellerhead combined granular synthesis and wavetable synthesis to create its own Graintable synthesis, which is the basis of the Malström's oscillators. Thor is the first Reason synth to offer a straight-up wavetable oscillator.

Imagine a WAV file of a gong crash sliced up into 100 equal slices. Each slice is a separate waveform, a tiny slice of a gong crash. String them all together and they make a wavetable. With Reason's wavetable oscillator, the Position knob is used to choose which little waveform (slice) in the wavetable will be played when you play a note. It stays stuck looping that single waveform and will play through the entire wavetable only if you move the Position knob all the way from right to left as you play the note.

1 In a freshly initialized Thor, click the arrow in the upper left corner of Oscillator 1 and select Wavetable from the menu.

2 Use the down arrow to click through the 32 wavetables one at a time, trying each one on your MIDI keyboard as you go.

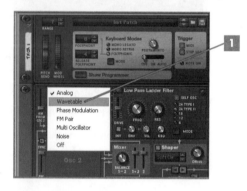

3 Click in the Wavetable display and choose Sine Harmonics. Then play your MIDI keyboard, and you will hear a basic sine wave.

4 While playing your MIDI keyboard with one hand, slowly turn the Position knob all the way to the right and then all the way back to the left (a value of zero). Now when you play your MIDI keyboard, you will hear a basic sine wave.

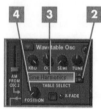

5 Click in the first Modulation Bus 1 Source cell and select Mod Env (modulation envelope).

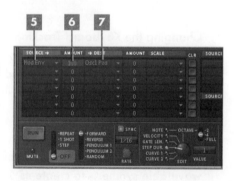

6 Click and drag the amount up to a value of 100.

7 Select Osc 1 Pos (oscillator 1 position) for the Destination. Play your MIDI keyboard, and you will hear a smooth sweep from end to beginning of the wavetable each time you play a key.

8 On Oscillator 1, click the X-fade (crossfade) button to turn crossfade off. Now when you play your MIDI keyboard, you will hear the sharp edges of each waveform in the wavetable.

Phase Modulation Oscillator

If anyone out there remembers the Casio CZ series of keyboards (like the CZ-1 or the CZ-101), then Thor's phase modulation oscillator may bring back memories, since it was modeled after that line of synthesizers. Thor's phase modulation oscillator can actually generate two waveforms, but instead of playing both at exactly the same time, it plays one after the other. What you hear when this happens is a second simultaneous tone that is one octave below the first tone. There is also a Phase Modulation knob that, when swept, simulates a filter sweep. This oscillator has its own unique character, providing another group of colors on Thor's palette.

1 In a freshly initialized Thor, choose Bypass for Filter 1, so you can hear Oscillator 1 with no filtering.

2 Choose Phase Modulation for Oscillator 1.

3 Play your MIDI keyboard while slowly turning the Oscillator 1 Phase Modulation knob all the way to the right, then all the way to the left, and ending back at 12 o'clock.

4 By default, the second waveform is off. Play your MIDI keyboard while using the up arrow to try each of the choices for the second waveform. When you are done, select the sawtooth wave for the second waveform.

5 Choose Wave number 5 for the first waveform so that your Parameter Value tooltip says OSC 1 Phase Modulation Wave 1:5 when you mouse over the waveform.

6 Turn the Phase Modulation knob all the way down to the left.

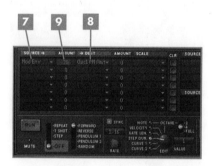

7 Set Modulation Bus 1 Source to Mod Envelope.

8 Set Modulation Bus 1 Destination to Osc 1 PM Amount.

9 Set Modulation Bus 1 Destination Amount to 70, and play your MIDI keyboard in the bass register.

10 Turn the Mod Envelope Decay slider down to 552ms (milliseconds), and play your MIDI keyboard in the bass register.

11 Continue to play your MIDI keyboard in the lower octaves while slowly turning the Oscillator 1 Pulse Modulation knob up and down through a full sweep.

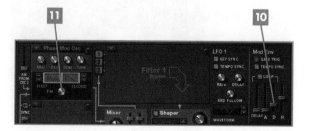

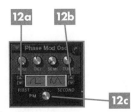

12 Select Wave 4 for the first waveform and Wave 4 for the second waveform (they have the same number but are different waveforms), and set Phase Modulation Amount to 9 o'clock (a value of 20). Now you have another serviceable bass sound.

I encourage you to mix and match waveforms and Phase Modulation knob settings to hear all the different sonic characters you can come up with.

FM Pair Oscillator

Digital FM (frequency modulation) synthesis was made famous by Yamaha's hugely successful DX7 synthesizer. It can be used for all sorts of metallic or bell-like tones and can be used in combination with other oscillators to add a bit of this character, as in the following example.

1 In a freshly initialized Thor (with Programmer showing), choose FM Pair for Oscillator 1.

2 Turn up the Amp Envelope Release slider to a value of about 3 seconds so that it is even with the Amp Envelope Sustain slider.

3 As you play your MIDI keyboard, use the up arrow to step through the Carrier values (one at a time) up to number 5 and leave it there.

4 As you play your MIDI keyboard, use the up arrow to step through the Modulator values up to number 17, and leave it there.

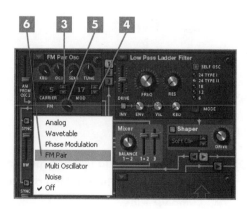

5 As you play your MIDI keyboard, slowly turn the Frequency Modulation knob all the way up to a value of 119 (almost all the way to the right). You should have a clangy, chime-like tone now.

6 Select FM Pair for Oscillator 2.

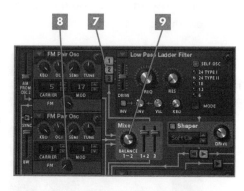

7 Click the Osc 2 to Filter 1 Enable button.

8 Turn the Oscillator 2 FM Amount knob all the way down.

9 Turn the Mixer knob to 3 o'clock, and play your keyboard a bit to see where you're at with this patch.

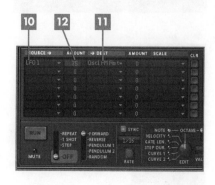

10 Set Modulation Bus 1 Source to LFO 1.

11 Set Modulation Bus 1 Destination to Osc 1 FM Amt.

12 Set Modulation Bus 1 Destination Amount to a value of 75, and play your MIDI keyboard to hear the effect.

13 Click the Chorus button to activate the Chorus effect. Now you should have a pretty sound to play with. But if you want to go even further into DX7 Land, go on to the next step.

14 Set Modulation Bus 2 Source to Mod Envelope.

15 Set Modulation Bus 2 Destination to Osc 2 FM Amount.

16 Set Modulation Bus 2 Destination Amount to a value of 75.

17 To make this patch more expressive, turn the Amplifier Velocity knob up to 3 o'clock. Now the volume of your patch depends on how hard you play.

Wow. I feel like I'm in the 1980s. Of course, if you liked the mellower sound you had before Step 16, you can simply turn Modulation Bus 2 Destination Amount back down to zero or somewhere in between.

Multi Oscillator

Thor's multi oscillator generates its sound with multiple detuned waveforms of the same type. If you select a square wave, the multi oscillator will play multiple square waves, detuned from each other in a manner determined by the Detune Mode menu, to a degree determined by the Detune Amount knob. Of course, you are free to experiment with the five different waveforms the multi oscillator has to offer, but this exercise is focused on what makes the multi oscillator unique, which is the use of its different detune modes, so you will be sticking with the default sawtooth wave in the following easy tutorial.

1 In a freshly initialized Thor, click the arrow in the upper left corner of Oscillator 1 and choose Multi Oscillator. Then play your keyboard to hear the sound of Random 1, the default detune mode.

2 Turn the Detune Amount knob all the way to the right. Now play some very high keys. Can you hear how this could be used to add a bell-like or metallic texture to a sound?

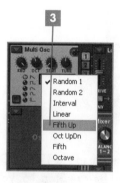

3 Click in the Detune Mode display window and select Fifth Up from the menu. Then play your keyboard to hear the sound.

4 Click the down arrow once to select Oct UpDn for the detune mode, and play your keyboard to hear the sound.

5 Click the down arrow once more to select Fifth for the detune mode, and you will hear a big mess when you play your keyboard.

6 Turn the Detune Amount knob down all the way to the left, and you will find that the Fifth detune mode starts with the waveforms a fifth apart (unlike the Fifth Up mode, which requires a maximum Detune Amount setting to produce a fifth interval).

7 Turn the detune amount up to 9 o'clock, and you will hear a chorusing effect.

8 Click the down arrow to choose Octave for the detune mode. The Octave mode starts with the waveforms an octave apart (unlike the Oct UpDn detune mode, which requires a maximum Detune Amount setting to produce an octave interval).

Noise Oscillator

What is more fun to play with than straight-up noise? Thor is the first Reason synth to offer anywhere near this degree of musical sculpting of noise. The results can be subtle, eerie, atmospheric, beautiful, or all of the above. By the way, Step 9 is my favorite part (I saved the best for last).

1 In a freshly initialized Thor, click the arrow in the upper left corner of Oscillator 1 and choose Noise Oscillator.

2 Click the arrow in the upper left corner of Filter 1 (currently a Low Pass Ladder filter) and choose Bypass from the menu, so you can hear Oscillator 1 with no filtering.

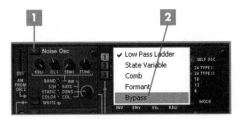

3 Turn the Amp Envelope Decay slider all the way to the top.

4 Turn Amp Envelope Release up nearly halfway so it's even with the Sustain slider, and then play a few notes on your MIDI keyboard to hear pure white noise.

5 Choose Color for the noise type.

6 Sweep the Modulation knob as you play your MIDI keyboard. Turning the knob toward the left produces darker noise color settings, while turning the knob all the way to the right produces white noise.

7 Choose Static for the noise type, and sweep the Modulation knob while playing your keyboard. Settings to the left produce lower density static similar to turntable pops.

8 Choose S/H (Sample and Hold) for the noise type, and sweep the Modulation knob all the way from left to right and back again while holding down a note on your MIDI keyboard. This adjusts the rate of the randomly generated S/H signal.

9 Choose Band for the noise type. Play your MIDI keyboard and sweep the Modulation knob all the way from left to right and back again.

When the noise type is set to Band, the Modulation knob controls the bandwidth, with the narrowest bandwidth at the far left. My favorite bandwidth setting is at 9 o'clock. It has sort of an ethereal, underwater sound.

AM from Oscillator 2

You are no doubt familiar with AM (amplitude modulation) from your work with Subtractor and the Malström. With Thor, AM is especially quick and easy, as you will experience with the following exercise.

1 In a freshly initialized Thor, select a sine wave for Analog Oscillator 1. (You could use another wave type, but sine will be nice for this.)

2 Click the arrow in the upper left corner of the Oscillator 2 slot and select Analog Oscillator.

3 Select a sine wave for Oscillator 2. You will not hear anything change because Oscillator 2 is not routed to either filter.

4 Turn the Keyboard Tracking knob all the way down on Oscillator 2.

5 While playing your MIDI keyboard, slowly move the AM from OSC 2 slider all the way to the top.

6 For a different effect (sort of like a touch-tone phone sound), turn Oscillator 2 Keyboard Tracking up to 12 o'clock, and turn the Oscillator 2 Octave knob up to a value of 6. Then play the lower octaves of your MIDI keyboard.

Oscillator Sync

You may have noticed some patches in the Reason synths with "sync" in the patch name. You also may have noticed that these patches have a certain sound in common. They are all using a technique called *oscillator sync*. When you use oscillator sync with Thor, Oscillator 1 is the master, and it controls the pitch that you hear. When you sync Oscillator 2 or 3 to Oscillator 1, you will not hear the sync effect until you modulate (change) the frequency (pitch) of Oscillator 2 or 3. To hear this effect immediately, you will try out the patch called Big Sync.

1 In an empty rack, create an MClass Mastering Suite, followed by Mixer 14:2 and an instance of Thor. Then load the following patch into Thor: Reason Factory Sound Bank > Thor Patches > Lead Synths > Big Sync.

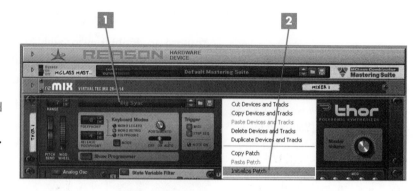

2 Hold a few long notes on your MIDI keyboard to hear the oscillator sync effect, which sounds kind of like the sweep of a comb filter. Then right-click on Thor and choose Initialize Patch from the context menu so that you can start building your own sync patch.

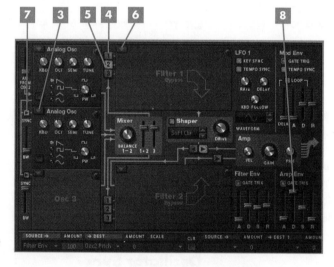

3 Click the arrow in the upper left corner of Oscillator 2 and choose Analog from the pop-up menu.

4 Click the Oscillator 1 to Filter 1 Enable button to turn it off so that the audio signal from Osc 1 will not pass into the filter.

5 Click the Oscillator 2 to Filter 1 Enable button to turn it on so that the audio signal from Osc 2 will pass through the filter.

6 Click the arrow in the upper left corner of Filter 1 and choose Bypass from the pop-up menu. Signal will pass through, but it will not be filtered.

7 Click the Oscillator 2 Sync to Oscillator 1 button. You will not hear much change in the sound if you play your MIDI keyboard right now.

8 Turn the Amp Envelope Decay slider all the way up to the top.

9 Set Mod 1 Source to Filter Envelope.

10 Set Mod 1 Destination Amount to 100.

11 Set Mod 1 Destination to Oscillator 2 Pitch. Now when you play your MIDI keyboard, you will hear a strong oscillator sync effect.

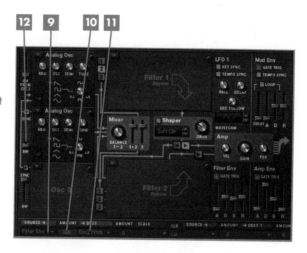

12 Turn the Oscillator 2 Sync Bandwidth slider all the way down. Play a key on your MIDI keyboard, and you will hear a slightly different effect (which will also make the higher notes quieter).

Note that the Sync Bandwidth sliders will set the bandwidth at maximum at the top and minimum at the bottom. It just says "sync" at the top, and "bw" at the bottom because there wasn't room to print "sync bandwidth" in one small space.

Using Thor's Filters

Thor's filters all have a drive control (which controls the signal level going into the filter), an Envelope Invert button (which you learned about in the Filter Envelope section of Chapter 5, "Malström"), an Envelope Amount knob, a Velocity knob, which determines how much the envelope amount will be affected by how hard you play, and a Keyboard Tracking knob. Although slightly different than the filters on other Reason devices, the Low Pass Ladder filter, the State Variable filter, and the Comb filter should all feel somewhat familiar to you. The one filter type Thor offers that is radically different from anything you've seen yet in Reason is the Formant filter.

Formant Filter

The word "formant" refers to the vowel sound resulting from a filter setting. Examples of formant filters would include the rubber end of a toilet plunger used on the bell of a trombone or trumpet, the way your mouth is positioned when playing a Jew's harp or when using a talk box for guitar, or a wah-wah pedal. You will understand what I mean just as soon as you start using this thing.

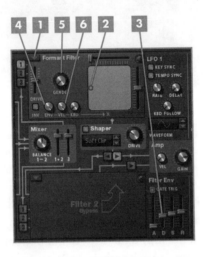

1 In a freshly initialized Thor, click the arrow in the upper left corner of Filter 1 and select Formant Filter from the menu.

2 While playing your MIDI keyboard in the lower octaves, drag the little "dot" inside the gray rectangle panel up, down, and all around every which way. When you are done, leave it in the far left of the gray rectangle, in the vertical middle.

3 Turn the Filter Envelope Decay slider down just a bit to a value of 1.9 seconds.

4 Turn the Filter 1 Envelope Amount knob all the way up to the right.

5 As you play your MIDI keyboard, slowly turn the Gender knob all the way to the right, then all the way to the left to hear its effect.

6 Turn the Velocity knob all the way up, and alternate playing your keyboard very softly and very hard to hear the effect of velocity on the filter frequency.

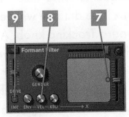

7 Move the dot all the way to the right, leaving it in the vertical middle.

8 Turn the Velocity knob all the way down (all the way to the left).

9 Click the Envelope Invert button. Play your MIDI keyboard, and you will hear very clearly how the filter envelope has been "flipped."

Self Oscillation: The Original Gangsta Le

One feature in Thor that none of the other Reason insn
is self-oscillating filters. Thor's Low Pass Ladder filter and the
Variable filter both have this feature.

When you turn up the resonance control on a filter, you are feeding
back the output of the filter into the filter's input. This is the same as
when a guitar feeds back with an amplifier (the guitar pickups and
strings are part of the filter there) or when a mic feeds back with
a PA system. That's why when you turn the resonance control all
the way up, the filter starts to scream. When a filter goes into self-
oscillation, it feeds back on itself, even without any external input
signal present. You can turn off your oscillator (sound source), and
the filter will scream on its own. Specifically, it will produce a very
pure sine wave.

I cannot prove this, but the word on the street is that Dr. Dre used
this effect (made with an old analog synth with a self-oscillating
filter) for some of the lead sounds on his highly influential solo debut
album, *The Chronic*, including the hit "Let Me Ride." This lead sound
became part of the musical vocabulary of rap and hip-hop. I am
going to show you how to make this sound with Thor now, and if
you compare it to the sound on the Dr. Dre tracks, you will find that
it is about as close as it can be.

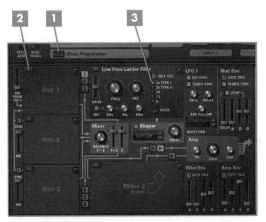

1 In an empty rack, create an instance of Mixer 14:2, followed by an instance of Thor. Right-click on Thor and choose Initialize Patch, and then click the Show Programmer button.

2 Turn off Oscillator 1 by clicking the arrow in the upper left corner and choosing Off from the menu. You will not hear anything when you play your keyboard now.

3 Set the Filter 1 mode to 24 Type 1.

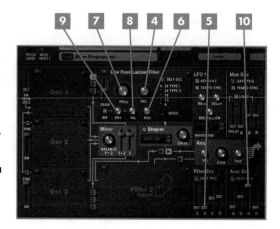

4 Turn up the Filter 1 Resonance knob all the way. Now when you play your keyboard, you will hear a high, falling note.

5 Turn the Filter Envelope Decay slider all the way down. Now the note you hear remains at a constant pitch, and every key plays the same note.

6 Turn the Filter 1 Keyboard knob all the way up. Now every key plays a different note, in semitone steps, and if you have a dog he's probably getting a bit irritated by now.

7 Turn the Filter 1 Frequency knob down to 521Hz. Now the note is one octave lower.

8 So that velocity (how hard you play a note) does not affect the filter envelope amount (and thus affect the filter frequency), turn the Filter 1 Velocity knob all the way down to zero.

9 To fine-tune the pitch, turn the Filter Envelope Amount knob down to a value of 8.

10 Turn the Amp Envelope Sustain slider all the way up.

Now you are absolutely ready to play the lead synth part from "Let Me Ride." But what if you want to add a little pitch bend, like in "B****es Ain't S***?" If you try your pitch bend right now, it won't do anything, because it defaults to bending oscillator pitch, and you're not even using any oscillators. (The filter is producing the tone through self-oscillation.) No problem, thanks to Thor's Modulation Bus Routing section. This next bit picks up at the end of the last exercise.

❈ ❈ ❈

1 In the Modulation Bus Routing section, click in the Source column in the first cell in the upper left and set Mod 1 Source to Performance > Pitch Bend.

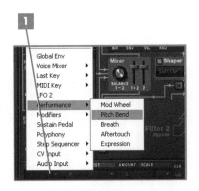

2 Set Mod 1 Destination to Filter 1 > Frequency.

3 Set Mod 1 Destination Amount to a value of 70. Then try playing with the pitch wheel on your MIDI keyboard.

4 (Optional) Turn Portamento on.

5 (Optional) Switch the Keyboard mode to Mono Legato, and play your MIDI keyboard to hear what you've got.

There is another popular flavor of classic hip-hop lead sound that you are no doubt familiar with, which is produced with a sawtooth wave instead of a sine wave. You can probably think of numerous examples where this sound has been used, but if you already have a copy of *The Chronic* handy (or YouTube.com), then one track that uses the sound is "High Powered." There's already a Thor preset that comes pretty close (Gangsta Lead 3).

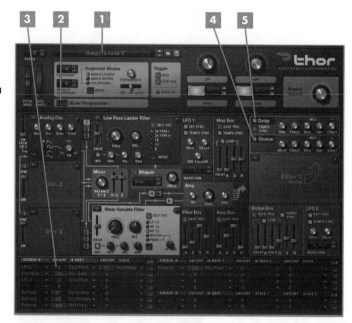

1 Load the following patch into Thor: Reason Factory Sound Bank > Thor Patches > Gangsta Lead 3.thor. (This patch is also in Thor Patches > Lead Synths.)

2 If you want to get rid of the vibrato (I do), click Show Programmer, and proceed to Step 3.

3 Turn Mod 1 Destination Amount down to zero.

4 If you want it to sound a little grittier and less polished, turn off Chorus.

5 If you really want to go dry as a bone, turn off Delay as well.

Thor's Shaper

Although Thor's Shaper is very similar in function to the Malström's Shaper, I will still take a moment here to introduce it to you. The Shaper provides a way to add different distortion types to a signal in Thor. It receives its signal from the output of Filter 1. I find that the more complex the signal you feed into the Shaper, the more interesting the result. I will leave much of that complexity up to your imagination and experimentation. The following example is rather simple.

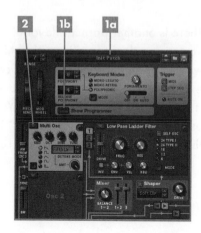

1 In a fresh rack containing Thor, right-click on Thor and choose Initialize Patch, then click the Show Programmer button.

2 Click the arrow in the upper left corner of Oscillator 1 and choose Multi Oscillator.

3 Choose Fifth Up for the Oscillator 1 Detune mode.

4 Turn the Oscillator 1 Detune Amount knob all the way up, and play some medium to low notes on your MIDI keyboard to hear the sound.

5 Click on the Shaper On button to activate the Shaper.

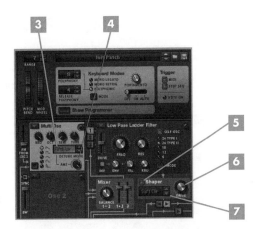

6 Turn the Shaper Drive knob up to 3 o'clock and play your MIDI keyboard to hear the sound.

7 Use the up/down arrows to try all the different Shaper modes while you play your keyboard. Be careful. The Wrap mode is quite loud.

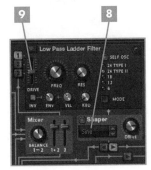

8 Select Sine for the Shaper mode.

9 While playing a low note on your MIDI keyboard, smoothly move the Filter 1 Drive slider all the way down, then all the way up, and finally back to the middle to hear the effect.

The Shaper is just one more thing you can try if you are looking to add a little extra something to your sound. You can use it to warm up your sound subtly or to not so subtly completely shred and obliterate your sound.

Basic Audio Signal Routing in Thor

You probably are already getting a feel for the audio signal routing in Thor, but if you ever get a bit confused, I hope the following tutorial will help set things straight in your brain. Also, just remember that Thor has little arrows all over the place showing the direction and path of the audio signal, so it's all pretty self-explanatory anyway.

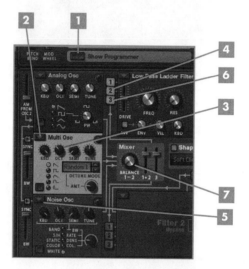

1. In a fresh rack containing Thor, right-click on Thor and choose Initialize Patch, then click the Show Programmer button. Play a few notes on your keyboard to hear Oscillator 1 going through Filter 1.

2. Choose Multi Oscillator for Oscillator 2.

3. Turn down the Oscillator 2 Octave knob one notch to a value of 3. You will not hear anything new because Oscillator 2 is not routed anywhere yet.

4. Click the Oscillator 2 to Filter 1 Enable button. Now you will clearly hear Oscillator 2 added to the mix.

5. Choose Noise for Oscillator 3. You will not hear anything new because Oscillator 3 is not routed anywhere yet.

6. Click the Oscillator 3 to Filter 1 Enable button. Now you will clearly hear Oscillator 3 added to the mix.

7. Play your MIDI keyboard as you turn the Mixer Balance knob all the way to the left. You will only hear Oscillators 1 and 3.

8. Play your MIDI keyboard as you turn the Mixer Balance knob all the way to the right. You will only hear Oscillators 2 and 3.

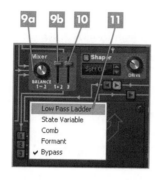

9 Turn the Balance knob back to the center, then turn down the Oscillator 1 + 2 Level slider, and you will only hear Oscillator 3 when you play your keyboard. When you are done, turn the 1 + 2 slider back up.

10 While playing your MIDI keyboard, move the Oscillator 3 Level slider all the way down and then back up again.

11 Select Low Pass Ladder for Filter 2.

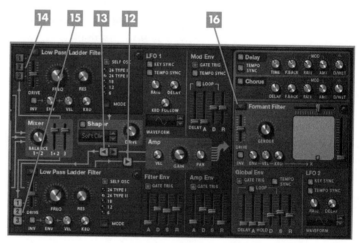

12 Click the Filter 2 to Amplifier Enable button to route Filter 2 to the amplifier. You will not hear anything different because nothing is routed to Filter 2 yet.

13 Click the left routing arrow just below the Shaper. Play your MIDI keyboard, and you will hear a mellower sound because the signal from Filter 1 is passing through Filter 2 on its way to the amp. The signal from the oscillators is being filtered twice.

14 Turn off all three of the Oscillator to Filter 1 routing buttons. Now you won't hear anything.

15 Turn on all three of the Oscillator to Filter 2 routing buttons. Now the signal from the oscillators is going straight through Filter 2 and never touching Filter 1.

16 Click the arrow in the upper left corner of Filter 3 and choose Formant Filter. Anything coming out of the amp goes through Filter 3. Play your MIDI keyboard and you will hear obvious proof that I am telling the truth.

The last two stops on the signal's path after Filter 3 are Chorus and Delay. Feel free to turn those on at the end of the last exercise if you want. After Delay, there is only Thor's Master Volume and then out to Thor's audio outputs. Also (going back a few steps), remember that the Shaper (not used in the preceding exercise) only processes the signal from Filter 1. It will not touch the signal from Filter 2.

Modulation Bus Routing Section

The last section dealt with audio routing. This section deals primarily with modulation routing (although Thor's Modulation Bus Routing section can actually be used to route both modulation *and* audio). You have already been using the Modulation Bus Routing section throughout this chapter, but I want to take a moment to focus on it. The Modulation Bus Routing section allows you to modulate (control) any part of Thor with any other part of Thor in nearly any way you can think of, and it also allows you to create audio signal paths beyond those available using Thor's routing buttons.

Each row in the Modulation Bus Routing section is a separate modulation bus. For our purposes, the word "bus" simply refers to a circuit where multiple devices share the same connection. It may look complicated, but once you understand its concept, you will realize it is actually quite simple, but powerful at the same time.

Here are the terms you will see all over the Modulation Bus Routing section.

Source: The modulator that will modulate the destination. For example, if LFO 1 is modulating Oscillator 1 Pitch, then LFO 1 is the source, and Oscillator 1 is the destination.

(Destination) Amount: The amount by which the destination will be modulated by the source.

Destination: The parameter that will be modulated.

(Scale) Amount: The degree to which the destination amount will be affected by another parameter, such as Modulation Wheel or Amp Envelope.

Scale: Allows you to modulate the destination amount with another parameter, such as Modulation Wheel, LFO1, and so on.

Once you try a few simple examples, you are sure to get it. As we go through the exercises, I will refer to Modulation Bus 1, Modulation Bus 2, and so on. But you will notice that the busses do not appear to be numbered. As long as you have Show Parameter Value Tool Tips selected on the General page of your Reason Preferences, then you can mouse over any Amount value and see Mod 1 or Mod 2 pop up, so you will know which bus you are on without having to count.

Modulation Busses 1 Through 7

The first seven busses (rows) on the left are the simplest, so we'll start with those.

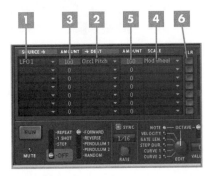

1 In a freshly initialized Thor with the Show Programmer button activated, click on Modulation Bus 1 Source and choose LFO 1 from the pop-up menu.

2 Click on Modulation Bus 1 Destination and choose Osc1 Pitch from the pop-up menu.

3 Hold down a note or chord on your MIDI keyboard while you click and drag upward on Modulation Bus 1 Destination Amount, setting it to a value of 100. Sounds pretty whacky now.

4 Set Modulation Bus 1 Scale Source to Performance > Mod Wheel.

5 Hold down a note or chord on your MIDI keyboard while you click and drag upward on Modulation Bus 1 Scale Amount, setting it to a value of 100. Then try using the modulation wheel (or joystick) on your MIDI keyboard to control the amount of LFO 1 to Osc 1 pitch.

6 Click the Clear button on Modulation Bus 1, and it will be as though Steps 2 through 5 never happened.

Modulation Busses 8 Through 11

The second group of four modulation busses (8 through 11) allows a second destination to be modulated by the same source. You will be using LFO 2 in this exercise, which is in the brown Global section of Thor's Programmer.

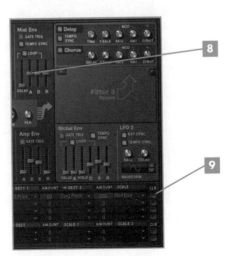

1 In a freshly initialized Thor, choose LFO 2 for Modulation Bus 8 Source.

2 Set Modulation Bus 8 Destination 1 to Filter 1 Frequency.

3 Hold down a note or chord on your MIDI keyboard while you click and drag upward on Modulation Bus 8 Destination 1 Amount, setting it to a value of 100.

4 Set Modulation Bus 8 Destination 2 to Oscillator 1 Pitch.

5 Hold down a note or chord on your MIDI keyboard while you click and drag upward on Modulation Bus 8 Destination 2 Amount, setting it to a value of 60.

6 Set the Modulation Bus 8 Scale parameter to Mod Env.

7 Click and drag upward on Modulation Bus 8 Scale Amount, setting it to a value of 100. Play a key or chord on your MIDI keyboard, and you will hear the modulation amount decrease as the modulation envelope (Mod Env) goes through the decay portion of its envelope.

8 Turn up the Mod Envelope Attack slider so it is even with the Decay and Release sliders. Then play a note on your MIDI keyboard, and you will hear the attack portion of the modulation envelope scaling the effect of LFO 2.

9 Click the Clear button on Modulation Bus 8 to erase any evidence.

Modulation Busses 12 and 13

Each of the final two modulation busses has only one destination but includes an extra Scale parameter. Here is a very simple example of how this might be used.

1 In a freshly initialized Thor, choose LFO 1 for Modulation Bus 12 Source.

2 Select Oscillator 1 Pitch for Modulation Bus 12 Destination.

3 Click and drag upward on Modulation Bus 12 Destination Amount, setting it to a value of 100.

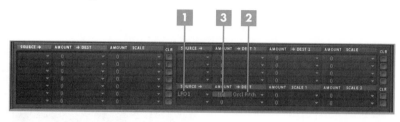

4 Turn up the LFO 1 Rate knob to a value of 10.1Hz (just past 2 o'clock) and play a note on your MIDI keyboard. It sounds like a sound effect from a 1970's anime.

5 Turn the LFO 2 Rate knob down do a value of 0.20Hz (almost 9 o'clock).

6 Choose LFO 2 for Modulation Bus 12 Scale 1.

7 Click and drag upward on Modulation Bus 12 Scale 1 Amount, setting it to a value of 100. Play and hold a note on your MIDI keyboard to hear LFO 1's amount being modulated by the slow sine wave from LFO 2.

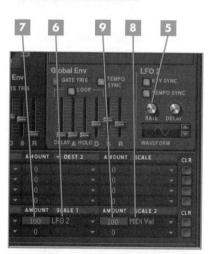

8 Choose MIDI Key > Velocity (MIDI Vel) for Modulation Bus 12 Scale 2.

9 Click and drag upward on Modulation Bus 12 Scale 2 Amount, setting it to a value of 100.

After you complete Step 9, playing your MIDI keyboard very gently will produce a smaller modulation effect, while playing it harder will produce a stronger effect.

❊ ❊ ❊

Routing Trick: Backward Thor

This last trick is some pretty fancy routing. It might not get you a record deal, but you may be able to win $5 off your friend if you bet him $5 you can make your keyboard play backward.

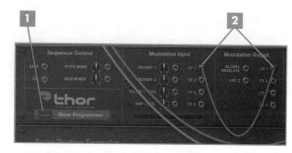

1. With a freshly initialized Thor, hit the Tab key on your computer keyboard to flip your rack around, and click the Show Programmer button.

2. Click and drag to create a cable connection between Thor's CV 1 Modulation Output and the CV1 Modulation Input.

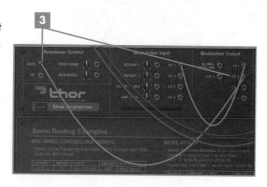

3. Connect CV 2 Modulation Output to the Sequencer Control Gate Input.

4. Hit Tab to flip your rack back around, and click on the Note Trigger MIDI button to disable it.

5. Select CV Input > 1 for Modulation Bus 1 Source.

6. Choose Oscillator 1 Pitch for Modulation Bus 1 Destination, and set Modulation Bus 1 Destination Amount to 100.

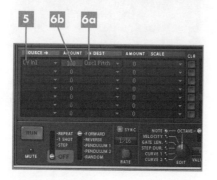

✳ ✳ ✳

7 Select MIDI Key > Note for Modulation Bus 2 Source.

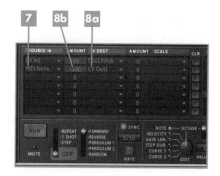

8 Select CV Output > 1 for Modulation Bus 2 Destination, and click and drag *down* on Modulation Bus 2 Destination Amount, setting it to a value of –100.

9 Select MIDI Key > Gate for Modulation Bus 3 Source.

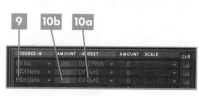

10 Select CV Output > 2 for Modulation Bus 3 Destination, and set Modulation Bus 3 Destination Amount to a value of 100.

11 Turn up Amp Envelope Sustain all the way.

Now play your MIDI keyboard, and up will be down and down will be up. It will be monophonic (because CV Gate is monophonic), but you still deserve to win the $5. But remember that if you try to *save* the patch, the cable connections in the back will not be saved (unless you right-click on Thor, choose Combine, and then save the patch as a Combinator patch instead of a Thor patch). More on saving rear panel routing in Combinator patches in Chapter 8, "Combinator."

I hope these exercises have taken some of the mystery out of the Modulation Bus Routing section. By the way, I truly have too much to cover in this chapter to get into it here, but the Rotary 1 and Rotary 2 knobs, as well as Button 1 and Button 2 on Thor's Controller panel (the top panel), are assignable within the Modulation Bus Routing section. They can be assigned to control whatever parameters you want. This is explained on the very first page of the Thor chapter in the Reason Operation Manual in the section entitled "About the Virtual Controls" if you are curious.

LFO 1 versus LFO 2

Thor's low frequency oscillators are small but mighty. Their function should feel familiar to you. Before getting into the exercises, here are a few brief notes on Thor's LFO controls.

The Tempo Sync button found on LFO 1 and 2 is just like the Sync button on Subtractor's LFOs and the Malström's modulators. It simply syncs the LFO to the song tempo. The Delay knob found on LFO 1 and 2 works exactly the same way as the Delay knob on Subtractor's LFO 2. It causes the LFO to wait a second or two before it starts modulating, allowing a note to sound purely for a second before vibrato is applied, for example. The Waveform selector is similar to the Waveform selector in the Malström's modulators A and B. Of course, the Rate knob controls how fast the LFO modulates. There is no LFO Amount knob because in Thor, this will be set in the Modulation Bus Routing section.

Key Sync

The ability to turn Key Sync on and off is a feature unique to Thor. If Key Sync is off, the LFO modulation may start at any point in the LFO waveform cycle when you play a note. If Key Sync is on, each time you play a note, the LFO cycle is reset, and modulation starts from the beginning of the LFO waveform cycle. This is easy to understand if you try it out.

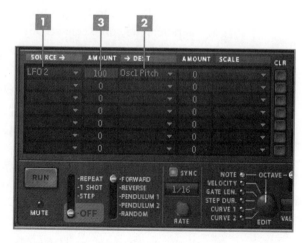

1 In a freshly initialized Thor, set Modulation Bus 1 Source to LFO 2.

2 Set Modulation Bus 1 Destination to Oscillator 1 Pitch.

3 Click and drag upward on Modulation Bus 1 Destination Amount, setting it to a value of 100.

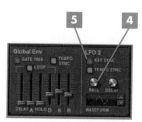

4 Turn the LFO 2 Rate knob down to 9 o'clock (value of 0.22Hz). Then play a note on your MIDI keyboard and let go, over and over again, about once every second. You will hear the note start at a different point in LFO 2's slow sine wave each time.

5 Click the LFO 2 Key Sync button to activate it. Then play your MIDI keyboard as you did in Step 4, and this time it will start at the same pitch each time. In fact, if you look at the picture in the LFO 2 Waveform Display, you can see the shape you're hearing.

It is interesting to note that the Malström's modulators A and B (the Malström LFOs) are always "key synced," while Subtractor's LFOs are not key synced; rather, they are always free running.

LFO 1 Keyboard Follow

Keyboard tracking is a feature you find in various forms throughout the Reason synths. In an oscillator, it determines to what extent pitch is affected by which key you play. In a filter, it determines to what extent the filter frequency is affected by which key you play. The LFO 1 Keyboard Follow knob on Thor works exactly the same way as the LFO 2 Keyboard Tracking knob on Subtractor. It determines to what extent the LFO rate is affected by which key you play. Low keys will have a slower rate, and high keys will have a faster rate.

1 In a freshly initialized Thor, set Modulation Bus 1 Source to LFO 1.

2 Set Modulation Bus 1 Destination to Filter 1 Frequency.

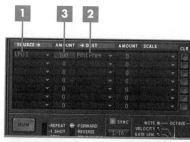

3 Click and drag upward on Modulation Bus 1 Destination Amount, setting it to a value of 100. Play some keys on your MIDI keyboard, and you will hear that the filter frequency is modulated at the same rate, no matter what key you play.

/board

e way to the

you play your

low keys will
have the fire. equency modulated slowly, while high keys
will have faster modulation.

Thor, Meet the BV512 Digital Vocoder

Used through the years by musical acts including Kraftwerk, Pink Floyd, Herbie Hancock, Wendy Carlos, Laurie Anderson, and Earth, Wind, and Fire, the vocoder has been part of music since the 1970s. You may be surprised to find out that the technology (in its original, non-musical form) has been around since the 1930s.

Typically, a vocoder is used in the following way: A carrier signal (created by a synthesizer and controlled with a keyboard) is modulated by another signal (created by a human voice speaking or singing into a microphone). This creates the musically pitched "robot voice" with which we are all familiar. Reason's BV512 Digital Vocoder can work in the same way (provided you use a sampled voice). However, in the following examples, you will be doing something a little different: You will be using Thor for the carrier signal (which is perfectly normal), but you will be modulating that signal with a beat from Dr.Rex instead of a voice.

1 In an empty rack, create an MClass Mastering Suite, followed by Mixer 14:2 and an instance of Thor. Then load the following patch into Thor: Reason Factory Sound Bank > Thor Patches > Lead Synths > Combing Lead.

2 Set **Thor's** Keyboard mode to Polyphonic.

3 Turn up Polyphony and Release Polyphony to a value of (at least) 8. Then play a few notes to hear this sound.

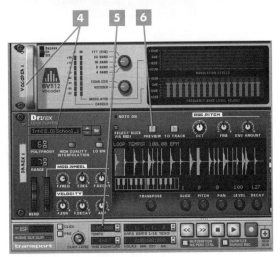

4 Underneath Thor, create a BV512 Digital Vocoder **followed by an instance of** Dr.Rex. **Then** load **the following** patch **into Dr.Rex: Reason Factory Sound Bank > Dr Rex Drum Loops > Abstract HipHop > Trh18_ OlSchool_100eLab.rx2.**

5 In the Reason Sequencer, turn the tempo **down to 100.**

6 Click **the** Preview button **on Dr.Rex to hear the beat, and then** click Preview **again once you've heard the beat (so that Preview will stop).**

7 Press Tab **to flip the rack around, and then** drag **the** cables **out of Dr.Rex's audio outputs. The cables should disappear.**

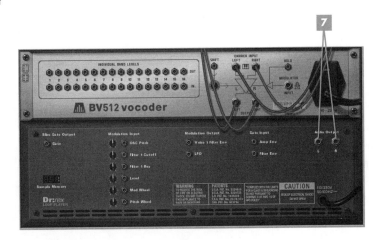

8 Drag a cable from Dr.Rex's left audio output to the BV512 Vocoder's Modulator Input.

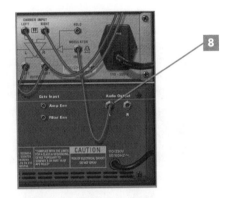

9 Press Tab to flip the rack back around facing front, and then click the Preview button on Dr.Rex to activate it. You will not hear anything yet.

10 Select the Thor 1 track in the Reason Sequencer by clicking on the Thor keyboard icon, and then play some chords on your MIDI keyboard. You should hear a vocoded drum beat.

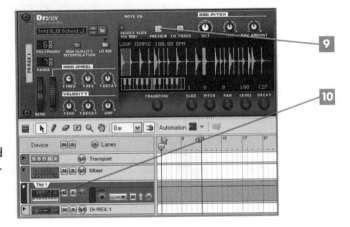

Now let's set things up so that you can have a sequence playing hands-free while you twiddle knobs elsewhere. The next bit picks up where the last bit left off.

1 Drag the Horizontal Zoom handle to the left to increase zoom until you have a nice view of individual bars and quarter note marks.

2 Alt+click on the timeline at bar 3, and the right locator will jump there.

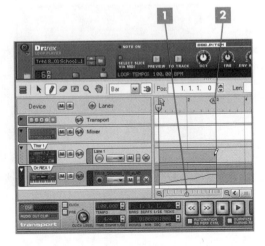

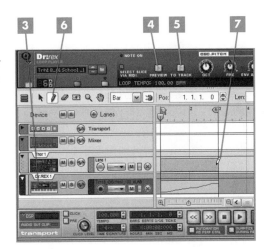

3 Select the Dr.REX 1 Sequencer track by clicking on the Dr.Rex icon.

4 Turn off Preview on Dr.Rex.

5 Click the To Track button on Dr.Rex.

6 Select the Pencil tool.

7 On the Thor 1 track in the Reason Sequencer, draw in a 2-bar clip starting at bar 1.

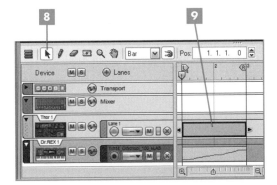

8 Choose your Selection tool.

9 Double-click on the clip you just created.

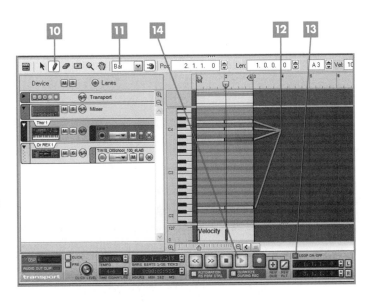

10 Select the Pencil tool.

11 Set the Snap value to Bar.

12 Draw in notes on bar 1 and bar 2 at D4, C4, A3, and D2.

13 Make sure Loop is on in the Reason Sequencer.

14 Click the Play button, and you should hear your vocoded beat.

Now while you are listening to your beat:

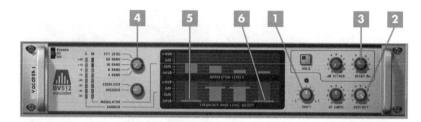

1 Slowly turn the BV512's Shift knob all the way to the right, all the way to the left, and then back to center to hear the effect.

2 Slowly turn the BV512's Dry/Wet knob all the way to the left and then back all the way to the right.

3 Slowly turn the BV512's Decay knob all the way to the right and then back to its original value of 42 (just past the 3 mark).

4 Switch the Band Count selector knob to the 4 Band position.

5 Drag the first band on the left all the way down in the Frequency Band Level Adjust section.

6 Drag the fourth band all the way down.

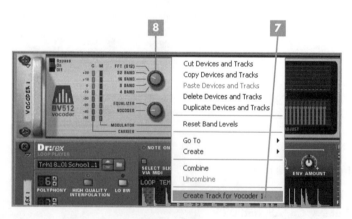

7 Turn all the frequency bands back up where they were, then right-click on the BV512 Vocoder and select Create Track for Vocoder 1.

8 Turn the Band Count selector knob to the 32 Band position, then one key at a time, play the notes on your keyboard between C1 and G3. Be careful. The closer you get to G3, the more dangerously loud the sound will become. When you play up near G3, play as softly as you can.

Besides being a fun way to make cool sounds, being able to play the vocoder's individual bands on the keyboard is helpful for deciding which bands you want to boost or cut. This could be useful when using a voice recording (instead of a drum beat) as a modulator, as you may find that cutting or boosting certain bands will make the vocoded signal more intelligible or help it to fit into (or cut through) the mix better.

The last vocoder trick I want to show you may seem rather novel. Instead of using a melodic sound for the carrier signal, you will use noise. Here is a chance to try Thor's Noise Oscillator. This exercise picks up where the last exercise left off.

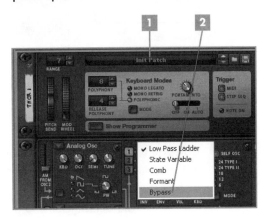

1. With your sequence playing, right-click on Thor and choose Initialize Patch.

2. Click the arrow in the upper left corner of Filter 1 and choose Bypass from the pop-up menu.

3. Click the arrow in the upper left corner of Oscillator 1 and choose Noise from the pop-up menu. The noise type will be White Noise by default.

4. Click the Oscillator 2 to Filter 1 Enable button so that it lights up red.

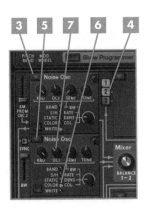

5. Click the arrow in the upper left corner of Oscillator 2 and choose Noise from the pop-up menu.

6. Choose Color for the Oscillator 2 Noise Type.

7. Turn the Oscillator 2 Octave knob down to a value of 3.

8. Move Thor's Amp Envelope Decay slider all the way up to the top.

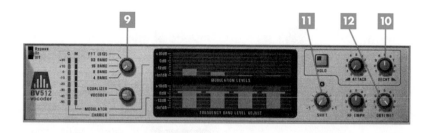

9 On the BV512, switch the Band Count knob to **4 Band**.

10 Turn Vocoder Decay up to **5** (halfway up).

11 Turn Vocoder Shift down all the way to **– 1**.

12 Turn the Dry/Wet knob all the way to the Dry position to hear what you started with, and then turn it back to the Wet position to hear how far you've come.

Can you believe that all that sound is really just coming from Thor's noise oscillators? Sounds pretty heavy. By the way, if you turn the BV512 Decay knob all the way up, it will really sound like noise—kind of like the ocean (but with a straighter beat).

❄ **BUT WHAT IF I WANT TO USE MY VOCODER FOR VOICE?**

Obviously, Reason does not have an audio input, so you cannot plug in a mic and vocode your voice live through Reason. What you *can* do is record yourself in another program (for free, there's Windows Voice Recorder built into your PC, or GarageBand included with your Mac). Record yourself saying "domo arigato Mr. Roboto" or "by your command" and save it as a WAV file. Browse to that WAV file from one of Reason's sample browsers (a Redrum channel or NN-19 would be simplest) and load the WAV file into the device. In the exercises you just completed, Redrum or NN-19 would take the place of Dr.Rex as the modulator, while Thor would remain the carrier. You will need MIDI info for the notes or chords Thor will play, as well as for the trigger note for Redrum or the NN-19.

Before you move on to learning about Reason's sample players, there's one last tip I have for you. If you enjoy making your own sounds with Thor and messing around "under the hood," then flip your rack around, make sure you have clicked Thor's Show Programmer button, and go through the routing examples printed on the back of Thor. They are really cool and useful.

7 } The Reason Samplers: NN-19 and NN-XT

For electronic sounds, you are most likely to use Thor, Subtractor, or the Malström. For realistic acoustic instrument sounds (such as pianos, orchestral instruments, and the like), the NN-19 and NN-XT samplers are the way to go.

Technically speaking, a true sampler has the capability to sample. That is, it is able to record a sound and then play it back. The hardware samplers from which the Propellerhead programmers drew their inspiration had that feature. However, the NN-19 and the NN-XT cannot record sounds. They can only play back sounds. So they should really be called "sample players." However, since they are referred to as samplers within the software, I will use this term as well.

Both Reason samplers have extensive ways to tweak the sounds once you have loaded them. And of course you could always record a sound in another program and load it into one of the Reason samplers. Any WAV, AIFF, REX, or SoundFonts (.sf2) file can be loaded into either of the Reason samplers. Reason comes with loads of great sample patches in the Reason Factory sound bank and the Orkester sound bank.

In this chapter you will learn how to:

* Load single samples into the NN-19 and NN-XT and assign them to specific keys
* Create keyboard splits so that part of the keyboard triggers one sample, while another part triggers another sample
* Create velocity layers in the NN-XT so that playing softly triggers one sample, while playing harder triggers another sample
* Tweak the tuning, looping, root key, and start/end points of your samples

NN-19

The NN-19 is the older of the two Reason samplers. It has basic and familiar synth parameters, and although you may end up using the more powerful NN-XT much of the time, you may still find a place in your heart for the ol' NN-19.

Loading Samples into the NN-19

The Reason sound banks come with numerous patches for the NN-19 and NN-XT. These patches contain multiple samples mapped all over the keyboard, and I'm sure you will have no problem loading those preset sample patches. It is just like loading Malström or Subtractor patches. What you are going to do now is load an individual sample.

1. In a fresh rack containing an NN-19, right-click on the NN-19 and choose Initialize Patch.

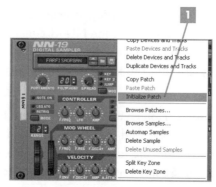

2. Click on the Browse Sample button and select Orkester Sound Bank > Percussion > Gong GNG > GNG_F.aif. Then play your MIDI keyboard to hear the gong automatically repitched for each key.

3. Right-click on the NN-19 and choose Split Key Zone. You will not hear the gong on any keys above D#3 anymore, and you will see the Key Zone Handle.

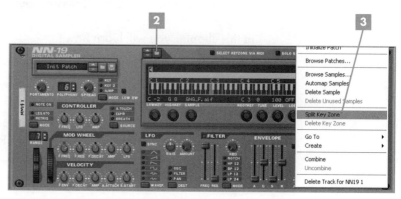

4 Click to select the key zone for the left half of the keyboard. It will turn bright blue.

5 Turn the High Key knob down to a value of C3 (which is also the root key). You will now hear the gong only when you play C3 and below.

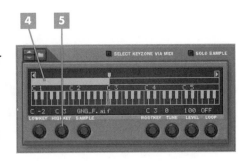

6 Click to select the key zone for the right half of the keyboard. It will turn bright blue.

7 Click on the Browse Sample button and select Orkester Sound Bank > Percussion > Cymbals > CYM_18brtswel2.aif.

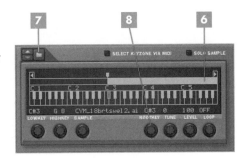

8 Change the root key to C#3. The cymbal sample will now play at its original speed when you play C#3 and will play faster with each key higher than that.

Now you have gongs on the left and cymbal swells on the right. By the way, think of a key zone as a container for a sample. A key zone contains only one sample. However, several key zones may be set to have the same key range (keys C0 to C6, for example).

Assigning a Single Sample to a Single Key

There are times when you want a single sample on a single key. Maybe you want to play one key and have it trigger a long sample (like a piece of a song or beat, or even an entire song). Or you might want to trigger a vocal sample or a sound effect. Also, if you are building a drum kit, you will probably want a different sample on each key. This would be the same if you were assigning samples to drum pads (like those found on an M-Audio Trigger Finger or on the Akai MP series controllers). All you have to do is make the key zone include only a single key.

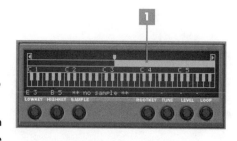

1 In a fresh NN-19 for which you have applied Initialize Patch, right-click on the NN-19 and choose Split Key Zone. Do this four times. Then click in the key zone to the right of the Key Zone Handle to select the key zone starting at E3.

2 Turn the High Key knob down to E3. Now you have a single-note key zone.

3 Click in the big key zone to the right of the Key Zone Handle at E3 to select it.

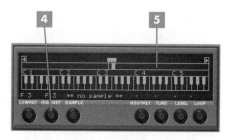

4 Turn the High Key knob down to F3. Now you have a second single-note key zone.

5 Click in the big key zone to the right of the Key Zone Handle at F3 to select it.

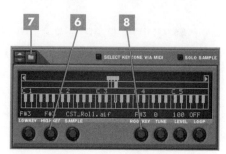

6 Turn the High Key knob down to F#3. Now you have a third single-note key zone.

7 With the F#3 key zone still selected, click the Browse Sample button and load Orkester Sound Bank > Percussion > Castanets CST > CST_Roll.aif.

8 Turn the root key up to F#3 (so it matches the low/high key of your key zone).

❄ ❄ ❄

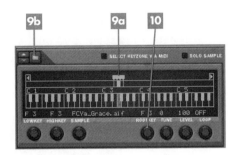

9 Click in the F3 key zone (the one in the middle) to select it and then load the sample Orkester Sound Bank > Percussion > Fingercymbals FCY > FCYa_Grace.aif.

10 Turn the root key up to F3 (so it matches the low/high key of your key zone).

11 Click in the E3 key zone to select it and then load the sample Orkester Sound Bank > Percussion > Cymbals CYM > CYN_20swpbrsh2.aif.

12 Turn the root key up to E3 (so it matches the low/high key of your key zone). Now you have three correctly pitched samples mapped to the individual keys of your choosing (E3, F3, and F#3).

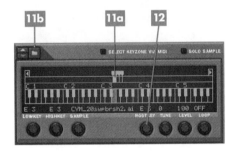

Note that by default, the root key (the key on which the sample plays at its original speed) of any sample you load is C3 unless the sample file actually has a root key in parentheses in the filename, such as a harp sample named HRP_F(A#5).aif. In that case, the NN-19 will correctly assign the root key as A#5.

NN-19 Synth Parameter Exercise: Precise LFO Pitch Modulation

I would assume that most people use the Reason samplers for orchestral and other "real" sounds, and they use Subtractor, Malström, and Thor for synth stuff. Those synths use mathematical algorithms to emulate synth sounds. However, the Reason Factory sound bank includes samples (actual recordings) of vintage synths, including Minimoog, ARP 2600 and Odyssey, Prophet V, Roland SH101, Mellotron, and Solina (Arp String Ensemble) string machine. You could argue that these short recorded samples of the original instruments contain some audio information not found in emulations.

Here is a fun thing you can do with the NN-19's LFO. Kraftwerk uses nearly the same idea on their track "Vitamin," although they are not using a sine wave as you will here.

1 In a fresh NN-19 for which you have applied Initialize Patch, load the following patch: Reason Factory Sound Bank > NN19 Sampler Patches > Synth Raw Elements > Raw_2600_Sine.

2 Turn up Polyphony to at least 10.

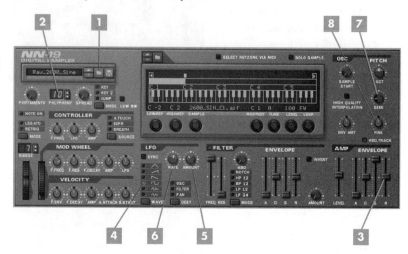

3 Turn the Amp Envelope Release slider halfway up to a value of 64. Play a few notes to hear this sound.

4 Set LFO Waveform to square.

5 Turn the LFO Amount knob up to a value of 53.

6 Turn the LFO Rate knob up to a value of 75. (If you want it a little faster, that's OK, but I don't think it sounds too cool much faster than 80.)

7 Turn the Oscillator Semitone knob up to a value of 2.

8 Turn the Oscillator Fine Tune knob to 12 o'clock.

❋ **A NOTE ABOUT USING REX FILES WITH THE REASON SAMPLERS**

Although I will not be using REX files in any of the examples in this chapter, I want to point out that they can be loaded two ways. If you load a REX file as a patch (using the sampler's Patch Browser), all slices in the REX file will be automatically mapped sequentially across the keyboard (from left to right chromatically). If you use the sampler's Sample Browser to open a REX file, you will be able to load a single REX slice of your choosing onto a single key (or key zone).

NN-XT

For loading a single sample and having it automatically mapped across all keys, the NN-19 is the fastest way to go. However, the NN-XT offers so much more, and it is likely to be your main sampler. Not only does it offer many more synth parameters than the NN-19, several functions are easier to use. Also, unlike the NN-19, it allows you to use multilayered samples, so that when you hit a key softly, it plays one sample, but when you play it harder, it plays another sample. For example, the highest-quality piano libraries have several samples for each key, which increases realism.

You already learned how to set up single samples on each key with the NN-19, but now let's see how much easier it is to do this on the NN-XT.

1 In a fresh NN-XT for which you have applied Initialize Patch, unfold the Remote Editor by clicking the little triangle on the left side of the Remote Editor.

2 Right-click in the display window and choose Add Zone. Do this three times.

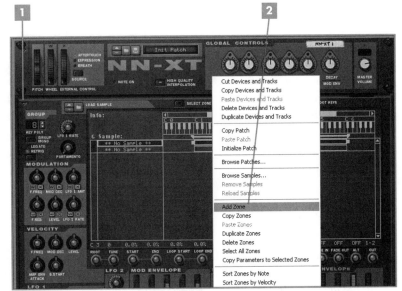

3 Click the third (bottom) zone to select it and then click the Browse Sample button and load Orkester Sound Bank > Percussion > Belltree BLT > BLT_FastStroke.aif.

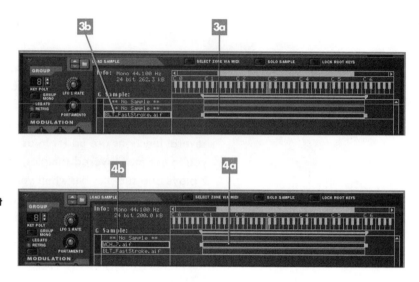

4 Click the middle zone to select it (you can click in the sample column if you want), and then click the Browse Sample button and load Orkester Sound Bank > Percussion > Wind Chimes WCH > WCH_7.aif.

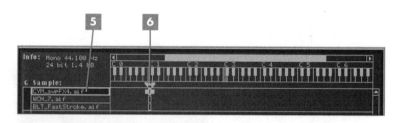

5 Click the top zone to select it and load in the following sample: Orkester Sound Bank > Percussion > Cymbals CYM > CYM_swpFX4.aif.

6 Drag the right zone boundary handle (on the tab bar) all the way to the left so that the low key and hi key for all three samples are C1 (you will also see this displayed above the Lo/Hi Key knobs at the bottom of the display window).

7 Click to the left of one of the samples in the Group column (labeled G) to select the whole group of all three samples.

8 Set the root to C1. This sets the root for all three samples because all three samples are selected.

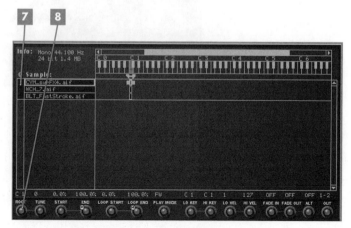

9 Click in a blank area of the display to deselect everything.

10 Drag the middle sample's entire zone to C2. Notice that the root automatically changes to C2.

11 Drag the bottom sample's zone to C3, and notice that the root automatically changes to C3.

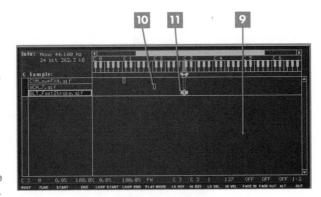

When you are done, you should hear a weird cymbal scrape when you play C1, an upward-sweeping wind chime when you play C2, and a downward-sweeping bell tree when you play C3. All other keys will be silent. You can move the key zones for the individual samples anywhere you want and the root will follow automatically, unless you activate the Lock Root Keys button in the upper-right corner.

Please leave this exercise as is, since you will be using it in the next exercise.

Velocity Layers

With the NN-XT, it is possible to have two or more key zones (with a separate sample in each zone) that are triggered by exactly the same range of notes. If each zone has the same velocity range, you will hear all the samples at the same time when you play a key. But if each sample has its own velocity range, you can play softly and hear one sample and play harder to hear another sample. This exercise picks up where the last exercise left off.

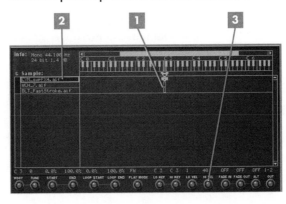

1 Move the zones for the top and middle samples to C3 so that all three samples are on C3.

2 Click on the top sample (CYM_swpFX4.aif) to select it.

3 Turn the Hi Vel (high velocity) knob down to 40.

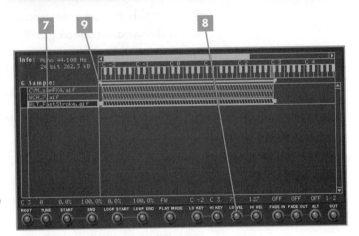

4 Click on the middle sample (WCH_7.aif) to select it.

5 Turn the Lo Vel (low velocity) knob up to 41.

6 Turn the high velocity knob down to 70.

7 Click on the bottom sample (BLT_FastStroke.aif) to select it.

8 Turn the Lo Vel (low velocity) knob up to 71.

9 So that you can play the sounds on all notes C3 and below, on the tab bar, drag the left zone boundary handle all the way to the left (C–2).

Now if you play the C3 key (or any key below that) very softly, you will hear the cymbal scrape. If you play just a bit harder, you will hear the wind chime, and if you play very hard, you will hear the bell tree. By the way, the stripes on the key zones are there to alert you that they do not have the full velocity range of 1–127.

Velocity Crossfades

It is possible to set up velocity crossfades manually (using the Fade In and Fade Out knobs) to create smooth transitions between the samples in an overlapping zone. Here is a simple example of how to do this.

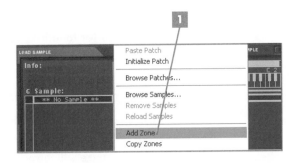

1 In a fresh NN-XT to which you have applied Initialize Patch, with the Remote Editor unfolded, right-click in the display window and choose Add Zone (do this twice to create two zones).

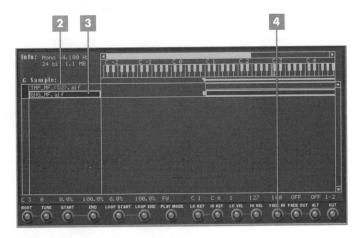

2 Select the top zone (by clicking on the zone or by clicking where it says No Sample) and load the following sample: Orkester Sound Bank > Percussion > Timpani TMP > TMP_MF_(D2).aif.

3 Select the bottom zone and load the following sample: Orkester Sound Bank > Percussion > Gong GNG > GNG_MF.aif.

4 With the bottom zone (containing the gong sample) selected, turn up the Fade In knob to 100.

5 Select the top zone (containing the timpani sample) and turn the Fade Out knob down to 30.

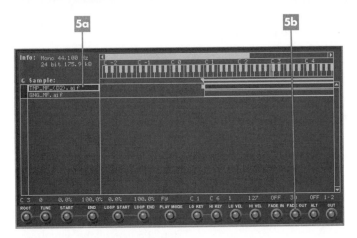

Now when you play just as softly as you can, you will hear mostly timpani and hardly any gong. As you play harder you will hear more gong, and if you play very hard you should hear no timpani at all.

If you are interested in checking out more examples of how to use velocity crossfades (or to learn about the Create Velocity Crossfades option in the Edit menu), please see the Reason Operation Manual.

A Few More Sample Parameters

We've already covered some of the NN-XT sample parameters, including Lo/Hi Key, Lo/Hi Velocity, Play Mode, and Fade In/Out. The following exercise will introduce you to Sample Tune, Sample Start/End, and Loop Start/End.

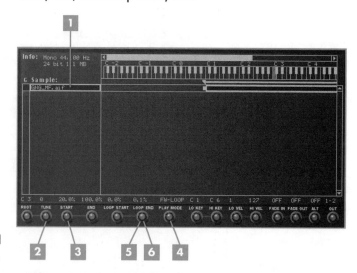

1 Right-click on a freshly initial-ized NN-XT (with the Remote Editor unfolded) and choose Add Zone. Then load the following sample: Orkester Sound Bank > Percussion > Gong GNG > GNG_MF.aif.

2 While playing your MIDI keyboard, turn the Tune knob (used to fine-tune samples) to the left all the way to –50 and then all the way to the right to a value of 50. When you are done, set it back to zero.

3 Play a note on your MIDI keyboard over and over as you slowly turn up the Sample Start knob to a value of 20%. You will hear the attack disappear, since you are starting the sample later (after the initial attack).

4 Change the Play mode to FW-LOOP.

5 Hold down a key on your MIDI keyboard and turn down the Loop End to 10%; then, while holding down the note, slowly turn it down to 1%.

6 Keep holding the note, and very slowly turn down the Loop End one step at a time all the way down to 0.1%, and you will hear a familiar "glitch" sound.

You will definitely want your mouse range in the General Preferences set to Very Precise for Step 6.

Backward Piano!

Here's a fun and easy trick to wrap up this chapter.

1 Load a fresh NN-XT into a rack, and it should have B Grand Piano 1.0.sxt loaded by default. Unfold the Remote Editor, and then right-click on the NN-XT and choose Select All Zones.

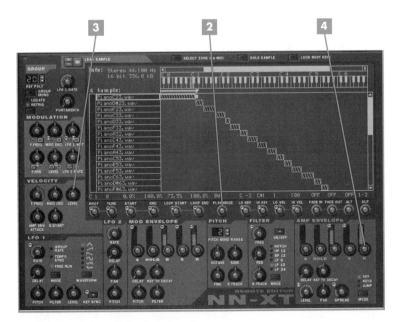

2 Change the Play mode to BW (backward).

3 In the Velocity section, turn down the Level knob to 12 o'clock.

4 In the Amp Envelope section, turn Release all the way up.

Now play your MIDI keyboard, and enjoy that backward piano sound. (Note that the samples take several seconds to fade in completely.)

If you really want to get deep into the NN-XT, you will want to spend some time with your Reason Operation Manual. Still, many of the NN-XT's synth parameters should already look familiar to you, such as the Mod Envelope, Amp Envelope, Filter, and LFO sections. If you want to learn just about everything there is to know about creating your own sample patches with the NN-XT and NN-19, you may want to check out my book *Using Reason's Virtual Instruments*, which includes a CD-ROM complete with samples and contains in-depth how-tos for power users!

8 } The Combinator

First introduced in Reason version 3.0, the Combinator is a huge step forward in the power and functionality of the program. It allows you to put any number of synths and effects together, control them all with one keyboard, and save the whole thing as one patch. It saves any routing you have done with rear panel patch cables (which could not otherwise be saved with an individual Malström or Thor patch, for example). It can be used for super-fat synth sounds built with a tower of synths or for complex effects processing (as in the MClass Mastering Suite Combi). It also allows you to create split or multilayered instruments. So you could create a Combinator patch (or Combi, for short) where when you play low notes you hear a Subtractor bass sound, and when you play high notes you hear a Thor lead sound, or when you play really hard you hear a Malström sound as well. And for the cherry on top, it is the only Reason device that is custom skinnable.

In this chapter you will learn how to:

* ❋ Make fat synth patches using multiple synths inside one Combinator
* ❋ Use the MClass Master Suite Combi to make your mixes sound better (and louder)
* ❋ Create Split Keyboard patches so that one part of your keyboard plays one instrument, while another part of the keyboard plays another instrument
* ❋ Assign the Combinator's virtual knobs and buttons to control various Reason device parameters
* ❋ Use a single Redrum to control 10 Thors

Adding Devices to a Combinator

There are a few ways to add devices to a Combinator, as this first exercise will demonstrate. This is just an easy exercise to help you become familiar with how this works before you get on with the fun stuff in the rest of the chapter.

1. In a fresh rack, choose Combinator from the Create menu.

2. From the Devices pane of the Tool window, drag a Subtractor into the empty black space at the bottom of the Combinator, just under the red Insertion Line.

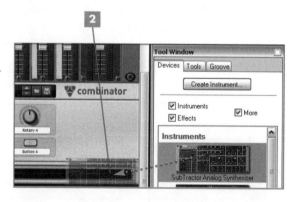

3. Right-click on the Subtractor and choose Create > Scream 4 Distortion.

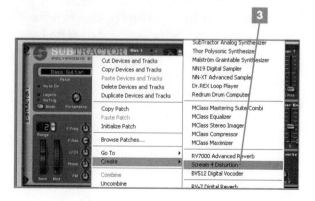

4 Click on any empty gray area of the Combinator anywhere above the Holder to highlight the Combinator. Then choose Subtractor from the Create menu. This makes a Subtractor *under* the Combinator. That's not what we want.

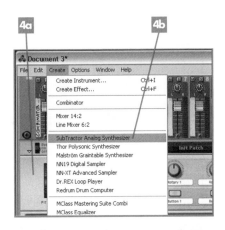

5 Click in the empty slot at the bottom of the Combinator, and you will see the red Insertion Line appear. (Devices inside the Combinator are folded in my picture, but yours will not be folded by default.)

6 Choose Subtractor from the Create menu. Now it shows up in the right spot inside the Combinator. (The screenshot shows the Subtractor already in place, but you won't see yours until you create it.)

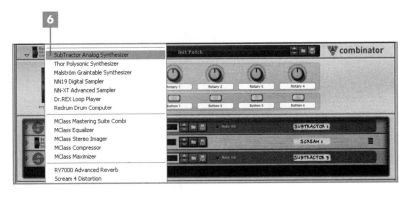

7 Right-click on the Combinator and choose Initialize Patch.

8 Click the Show Devices button to turn it off. The Holder (the area at the bottom of the Combinator that holds the devices) disappears. There is no way to add a device to the Combinator.

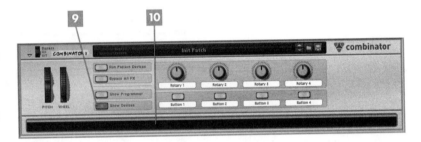

9 Click the Show Devices button again. You can see the Holder again.

10 Click inside the black space in the Holder, and you will see the red Insertion Line appear. Now you are ready to add a device to the Combinator.

Obviously, you can assume they call it the *Insertion Line* because when it is visible, any new device that is created (or that you drag from the Tool window into the Holder) will be inserted directly below that line.

OK, now that we have that basic bit of business out of the way, it's time to have some fun. You are about to find out how easy it is to make great sounds using the Combinator.

Fat Synth Sounds Made Easy

A really easy way to use the Combinator to make fat synth patches goes like this: Create or find a sound you like on a Reason synth. Create a Combinator containing a mixer plus two instances of the synth with your patch loaded. Pan one synth hard left and the other hard right, and then slightly change something about the sound of one of the synths. Instant fat synth patch. Let's give it a try.

1 In a fresh Reason Rack containing a Mixer 14:2, use the Create menu to create a Combinator, and then create a Line Mixer 6:2 inside the Combinator, followed by a Subtractor.

2 Load the following patch into the Subtractor: Reason Factory Sound Bank > Subtractor Patches > PolySynths > FatThang.zyp. Play around on your MIDI keyboard to familiarize yourself with this sound.

3 Right-click on the Subtractor and choose Create > Subtractor Analog Synthesizer from the context menu.

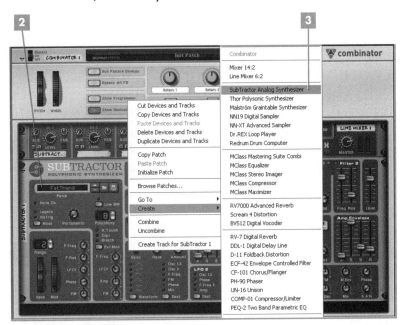

4 Load the same FatThang patch into the second Subtractor.

5 On the second Subtractor, turn Oscillator 1 Fine Tune up to a value of 20 cents.

6 On the second Subtractor, turn Oscillator 2 Fine Tune down to a value of –20 cents.

7 On the Line Mixer (micromix), turn Channel 1 Pan all the way to the left and Channel 2 Pan all the way to the right. Play your keyboard, and you will hear a nice wide stereo image.

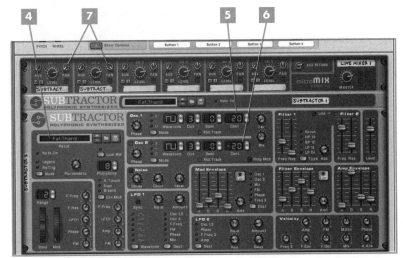

8 Right-click on the Line Mixer and choose Create > RV7000 Advanced Reverb from the context menu. It will be auto-routed to the Auxiliary Send/Return of the Line Mixer.

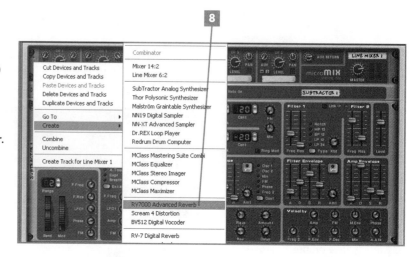

9 On the Line Mixer, turn the Auxiliary Send knobs on Channels 1 and 2 up to a value of 80.

10 If you like this patch, click the Save Patch button on the Combinator, and name it something like Extra Fat Thang.

One additional thing you might want to add to this patch: Turn Portamento on the second Subtractor up halfway and set the Key mode to ReTrig.

Since the Line Mixer and everything are already set up nicely, let's leave this Combinator as it is and load a different patch into the Subtractors for another quick example.

1 Load the following patch into
both Subtractors: Reason
Factory Sound Bank >
Subtractor Patches > Pads >
Sweeping Strings.zyp.

2 On the second Subtractor, turn
down Filter Envelope Decay to
a value of 88.

Now the filter sweep will happen just a bit faster on the second
Subtractor (right channel) than it will on the first Subtractor (left
channel).

To get a nice stereo spread this way, you could also use an entirely
different patch on one of the two synths, or you could vary another
parameter such as the speed of an LFO or even the octave of an
oscillator. I'm sure you get the idea.

❊ **PRECISION VALUES WHEN MOVING KNOBS AND FADERS**

If you have trouble getting precise values when dragging knobs and faders
with your mouse, try holding down the Shift key on your computer keyboard
while you click and drag. This will cause the knob or fader to move more
slowly (increasing or decreasing values in the smallest increments possible)
and will therefore allow you to select precise values. This works regardless
of the Mouse Knob Range setting on the General page of the Reason
Preferences. This trick also works when dragging up and down in the Amount
fields in Thor's Modulation Matrix or in the Min/Max fields in the Modulation
Routing section of the Combinator's Programmer window.

Combine/Uncombine

Throughout most of this chapter, you will be creating empty
Combinators and then creating devices within the Combinator.
However, that's not the only way to make a Combinator patch.

If you find that you have a group of devices in your Reason song that are working together in a useful way, you can combine them into a Combinator patch (Combi) that can be opened later in other songs as well. This comes in especially handy when using effects devices that have no Save Patch functionality.

1. In an empty rack, create an MClass Mastering Combi, followed by a Mixer 14:2 and Dr. Rex.

2. Load the following patch into Dr.Rex: Reason Factory Sound Bank > Dr Rex Drum Loops > Abstract HipHop > Trh36_ MiddleSkool_090_Grif.rx2. (It's the last patch in the folder.)

3. Turn the Tempo down to 90.

4. Click the Preview button on Dr.Rex.

5. (These drums are going to sound very big after the next few steps.) Create a Scream 4 Sound Destruction Unit under Dr.Rex, and turn the Body Type knob to D.

6. Turn the Scale knob up to 9 o'clock.

7. Turn the Auto knob up to 9 o'clock.

8. Turn the Resonance knob all the way up. That's what I'm talking about.

9 Shift+click on Dr.Rex and Scream 4. Then right-click on either device and select Combine from the context menu.

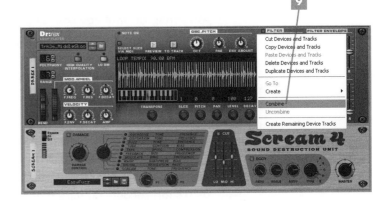

10 Click the Combinator's Save Patch button, and choose a name you'll remember (like Big Fat MiddleSkool Teacher).

11 To uncombine, right-click on the Combinator and choose Uncombine from the context menu.

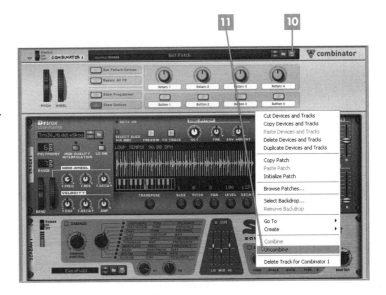

Using the MClass Mastering Suite Combi

The MClass Mastering Suite Combi can help you add the finishing touches that can turn an OK mix into one that really jumps out and reaches the listener. Normally, you will create this Combi above the main mixer so that the Mastering Suite Combi is the last thing the entire mix passes through on its way out of Reason. In fact, there is a song file in your Template Documents folder called Mixer and Mastering.rns that you can set as the default song on the General page of your Reason Preferences, if you like. That way, every time you open a new song, it will have an MClass Mastering Suite Combi followed by Mixer 14:2 at the top of an otherwise empty rack. (Of course, all the exercises in this book start with a completely empty rack.)

The following exercise will help you familiarize yourself with the function of the MClass Mastering Suite. Please leave everything as-is at the end of this exercise with the track playing, because there will be a short second exercise that picks up where this one leaves off.

❊ **IMPORTANT NOTE**

If you cannot find the Tutorial Song mentioned in Step 1 below, you can download it here: http://www.propellerheads.se/support/files/TutorialSong.zip. It's a tiny 44kb download. However, if you are running Reason version 4.0.1 or later, you should already have the file.

1 Open the Tutorial Song found in the Reason Program folder and click Play on the Reason Transport. The song will begin looping, which is perfect.

2 Right-click on Reason Hardware Device at the top of the rack and select Create > MClass Mastering Suite Combi from the context menu. You will hear a slight volume increase.

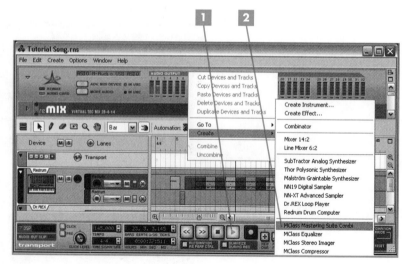

3 Click the Show Devices button on the Combinator.

4 Bypass the MClass Maximizer for now. Now all the devices in the Combinator are bypassed (not active) except for the MClass Equalizer.

5 Turn up the Low Shelf Gain to a value of 2.9dB. If your monitors or headphones are decent, you should hear an increase in bass.

6 Activate the High Shelf, and you will hear the cymbals ring out and "breathe" more.

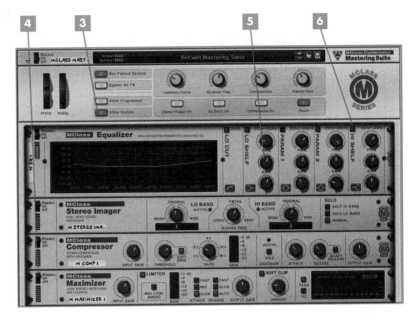

7 Turn on the MClass Stereo Imager, and turn the Lo Band Width knob all the way down to Mono.

8 Turn Hi Band Width all the way up to Wide.

9 Click Solo Hi Band to hear just the Hi Band. You can play with the X-Over Freq (crossover frequency) knob and return it to 1.28KHz when you're done.

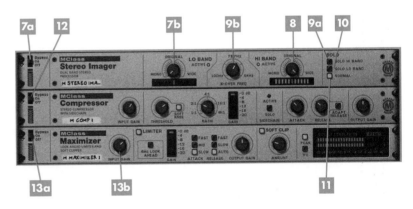

10 Now click Solo Lo Band to hear just the Lo Band (which is completely mono). You can play with the X-Over Freq (crossover frequency) knob and return it to 1.28KHz when you're done.

11 Click the Normal button on the MClass Stereo Imager.

12 Turn on the MClass Compressor to add a subtle bit of compression.

13 Turn on the MClass Maximizer, and turn Input Gain up to a value of 4.1dB.

14 Bypass the Mastering Suite Combi to hear the difference between what you started with and what you ended up with.

One big difference: It's much louder. And since everyone maximizes the hell out of their electronic music these days, perhaps you will want to do the same. This decreases dynamic range, but at least it ensures your track isn't way quieter than the other guy's before it. Now, I am not claiming to have done a brilliant job mastering here. I just wanted you to hear what each device in the Mastering Suite does.

In addition to the default Mastering Suite patch, there are several presets that may sound great on your song. With the Tutorial Song still playing, please do the following:

1 Click the Combinator's Browse Patch button.

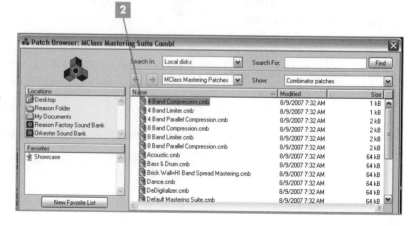

2 Click once on the top patch, called 4 Band Compression.cmb, to hear it previewed. Then use the down arrow on your computer keyboard to select and preview each of the patches in the MClass Mastering Patches folder.

Notice that several of these presets feature different configurations of the MClass devices. For instance, the 8 Band Compression patch contains eight MClass compressors and eight MClass Stereo Imagers. The Bass and Drum patch contains a Scream 4. Also, keep in mind that all the MClass devices can be created separately wherever you need them in your song or as part of other Combis.

Using the Programmer Panel

The Combinator's Programmer panel is where you can control the flow of MIDI messages for all the devices within the Combinator. You can use it for modulation routing (similar to Thor's Modulation Matrix), to create keyboard splits and velocity-layered sounds, and to decide what kind of MIDI information each device in the Combinator can receive. And as complex as that may sound, the good news is that the Programmer panel is set up very simply and logically.

Creating a Split Instrument with the Combinator

One easy thing you can do with a Combinator is create keyboard splits. This is especially useful for live performances. In the following example, you will create a Combi in which the lower keys play a bass sound, while the rest of the keyboard plays a dreamy synth piano sound.

1 In a fresh rack containing an instance of Mixer 14:2, create a Combinator. (This step is not pictured.)

2 From the Devices pane of the Tool window, drag a Line Mixer 14:2 into the Combinator, followed by two Thors. You will see the red Insertion Line appear as you drag so that you know you're dropping the new device in the right place.

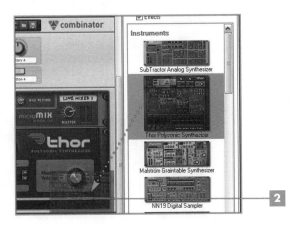

3 In the top Thor, load the patch
Fat Boy (found in the default
folder and also in Reason
Factory Sound Bank > Thor
Patches > Bass).

4 In the bottom Thor, load the
following patch: Reason
Factory Sound Bank > Thor
Patches > Poly Synths > IDM
Keys 1.thor.

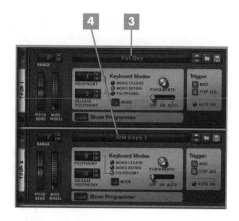

5 Click the Combinator's Show
Programmer button.

6 Drag the scrollbar at the top
of the Key Mapping section all
the way to the right.

7 Click in the Device area of the
Programmer where it says
Thor 1.

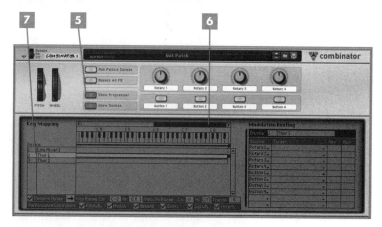

8 Drag the right edge of Thor
1's horizontal bar to the left
until the Key Range Hi value
reads E2.

9 Click in the Device area of the
Programmer where it says
Thor 2.

10 Click in the KeyRange Lo field
and drag upward until you
have a value of F2.

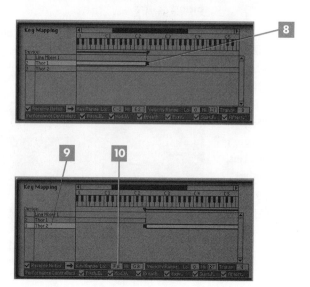

Now if you play your MIDI keyboard, notes E2 and below will trigger the Fat Boy sound in Thor 1, and notes F2 and above will trigger the IDM Keys 1 sound in Thor 2. Of course, if you want, you could add several synths to your Combinator, some with separate key ranges, and some with the same or overlapping key ranges.

Creating a Velocity-Layered Instrument with the Combinator

You should already be familiar with velocity layers from your experience with the NN-XT. In that context, hitting a drum sample, for example, at a lower velocity setting could trigger one drum sample, while striking the controller more sharply would trigger another drum sample. This can be done with the Combinator as well. In the next exercise, you will create a piano and strings patch where playing softly will get you piano only, and playing more forcefully will give you piano and strings at the same time.

1 In a fresh rack containing a 14:2 Mixer and a Combinator, load the following devices into the Combinator in this order: Line Mixer 6:2, RV7000 Advanced Reverb, and two instances of NN-XT. (This step is not pictured.)

2 The NN-XTs will have the B Grand Piano 1.0 patch loaded by default. In the second NN-XT, click in the Patch display window and choose Violin Section from the menu.

3 In the Line Mixer, turn Channel 1 Aux a little past 2 o'clock, and turn Channel 2 Aux all the way up. You should have a pretty piano and strings sound.

4 The violins might be a little too loud, so turn down the Channel 2 level to a value of 85 or so.

5 Click the Combinator's Show Programmer button.

6 In the Device area of the Programmer window, click where it says NN-XT 2.

7 Click in the Velocity Range Lo field and drag up to a value of 70.

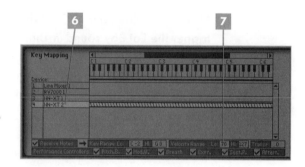

Now when you play very softly, you will hear piano only, and when you play more forcefully, you will hear the violins as well. Note that the horizontal bar representing the key range of NN-XT 2 now has stripes to indicate that it has a velocity range of less than 0–127. You can experiment with the Velocity Range Lo value until you find one that feels comfortable with your playing style (and with the velocity response of your MIDI keyboard). Please leave this patch up (and save it if you want) because we can use it in the next section.

MIDI Data Routing/Performance Controllers

By default, when your Combinator is selected as the active Sequencer track, all MIDI will be sent to all devices in the Combinator all the time. However, you can control this. Using your piano and strings Combinator from the previous exercise, please do the following:

1 My fingers are getting tired of playing hard to hear the violins, so with NN-XT 2 still selected in the Device list, let's drag that Velocity Range Lo parameter back down to zero. (Notice the stripes disappear.)

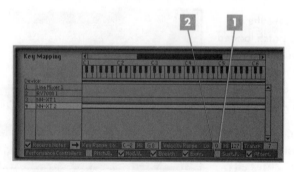

2 In the Performance Controllers section, click in the Sust.P. (Sustain Pedal) checkbox to deselect it. Now if you are using a sustain pedal with your MIDI keyboard, it will only sustain the piano sound, but it will cease making a mushy mess of your violins.

3 Uncheck Pitch Bend. Now your pitch wheel will affect only the piano but not the strings. Of course, this is a funny example since you normally wouldn't pitch bend piano, either.

4 Click in the Transpose field and drag up to a value of 7. Now play your MIDI keyboard, and the violins will be transposed up a fifth, making you sound all complex and stuff.

5 Uncheck Receive Notes. Now NN-XT 2 (Violin section) will not receive any MIDI note information, and you will hear only piano.

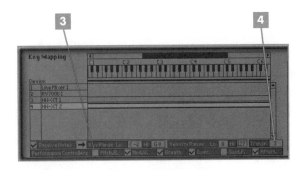

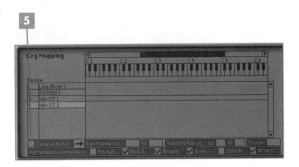

Step 5 may not be much fun for this patch, but it could be useful if you had a Combi containing a Redrum where you didn't want the drums to be triggered by your keyboard playing. This could also be useful in Combinators containing vocoders or other complex situations. Also, if you have a split with a bass sound and a lead sound, you might want pitch bend, mod wheel, and sustain to affect the lead sound only, but not the bass sound.

Assigning the Virtual Controls

The Combinator's Controller panel has four virtual knobs and four virtual buttons that can be assigned to control parameters of the devices inside the Combinator. By default, they are not assigned to anything. But if you want, you could make one knob (or one button) control up to 10 different parameters. You will notice that Thor has two similar virtual knobs and two virtual buttons as well. The following exercise should give you a feel for how to use these.

1. Create a Combinator, and create a Subtractor inside of it. Then click inside of Subtractor's Patch display window, and choose Synthol.zyp from the menu. (This patch is also in the Subtractor Patches > MonoSynths folder.)

2. Click the Combinator's Show Programmer button.

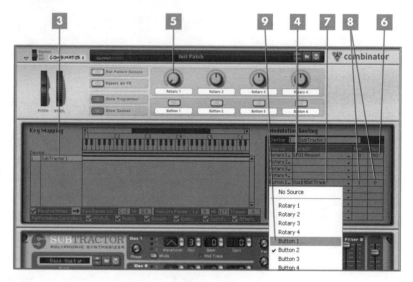

3. In the Device area of the Programmer, click where it says SubTractor 1.

4. In the Modulation Routing section, choose LFO1 Amount for the Rotary1 target. (You'll have to scroll down the pop-up menu to see the selection for LFO1 Amount.)

5. While playing your MIDI keyboard, drag the Rotary 1 knob back and forth and turn it all the way to the left when you are done.

6. If the effect is too crazy, drag the Rotary1 Max value down to 40. Now when you turn the Rotary 1 knob all the way up, the effect is tamer.

7. Choose Osc2 Kbd Track for the Button 1 target.

8. Set Minimum to 1 and Maximum to 0 for Button 1. Now when Button 1 is on, Oscillator 2 Keyboard Tracking will be off, and vice versa.

9. In the Source column, click on Button 2, and choose Button 1 from the menu. This is how you can have the same button control two different things.

❖ ❖ ❖

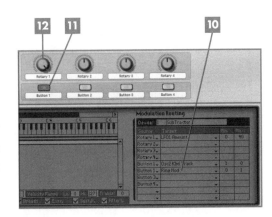

10 Choose Ring Mod for the second Button 1 target.

11 Click Button 1, and you will have a ring-modulated sound.

12 Turn the Rotary 1 knob all the way up, and people will think you are weird.

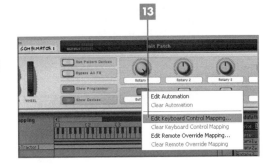

13 Right-click on Button 1, and choose Edit Keyboard Control Mapping.

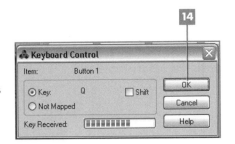

14 Press the Q key on your computer keyboard and then click OK. Now when you press the Q key on your computer keyboard, it will turn Button 1 on and off.

Of course, you can use that last trick on any button-style parameter in Reason. Similarly, you can right-click on any knob or button in Reason, choose Edit Remote Override Mapping, and map the knob or button to a knob or button on a MIDI controller. Your Reason Operation Manual can provide more details. It's pretty easy.

Sequencing with the Combinator

Sequencing with the Combinator is pretty much like sequencing with any other instrument in Reason, but there is one thing I'd like to point out. The Combinator track in the Reason Sequencer sends information through the entire Combinator. What if you want to automate a parameter in only one device inside of a Combinator? The following exercise shows how to do that. It also introduces you to the Create Instrument method of creating a Reason device. In the Create Instrument patch browser, patches are arranged by sound type instead of by device.

1 In a new rack containing Mixer 14:2, select Create Instrument from the Create menu.

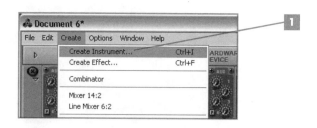

2 When the browser window opens, you should already see the contents of Reason Factory Sound Bank > ALL Instrument Patches. Select Performance Patches > Boutique > Renaissance Teebee Combi [Run].cmb, then click OK.

3 Click the Run Pattern Devices button (relabeled "Run/Stop" in this Combi). You should hear music.

4 Click the Show Devices button (relabeled "Show Synth/Seq" in this Combi).

5 Unfold Thor.

6 Slowly turn the Oscillator 1 and 2 Balance knob in the Mixer section from left to right and back again to hear what this sounds like.

7 Right-click on Thor, and select Create Track for Thor from the context menu.

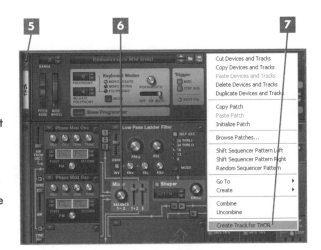

8 With the Thor Sequencer track still selected, click the Track Parameter Automation button and choose Osc 1 And 2 Balance from the menu. An automation lane will appear under the note lane.

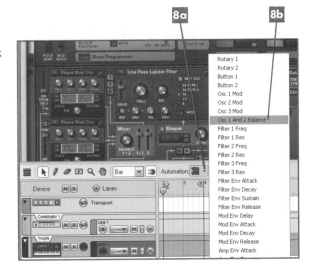

9 Select your Pencil tool.

10 Draw in a clip between bars 1 and 9 in the Osc 1 And 2 Balance parameter automation lane.

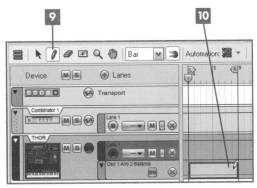

11 Alt+double-click on the clip, and then create three points in the shape of a "V," as shown. The high points of the "V" should have a value of 127, and the low point should have a value of zero.

12 Click Play on the Reason Transport. The Transport should be in Loop mode by default, and you should hear (and see) Thor's Mixer knob moving smoothly back and forth between its minimum and maximum values.

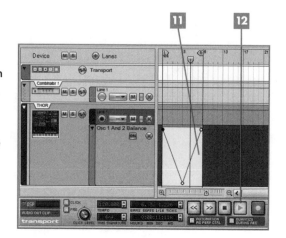

Keep in mind that you can right-click on any Reason device and choose Create Track For from the context menu, regardless of whether or not the device happens to be inside a Combinator.

In the exercise you have just completed, you used Create Instrument to create your Combinator. Of course, you could have created a Malström, Subtractor, or any other instrument device using the same command. You can tell what type of device you are loading by the file extension in the patch name. In the next exercise, instead of using Create Instrument, you will use Create Effect to add effects to your sequence.

Please leave the sequence you have just created running (so that you can still hear the Renaissance Teebee Combi).

1 Click on the Combinator to make sure it's highlighted. Then choose Create Effect from the Create menu.

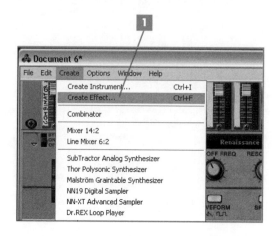

2 Expand the Modulation folder by clicking the plus symbol to the left of it (which will become a minus sign).

3 Click once on 4-Band PhaseEQ.cmb to hear the effects patch previewed. Then press the down arrow on your computer keyboard to hear the next patch. Keep using the down arrow until you have previewed all the effects Combis in that folder.

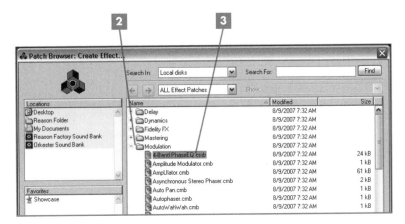

4 Expand the Fidelity FX folder. (If necessary, first drag the vertical scrollbar up to the top so that you can see this folder.)

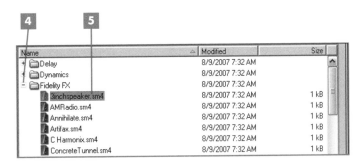

5 Click once on the first patch, entitled 3inchspeaker.sm4. (Careful, it's loud.) Then use the down arrow on your computer keyboard to preview the rest of the patches in that folder.

I realize the patches in the Fidelity FX folder are not Combis but are actually Scream 4 patches. I just thought they were pretty extreme and that you might enjoy checking them out. And at least we were processing the Renaissance Teebee Combi, so this leg of the exercise is still in the right chapter.

I should note that in Step 3 I was not able to hear anything when previewing the Tuned Thor Filters 1 & 2 patches. (I mention that in case you noticed the same thing and were wondering if your stuff was broken.) I should also note that moving the mod wheel (relabeled Shred) and also the first rotary knob (labeled Cut Off Freq) on the Renaissance Teebee Combi can yield pretty cool results.

Custom Skins for Your Combinator

Reason allows you to change the appearance of your Combinator. The following exercise requires that you use whatever image-editing program you have at your disposal to crop or resize a JPEG image to 754×138 pixels. The image must be in JPEG format (with a .jpg or .jpeg file extension).

1 Create a Combinator. Then right-click on it and choose Select Backdrop from the context menu.

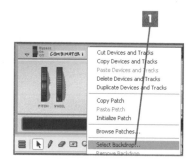

2 Double-click on the desired 754×138 JPEG image in the Image Browser window.

3 If you want to rename your Combinator, double-click on the piece of tape to the left of the display window and type in your text. (This works for any of the "console-tape style" labels in the Reason user interface.)

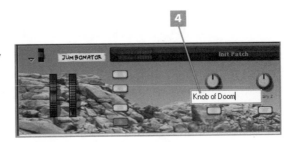

4 If you want to rename a rotary knob or button controller, double-click under it, type in the desired text, and press Enter.

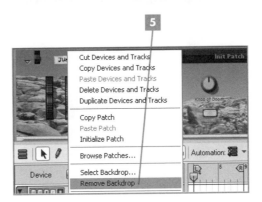

5 To remove the image, right-click on the Combinator and select Remove Backdrop from the context menu.

This is the quick and easy way to change the backdrop. You can try any JPEG image on your computer, but if it has the wrong dimensions, it may cover only part of the Combinator, or you may be able to see only a small portion of the image file.

If you know your way around Photoshop, you can use the Template Backdrop.psd file found in Reason\Template Documents\Combi Backdrops. It is a multilayer template. By using an image editor such as Photoshop, you will be able to add custom text as well. If you plan to include custom text for the knob and button labels in your image file, you will have to double-click on the existing label and delete the contents.

Backdrop image information is saved when you save your Combinator patch. It is also saved with the song in which the Combinator is used. For more information on creating your own custom Combinator look, please see the Read Me file located in Reason\Template Documents\Combi Backdrops.

Advanced Combi in Which Redrum Controls 10 Thors

In the following exercise, you will create a Combi in which Redrum controls 10 Thors. Since there are so many steps, I have broken up the exercise into two parts. In the first part, you will set up the devices in the Combinator. In the second part, you will load patches into all the Thors.

Setting Up Your Thor Drum Combi

1 In a fresh rack containing a Mixer 14:2, create a Combinator. Inside the Combinator, create a Mixer 14:2, followed by a Redrum.

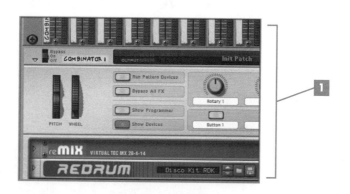

2 Press the Tab key to flip your rack around, drag the cables out of Mixer Channel 1 Left and Right inputs, and plug them into Mixer Channel 11 Left and Right inputs.

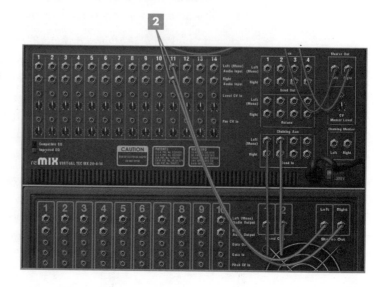

3 Press the Tab key to flip your rack around facing front, and mute Channel 11. Then create 10 Thors under Redrum. After creating each Thor, fold it.

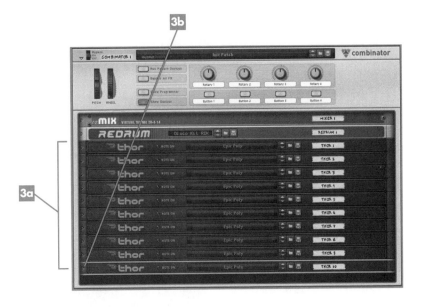

4 Flip your rack around, unfold Thor 1, and connect Redrum Channel 1 Gate Out to Thor 1 Sequencer Control Gate In.

5 Connect all remaining Redrum Gate outs to the remaining Thor Gate ins (Redrum Channel 2 Gate Out to Thor 2 Gate In, Redrum Channel 3 Gate Out to Thor 3 Gate In, etc.). Unfold as needed. Folding Mixer 14:2 helps.

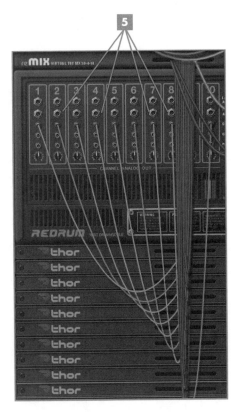

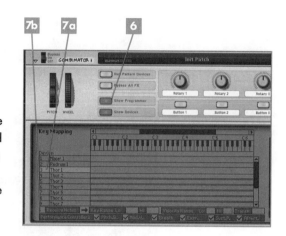

6 Flip your rack around facing front. Click the Combinator's Show Programmer button.

7 Click on Thor 1 (in the Device area of the Programmer) and uncheck Receive Notes. Then do the same for each of the remaining Thors in the Device list.

8 On the Mixer 14:2 inside the Combinator, mute Channel 11 (the one Redrum is plugged in to).

Remember that in Reason, Gate CV carries note on/note off information, as well as velocity information.

Selecting Sounds for Your Thor Drum Combi

Tastes vary widely, so you may find that my choices bear little relation to the music you want to make; however, you can certainly make your own modifications later. Of course, this picks up where the last bit left off.

1 Load the following into Thor 1:
Reason Factory Sound Bank >
Thor Patches > Percussion >
BassDrums > 808 BD.thor.

2 Load the following into Thor 2:
Reason Factory Sound Bank >
Thor Patches > Percussion >
SnareDrums > ER Snare
Construction.thor.

3 Load the following into Thor 3:
Reason Factory Sound Bank >
Thor Patches > Percussion >
Claps > HandClap 1.thor.

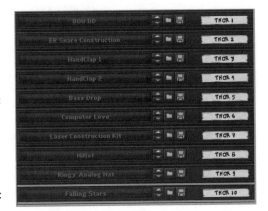

4 Load the following into Thor 4: Reason Factory Sound Bank >
Thor Patches > Percussion > Claps > HandClap 2.thor.

5 Load the following into Thor 5: Reason Factory Sound Bank >
Thor Patches > Percussion > Misc Percussion > Bass Drop.thor.

6 Load the following into Thor 6: Reason Factory Sound Bank >
Thor Patches > Fx > Computer Love.thor.

7 Load the following into Thor 7: Reason Factory Sound Bank >
Thor Patches > Fx > Laser Construction Kit.thor.

8 Load the following into Thor 8: Reason Factory Sound Bank >
Thor Patches > Percussion > HiHats > HiHat.thor.

9 Load the following into Thor 9: Reason Factory Sound Bank >
Thor Patches > Percussion > HiHats > Ringy Analog Hat.thor.

10 Load the following into Thor 10: Reason Factory Sound Bank >
Thor Patches > Fx > Falling Stars.thor.

Now that you've got your sounds all set up, you can save this
Combinator patch. (I'm going to call mine Throbinator. It throbs,
and the name reminds me of Thor.)

Here are some tips for using this Combi:

* You may want to build your beats with Mixer Channel 11 soloed (so that you can hear a regular kit as your make your beat) and then turn Channel 11 Solo off (so that Channel 11 is muted, and you can hear all your Thors instead).

* Another great starting point for making beats with this Combi is to leave Mixer Channel 11 muted so that you can hear the Thors. Then right-click on Redrum and choose Randomize Pattern.

* You may want to alternate left and right panning of Remix Channels 2 through 10 so that you have a nice stereo kit. Once you're happy with the sound, you can save the Combi again.

* If the 808 BD or the Bass Drop is not tuned to your liking, you can unfold the appropriate Thor, click on Show Programmer, and adjust the Octave and Semi knobs on the analog oscillators. The Tune knobs on Redrum will have no effect.

* If you don't like the sound in a particular Thor, you can use the arrows next to the Patch display window to scroll up and down between patches in the same folder as the currently selected patch.

* Remember that your pitch bender and modulation wheel will control all Thors simultaneously.

Something for Adventurers: Spider CV Merger and Splitter

This is definitely the most advanced exercise in this book, but if you're into it, it's just a matter of following the steps. Could be fun. This exercise uses the Throbinator you just constructed. Before beginning the exercise, please use Redrum's Pattern Sequencer to create a beat. If you need help, please refer to Chapter 3, "Redrum," or check your Reason Operation Manual. If you're in a hurry, you can use Randomize Pattern to create instant chaos. Once you have a beat, do the following:

1 Drag an ECF-42 Envelope Controlled filter into the Holder directly above the Mixer 14:2.

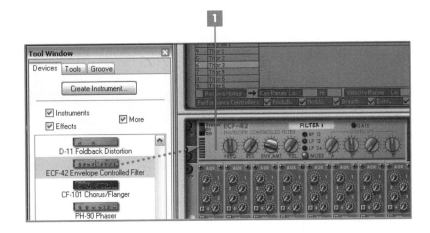

2 Flip your rack around and disconnect the cables going into the Left and Right inputs of the Envelope Controlled filter.

3 Disconnect the cables going out of the Mixer Master outs and into the Combinator's From Devices jacks.

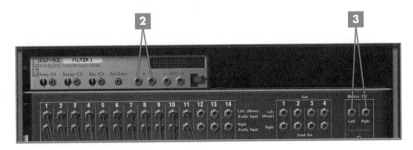

4 Connect the Left and Right Master outs of the Mixer 14:2 to the L /R In of the Envelope Controlled filter.

5 Create two DDL-1 Digital Delay Line devices after the Envelope Controlled filter and disconnect all cables from the Digital Delays.

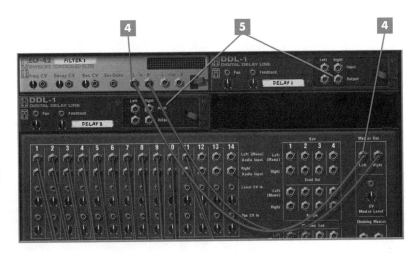

❋❋❋

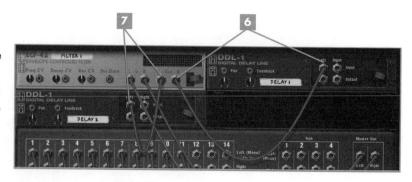

6 Connect the Right output of the Envelope Controlled filter to the Left input of the first Digital Delay, but disconnect the cable that automatically appears to connect the right channel.

7 Connect the Left output of the Envelope Controlled filter to the Left input of the second Digital Delay.

8 Connect the Left output of the first Digital Delay to the Combinator's Right From Devices input.

9 Connect the Left output of the second Digital Delay to the Combinator's Left From Devices input.

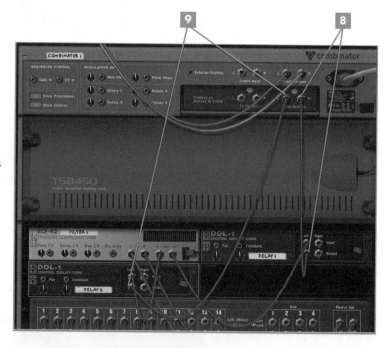

10 Flip your rack around, and change the delay time on the first Digital Delay to 4 Steps.

11 Turn the Dry/Wet knob on both delays down to 9 o'clock.

12 Play your beat while turning the Frequency knob on the Envelope Controlled filter back and forth. (You can play with Resonance, too, if you want. You've been good.)

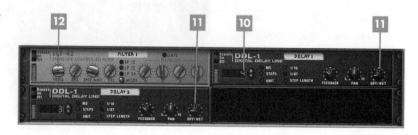

You may now be wondering where the Spider is. It's coming next. If you have been puzzling over the Envelope Controlled filter and wondering how you get the envelope to control it, the answer is that we haven't hooked that part up yet. We will in the next section of this crazy exercise. Picking up where we left off:

1 Create a Spider CV Merger & Splitter after the second Digital Delay, and then create a Matrix Analog Pattern Sequencer under that.

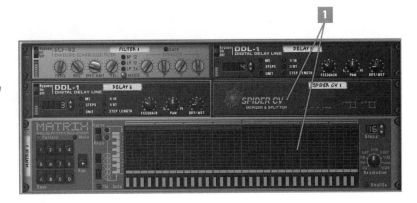

2 Flip your rack around and disconnect Redrum Channel 1 Gate Out from Thor 1 Gate In.

3 Disconnect **the** cables **coming out of the Matrix. Then** con- **nect Redrum Channel 1 Gate Out to Spider CV Split A input. (Click the L key to hide or show cables if the spaghetti is in the way.)**

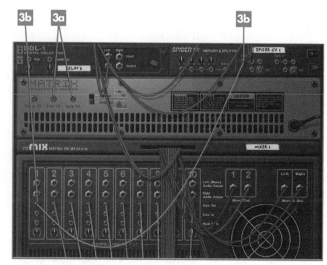

4 Connect Spider CV Split A Out 1 to Thor 1 Gate In.

5 Connect Spider CV Split A Out 2 to the Envelope Gate input of the Envelope Controlled fil- ter. Now Redrum's Channel 1 Gate Out is controlling Thor 1 (as before) plus the Envelope Controlled filter.

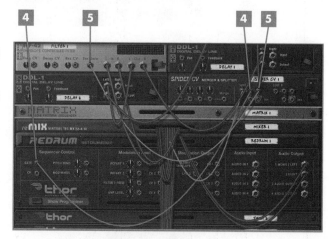

6 Switch **the** Matrix **to Bipolar Curve mode.**

7 Connect **the Matrix's** Curve CV output **to the Envelope Controlled filter's Freq CV input.**

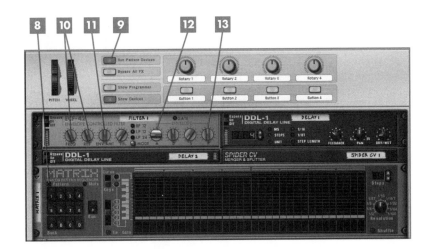

8 Flip your rack around, and turn off the Pattern Enable button on the Matrix. We're not using the Matrix yet.

9 Click Run Pattern Devices on the Combinator to start your beat (if it's not already playing).

10 Turn the Freq and Res knobs up to 11 o'clock on the Envelope Controlled filter.

11 Turn the Envelope Amount knob slowly all the way up and all the way down. Then set it at 12 o'clock.

12 Slowly turn the Envelope Attack knob up to 12 o'clock, and then down to 9 o'clock.

13 Slowly turn the Envelope Release knob all the way to the right, then all the way to the left, then back to 12 o'clock.

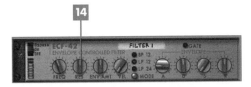

14 Slowly turn Resonance up all the way to the right and then back down to 12 o'clock. (It's fun to play with the filter frequency when Resonance is turned up, too. Be careful of your ears/speakers.)

Did I throw that Matrix in there just for looks? In the final leg of this mammoth exercise, you will use the Matrix to modulate the cutoff frequency of the Envelope Controlled filter, and you will also do a little bit of routing in the Combinator's Programmer.

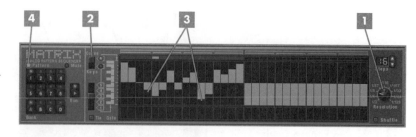

1. On the Matrix, turn the Resolution knob down to 1/8.

2. Set the Matrix's Edit mode to Curve.

3. Using your mouse, draw a random pattern in the first eight steps.

4. Click the Matrix's Pattern Enable button so it lights up red, and you should hear the Envelope Controlled filter's frequency being modulated by the Matrix.

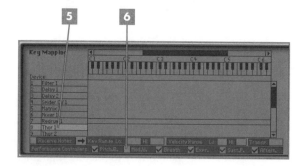

5. In the Combinator's Programmer, select Thor 1 from the Device list.

6. Turn off Mod.W. for Thor 1. Then do the same for the remaining nine Thors.

7. Select Filter 1 from the Device list.

8. In the Modulation Routing section, choose Mod Wheel for the first empty Source slot.

9. For Target, select Frequency.

10. Select a value of 38 for Minimum by clicking and dragging up in the Minimum box. Now you can control the Envelope Controlled filter frequency with the modulation wheel on your MIDI keyboard.

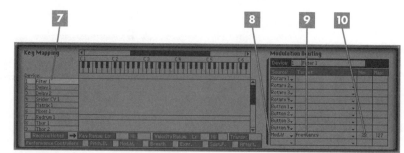

11 Select Matrix 1 from the Device list.

12 For the Button 1 Target, choose Pattern Enable.

13 Click Button 1 on the Combinator's Controller panel to turn the Matrix on and off.

14 Just so you will have touched every part of the Combinator in this exercise, click the Bypass All FX button on the Combinator, and the Digital Delays will be bypassed.

Whew. Did you make it through all that? If you did, I hope you enjoyed it, and I hope it gave you some ideas. By the way, there is also a Spider Audio Merger and Splitter that works the same way as the Spider CV, but it is used for merging and splitting audio signals instead of control voltage signals. Whenever you need one thing to go out to several things or several things to merge into one thing, the Spiders are there for you.

One last word about the advanced exercise: I hope you will take that idea with you regarding processing the left channel with a Digital Delay set to three steps and processing the right channel with a Digital Delay set to four steps (or two steps). This can be a very effective combination for processing rhythms in a variety of electronic music. You may even want to design a little Combi based on that idea.

External Routing Indicators

Here's the last little bit of the Combinator I want to tell you about before moving on to the next chapter. The Combinator includes external routing indicators (on both the front and the rear of the Combinator) to warn you if you have connected any of the devices inside the Combinator directly to a device outside the Combinator.

The following exercise shows how to do something that you normally want to avoid.

1. In a fresh rack containing a Mixer 14:2, create a Combinator with a Subtractor inside it. (This step is not pictured.)

2. Press Tab to flip your rack around, and then drag a cable connecting Subtractor's LFO 1 Modulation output to the Mixer's Channel 1 Pan CV in. The External Routing light will turn on.

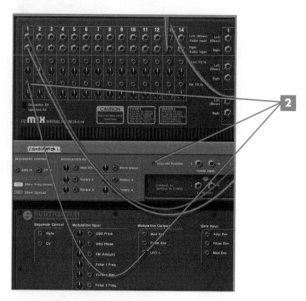

3. Press the Tab key to flip your rack back around, and you will see that external routing is indicated in the Combinator's display window as well.

Although using the Subtractor's LFO to auto-pan Channel 1 of the Mixer is a neat idea (and I wouldn't try to stop you), the reason it is generally good practice to avoid external routing is that those connections will not be saved with the Combinator patch. External routing is saved with the Reason Song file, however. If you choose to route externally in this manner, be aware that when you open that Combi in another song, you will be missing any external connections.

The Combinator is truly one of the most powerful tools in Reason. I hope that after making it through this chapter, you are comfortable and confident using the Combinator in your Reason songs.

Now it's time to move on to the next chapter and learn about the ReGroove Mixer.

9 The ReGroove Mixer

The ReGroove Mixer is a Reason 4 innovation that gives you unprecedented hands-on control over the rhythmic content of your Reason songs. It offers powerful real-time control of several rhythmic aspects of the individual tracks in your sequence, and it also controls the relationship between those tracks (using the Slide control).

In this chapter you will learn how to:

* Apply preset groove patches to a drum pattern
* Make your own groove patch
* Permanently apply your ReGroove Mixer settings to a MIDI track
* Apply Random Timing to a programmed beat to add a "human feel"
* Use the Slide control to move individual drum parts ahead of or behind the beat

Applying a Preset Groove Patch

The exercises in this chapter will be a bit long, simply because we have to set up a beat before we can apply the ReGroove Mixer to it. The first part of this next exercise will be setting up the beat, and the second half will be actually using the ReGroove Mixer. In this exercise, you will use the RPG-8 Arpeggiator to help you construct your beat.

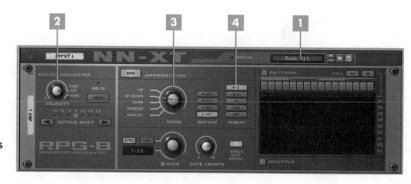

1 In a fresh rack containing a Mixer 14:2, create an NN-XT and load the following patch: Reason Factory Sound Bank > NN-XT Sampler Patches > Drums and Percussion > Drums and Kits > Rock Kit.sxt.

2 Under the NN-XT, create an RPG-8 Monophonic Arpeggiator and turn the Velocity knob to Fixed 127. Now all notes from the Arpeggiator will be at max volume, regardless of how hard you play.

3 Turn the Mode knob to Up + Down.

4 Turn the Insert mode to 4–2.

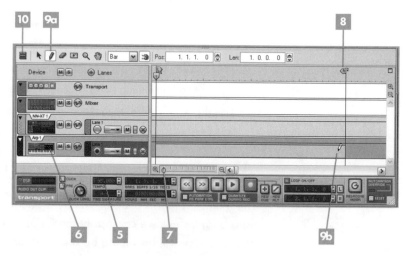

5 In the Reason Sequencer, turn Tempo down to 95.

6 Click on the Arp 1 device icon to select the track, and then hold down the C1 and D1 keys on your MIDI keyboard, just to hear the RPG-8 Arpeggiator in action. You can try other key combinations as well.

7 Move the Horizontal Zoom slider to the left until bar 1 takes up almost the entire window.

8 Alt+click on bar 2 to place the right locator there.

9 Select your Pencil tool and draw in a 1-bar clip on the Arp 1 track.

10 Click the Switch to Edit Mode button.

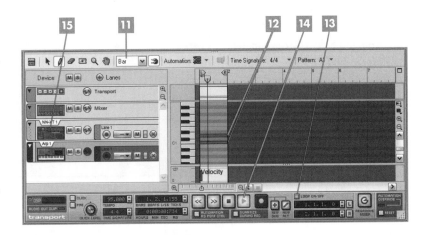

11 Make sure Bar is selected for the Grid mode.

12 Draw in notes at C1 and D1. You need only click once in the C1 and D1 grid squares, and the entire note will be drawn automatically, since you set the Grid mode to Bar already.

13 Make sure Loop is on.

14 Click Play, and you will hear a very robotic beat with a fixed velocity and perfect timing!

15 Select the NN-XT track by clicking its device icon.

16 Right-click on the RPG-8 and select Arpeggio Notes to Track. You will hear the sound of double-triggering.

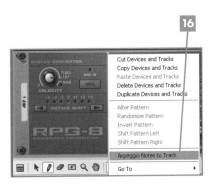

17 Mute the Arp 1 track in the Reason Sequencer. The double-triggering will go away.

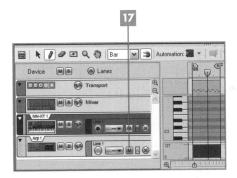

Now that your beat is set up, you can start using the ReGroove Mixer. You might want to save first, since you went to all the trouble of making this little beat.

1 Select Groove Channel A1 from the Select Groove menu on the NN-XT 1 track.

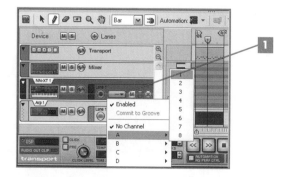

2 Show the ReGroove Mixer.

3 Click the Channel A1 Browse Groove Patch button and load the following patch: Reason Factory Sound Bank > ReGroove Patches > Drummer > Vintage Soul-RnB > Alkaholics.grov.

4 Click the Channel A1 Edit Channel button. This will open the Tool window to the Groove tab, with Groove Channel A1 already selected for editing.

5 If a shuffle was not what you had in mind, turn down the Timing Impact slider to about 31%.

6 To dial back the variation in velocity, turn down the Velocity Impact slider to 70%.

7 Slowly turn the Channel A1 Groove Amount slider all the way down until you have that stiff robo-drummer back behind the kit.

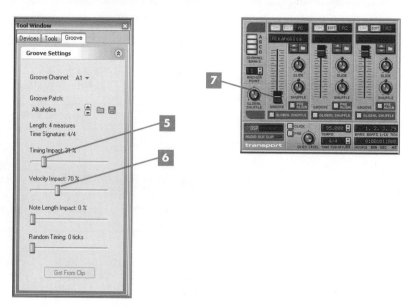

The next exercise picks up where this left off, so you might want to save again.

Get Groove from Clip (Making Your Own Groove Patch)

You are not limited to the groove patches in the Reason Factory Sound Bank. You can create your own groove patch from any MIDI clip in Reason. So if you play a keyboard bass part with a certain groove into the Reason Sequencer, or maybe you play a cymbal part on a drum pad controller that has a groove you want to use, you can turn the MIDI clip in the Reason Sequencer into a groove patch easily.

This exercise picks up where the last exercise left off.

1 Under the RPG-1, create a Dr.Rex and load the following patch: Reason Factory Sound Bank > Dr Rex Percussion Loops > Tabla 075 bpm > Tabla_04a_075.rx2.

2 Make sure the Dr.REX 1 track is selected in the Reason Sequencer, and then click the To Track button on Dr.Rex.

3 Mute the Dr.REX 1 track in the Reason Sequencer.

4 Select Groove A2 for the NN-XT 1 track.

5 On the Groove tab of the Tool window, select Groove Channel A2.

6 Using your Selection tool, click once on the clip on the Dr.REX 1 track to select it.

7 Click the Get from Clip button at the bottom of the Groove Settings window.

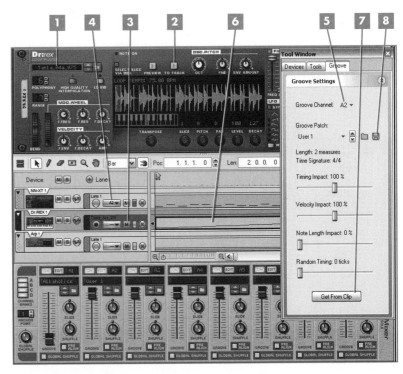

8 Click the Save button in the Groove Settings window if you want to save your groove patch in a user folder of your choosing (optional).

Now when you play your track, you will hear the shuffle timing you got from your Dr.Rex clip applied to your NN-XT 1 track. You won't hear the cool velocity performance in the tabla REX loop, however, since that was in the audio recording of the tabla player—not in the MIDI data of the REX loop. Of course, if you used Get Groove from Clip on a clip you had actually played into the Reason Sequencer, you'd have all the velocity, timing, and note length information from your performance in your new groove patch.

Note that instead of using the Get from Clip button in the Tool window, you can also right-click on any sequencer clip and select Get Groove from Clip from the pop-up menu. Whenever a clip is selected in the Reason Sequencer, you can also choose Get Groove from Clip from the Edit menu. In either case, the groove will be applied to whatever is the currently selected groove channel on the Groove tab of the Tool window.

Let's save once more, because the next exercise picks up where this one leaves off.

Commit to Groove

So far, everything we've done with the ReGroove Mixer has been nondestructive. That is, it is not actually changing the MIDI data in our sequencer tracks. Commit to Groove allows you to apply the groove to the MIDI track so that the track will sound "groovy" even if you do not have a groove channel enabled on the track. This exercise picks up where the last exercise left off.

1 Right-click on the Dr.REX 1 track and choose Delete Track and Device.

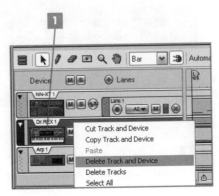

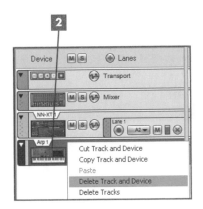

2 Right-click **on the** Arp 1 track **and** choose Delete Track and Device.

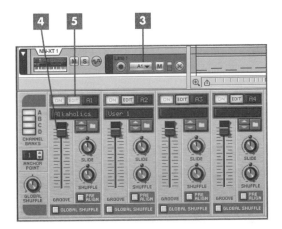

3 Assign Groove Channel A1 **for the** NN-XT 1 sequencer track.

4 Turn **the Channel A1** Groove Amount slider **all the way up.**

5 Click **the Channel A1** Edit Channel button.

6 In the Tool window, turn Timing Impact **up to 100%**

7 Double-click **on the** NN-XT 1 clip.

8 Drag the Horizontal Zoom slider to the left so that bar 1 takes up almost the whole window.

9 Use the vertical scrollbar so you can see the notes on C1 and D1. (If you don't see a vertical scrollbar, you need to drag the top of the sequencer window up by its handle to make it taller.)

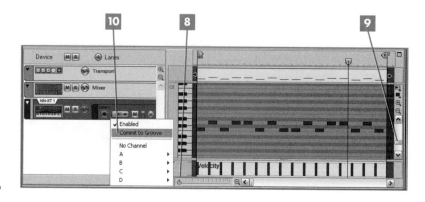

10 From the Select Groove drop-down on the NN-XT 1 sequencer track, select Commit to Groove. You will see the notes move in the clip, and the velocities become varied.

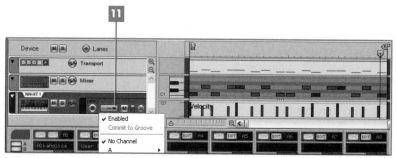

11 Notice that no groove channel is enabled anymore on the NN-XT 1 track. If you look in the Select Groove menu, you will see that after you selected Commit to Groove, No Channel was automatically selected.

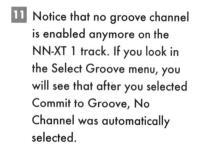

Of course the reason that No Channel is automatically selected when you use Commit to Groove is so that you don't have the groove applied twice (once to the actual MIDI data in the clip and once again through the ReGroove Mixer). Please save your song so that we can head into the last leg of this multipart exercise.

Random Timing

Random timing can be used to add a subtle amount of human-feel to a cymbal part or to drastically mess up a beat. This exercise picks up where the last one left off.

1 While playing the beat you've made, select Groove Channel A3 on the NN-XT 1 track.

2 Click the Channel A3 Edit button so you can adjust Channel A3's groove settings in the Tool window.

3 Slowly move the Random Timing slider all the way to the right, and listen as your drummer becomes ever more avant-garde!

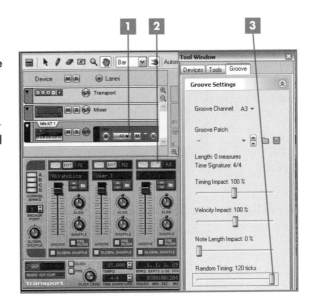

We are done with this setup (at long last!). The next exercise will start with a fresh rack.

Redrum, ReGroove, and the Slide Control

In the past, when using the Copy Pattern to Track feature in Redrum, you have been copying the entire pattern (kick, snare, cymbals, and all) to a single note lane in the Reason Sequencer. However, to get the most out of the ReGroove Mixer, it's nice to have each drum on a separate note lane so that you can apply shuffle, groove patches, and slide separately instead of to the entire drum kit. The next exercise shows you how to do this.

Also included in this exercise is use of the Slide control, which allows you to move an individual track slightly behind or slightly ahead of the beat. This allows you to build some tension by playing slightly on top of (or in front of) the beat or lay back slightly behind the beat.

1 In a fresh rack containing a Mixer 14:2, create an instance of Redrum. It will have Disco Kit RDK loaded by default. Click Redrum's Channel 8 Select button so you can program a hi-hat part.

2 Click and drag from left to right across all 16 step buttons so that they are all lit orange.

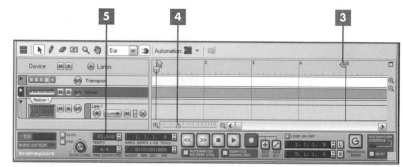

3 In the Reason Sequencer, drag the right locator to bar 5.

4 Increase the horizontal zoom until the first four bars fill up most of the Sequencer window.

5 Turn the Tempo down to 85.

6 Right-click on Redrum and choose Copy Pattern to Track.

7 Right-click on Redrum and choose Clear Pattern.

8 Double-click on the Redrum 1 note lane (where it says "Lane 1") and rename it "hi-hat." Then press Enter on your computer keyboard.

9 Click Play in the Reason Transport.

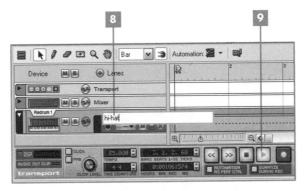

10 On Redrum, click the Channel 2 Select button so you can program a snare part.

11 Click step buttons 5 and 13.

12 Right-click on Redrum and choose Copy Pattern to Track (not pictured).

13 Right-click on Redrum and choose Clear Pattern (not pictured).

14 In the Reason Sequencer, double-click on the Redrum 1 Lane 2 label and rename it "snare."

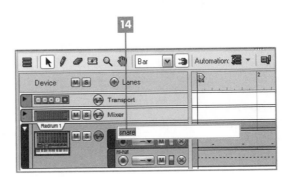

❅ ❅ ❅

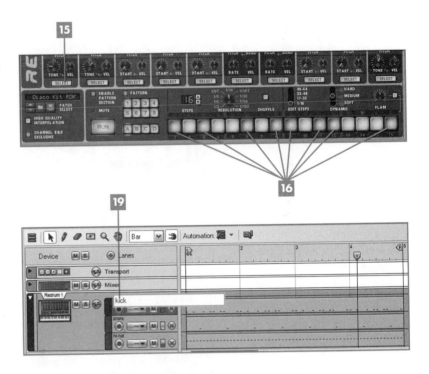

15 On Redrum, click the Channel 1 Select button so you can program a kick drum part.

16 Activate step buttons 1, 3, 6, 8, 9, 11, 12, and 16. Now you've got a fairly busy kick drum part.

17 Right-click on Redrum and choose Copy Pattern to Track (not pictured).

18 Right-click on Redrum and choose Clear Pattern (not pictured).

19 In the Reason Sequencer, double-click on the Redrum 1 Lane 3 label and rename it "kick."

OK, now you have a simple drum part set up with separate note lanes for each drum. You might want to save the song before going forward. You are now ready to start setting things up for the ReGroove Mixer. Of course, you will be picking up where you left off.

1 Select ReGroove Channel A1 from the Select Groove drop-down menu in the "kick" note lane.

2 Select ReGroove Channel A2 from the Select Groove drop-down menu in the "snare" note lane.

3 Select ReGroove Channel A3 from the Select Groove drop-down menu in the "hi-hat" note lane.

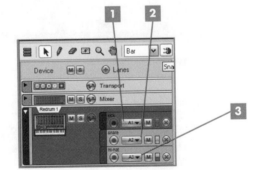

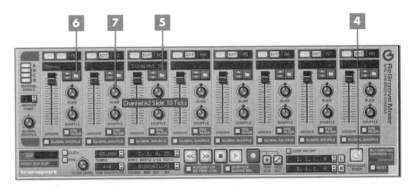

4 Click the ReGroove Mixer button in the Reason Transport to show the ReGroove Mixer.

5 Click the Channel A3 Browse Groove Patch button and load Factory Sound Bank > ReGroove Patches > Percussion > Shaker > Straight Shaker.grov. You will hear a difference in velocity emphasis and timing in the hi-hat track.

6 Click the Browse Groove Patch button on ReGroove Channel A1 and choose Factory Sound Bank > ReGroove Patches > Programmed > HipHop > Bones.grov.

7 On ReGroove Channel A2 (controlling the snare drum), move the Slide knob to a value of 10 ticks. This will make the snare hit just a bit late. (Hold down the Shift key as you drag the knob to get precise values.)

8 To go back to robot-feel, turn the Groove Amount sliders all the way down on ReGroove Channels A1 and A3 (kick and hi-hat).

9 Turn the Shuffle Amount knobs up to a value of 64 on ReGroove Channels A1 and A3.

10 To re-humanize the feel, turn the Groove Amount sliders all the way back up on ReGroove Channels A1 and A3.

11 Slowly turn the Channel A3 Slide Amount knob all the way to the right, and then slowly dial it back to a value of 40, which will leave the hi-hats just a bit behind the rest of the beat.

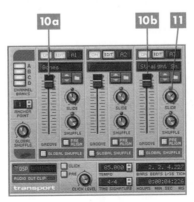

261

❄ ❄ ❄

Hmm…Sounds like the drummer could use some Red Bull or something!

We're done with that setup now. The next (and final!) exercise will start with a fresh rack.

Pre-Align

Pre-Align is a feature that nondestructively aligns (quantizes) the notes in a track to a 1/16-note grid so that when a groove patch is applied, it doesn't result in unpredictable results due to an imperfect live performance on the MIDI keyboard or drum pad.

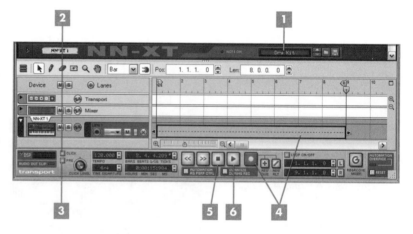

1 In a fresh rack containing Mixer 14:2, create an NN-XT and load the following patch: Reason Factory Sound Bank > NN-XT Sampler Patches > Drums and Percussion > Drums and Kits > Dry Kit.

2 Turn on Click.

3 Turn on Precount so that you will have a one-bar count-in when you press Record in the next step.

4 Press the F#1 key on your MIDI keyboard. You should hear a closed hi-hat. Click the Record button, and record a 1/8-note pattern for eight bars (filling the space between the L/R locators).

5 Click Stop.

6 Click Play.

7 Click the button to show the ReGroove Mixer.

8 Select Groove Channel A1 for the NN-XT 1 track.

9 Click the Channel A1 Pre-Align button. You should hear your hi-hat hits quantized right on the 1/8 notes, even though the MIDI notes don't actually move on the grid (if you were to look at them).

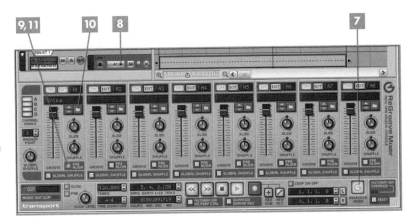

10 Click the Channel A1 Browse Groove Patch button and choose Reason Factory Sound Bank > ReGroove Patches > Drummer > Hiphop > Erika.

11 Turn off Pre-Align, and if your performance was less than perfect, you may hear some pretty weird stuff! Turn Pre-Align back on, and you should be good.

Congratulations! You have made it through all the exercises in this book! I hope you have a delicious cookie available at this time, because you deserve it.

} Index

INDEX }

INDEX }